JOURNAL FOR THE STUDY OF THE OLD TESTAMENT SUPPLEMENT SERIES
229

Sheffield Academic Press

Prophets and Paradigms

Essays in Honor of Gene M. Tucker

edited by
Stephen Breck Reid

Journal for the Study of the Old Testament
Supplement Series 229

Copyright © 1996 Sheffield Academic Press

Published by Sheffield Academic Press Ltd
Mansion House
19 Kingfield Road
Sheffield S11 9AS
England

Printed on acid-free paper in Great Britain
by Bookcraft Ltd
Midsomer Norton, Bath

British Library Cataloguing in Publication Data

A catalogue record for this book is available
from the British Library

ISBN 1-85075-630-9

CONTENTS

Part I
PROPHETS

Part II
PARADIGMS

PREFACE

Gene Tucker has been a pivotal person in the lives of people from around the world who come together to honor him with this Festschrift. For some of us he has been a teacher, for some an associate, for some a student, but to all of us he has been a respected and dedicated scholar. We present this volume to him as recognition of his work and service to the field of theology.

Every book project is a collaboration; a collection of essays in honor of a scholar and teacher requires even more collaboration than usual. I want to specifically thank the contributors for their attentiveness to detail and flexibility as we brought this project to a successful conclusion. The support of Austin Presbyterian Theological Seminary and its president Robert M. Shelton made the publication possible, through the good work of Jeanne French, Fern Davis, Lesley Blair, Dan Loomis and Gene Luna with the Stitt Library staff. Without their work this project would not have moved as smoothly. Finally my appreciation goes to the people of Sheffield Academic Press—Philip Davies with whom I initially broached the idea, Managing Editor Steve Barganski and Carol Smith who provided invaluable insight and direction. Thanks to you all.

A SHORT BIOGRAPHY OF GENE TUCKER

Gene Milton Tucker was born on January 8, 1935 in Albany, Texas. He graduated from McMurry College and married his high school sweetheart in 1957 (BA). He moved with his bride to New Haven, Connecticut and Yale Divinity School. He took three degrees (BD in 1960, MA in 1961, and PhD in 1963). During this time he was introduced to form criticism and imbibed a passion for the theological reflection on the Hebrew Scriptures. His major teachers at Yale were Brevard Childs and Marvin Pope, and such visiting scholars as Walther Zimmerli and Erhard Gerstenberger. His dissertation on 'Contracts in the Old Testament: A Form Critical Investigation' exhibits a preliminary foray into what would become his life's work.

He began his teaching career at the University of Southern California (1963–66). While in southern California he met Rolf Knierim, a student of Gerhard von Rad. The two of them would organize the form-critical project which produced the Forms of the Old Testament Literature series published by Eerdmans. He left southern California for the east coast and a teaching position in a major Methodist seminary, Duke Divinity School (1966–70).

Most of his teaching career was as a member of the faculty of Candler School of Theology at Emory University (1970–95). When he went to Emory the seminary Candler School of Theology had a long history but the PhD program was fairly new. He was one of the first faculty members of what has become a leading doctoral program in Hebrew Bible.

Early in his career he wrote a short introduction to form criticism of the Old Testament entitled *Form Criticism of the Old Testament* (Philadelphia: Fortress Press) in the Guides to Biblical Scholarship series of which he would soon become Old Testament editor, replacing J. Coert Rylaarsdam. His short introduction to form criticism in a succinct way defined his understanding of the method. At places it intentionally varied from the Biblischer Kommentar series, then the premier form-critical commentary, especially in the understanding of setting and structure as relevant for form-critical analysis.

One of his earliest publications was on the Joshua material ('The Rahab Saga: Some Form Critical and Traditio-Historical Observations', in *The Old Testament in the New and Other Essays* [Durham, NC: Duke University, 1972]). This led naturally to a collaboration on a Joshua commentary with J. Maxwell Miller (Cambridge: Cambridge University Press, 1974). Tucker, even though his research focused on form criticism and literary analysis, always remembered and told his students that biblical studies was a historical discipline. Therefore, collaborating on a commentary on Joshua fit his self-understanding, as a biblical scholar should participate in the debate about the ancient world. As part of this commitment Tucker maintained membership in the American Schools of Oriental Research and the American Oriental Society.

The modern biblical scholar is both a historian and a theologian. This comes through in his co-authored piece on 'Exegesis' in the *Interpreter's Dictionary of the Bible* (ed. G. Buttrick; Nashville: Abingdon Press, 1976). Also in keeping with this self-understanding Tucker was a member of the American Academy of Religion.

Not only did Tucker give of himself to his research, but he was also an active force in his professional society and in Candler School of Theology. As a member of the Candler faculty he exhibited leadership and served for a time as academic dean (1978–88). As a member and leader in the Society of Biblical Literature he served as a member and then chair of the research and publications committee for many years. In that capacity he helped promote research projects and edited works that investigated the history of the discipline of biblical studies, such as the *Hebrew Bible and its Interpreters*, as well as *Humanizing America's Iconic Book*. During that time he saw the Society blossom and grow from a meeting over Christmas, usually at Union Seminary in New York, to the huge gathering it is today. He continued to serve the society as President.

He edited projects outside of the Society of Biblical Literature as well. He was one of the editors of the Brevard Childs *Festschrift* entitled *Canon, Theology, and Old Testament* (Fortress Press). He and Rolf Knierim are piloting the FOTL commentary series. His contribution to the series will be a work on Amos and Hosea. Tucker's deep commitments to justice and theology have made the eighth-century prophets irresistible objects of study and conversation partners over the years.

ABBREVIATIONS

AAR	American Academy of Religion
AB	Anchor Bible
ABRL	Anchor Bible Research Library
ABD	*Anchor Bible Dictionary*
AJSL	*American Journal of Semitic Languages and Literatures*
ANET	J.B. Pritchard (ed.), *Ancient Near Eastern Texts*
ArOr	*Archiv orientálni*
ASOR	American School of Oriental Research
BA	*Biblical Archaeologist*
BARev	*Biblical Archaeology Review*
BASOR	*Bulletin of the American Schools of Oriental Research*
BDB	F. Brown, S.R. Driver and C.A. Briggs, *Hebrew and English Lexicon of the Old Testament*
BETL	Bibliotheca ephemeridum theologicarum lovaniensium
BHT	Beiträge zur historischen Theologie
BI	*Biblical Interpretation*
Bib	*Biblica*
BSac	*Bibliotheca Sacra*
BTB	*Biblical Theology Bulletin*
BWANT	Beiträge zur Wissenschaft vom Alten und Neuen Testament
BZAW	Beihefte zur *ZAW*
CBQ	*Catholic Biblical Quarterly*
CBQMS	*Catholic Biblical Quarterly*, Monograph Series
ConBOT	Coniectanea biblica, Old Testament
FOTL	The Forms of the Old Testament Literature
HAR	*Hebrew Annual Review*
HAT	Handbuch zum Alten Testament
HBT	*Horizons in Biblical Theology*
HSM	Harvard Semitic Monographs
HTR	*Harvard Theological Review*
HUCA	*Hebrew Union College Annual*
ICC	International Critical Commentary
IEJ	*Israel Exploration Journal*
Int	*Interpretation*
JAAR	*Journal of the American Academy of Religion*
JBL	*Journal of Biblical Literature*
JBR	*Journal of Bible and Religion*
JCS	*Journal of Cuneiform Studies*
JNES	*Journal of Near Eastern Studies*

JPOS	Journal of the Palestine Oriental Society
JQR	Jewish Quarterly Review
JR	Journal of Religion
JSOT	Journal for the Study of the Old Testament
JSOTSup	Journal for the Study of the Old Testament, Supplement Series
JSS	Journal of Semitic Studies
JTS	Journal of Theological Studies
NCB	New Century Bible
NRT	La nouvelle revue théologique
OBT	Overtures to Biblical Theology
OTL	Old Testament Library
OTS	Oudtestamentische Studiën
RevScRel	Revue des sciences religieuses
SBL	Society of Biblical Literature
SBLDS	SBL Dissertation Series
SBLMS	SBL Monograph Series
SBLSP	SBL Seminar Papers
SBS	Stuttgarter Bibelstudien
Sem	Semitica
SJT	Scottish Journal of Theology
ST	Studia theologica
TDOT	G.J. Botterweck and H. Ringgren (eds.), Theological Dictionary of the Old Testament
TQ	Theologische Quartalschrift
VT	Vetus Testamentum
VTSup	Vetus Testamentum, Supplements
WBC	Word Biblical Commentary
WMANT	Wissenschaftliche Monographien zum Alten und Neuen Testament
ZAW	Zeitschrift für die alttestamentliche Wissenschaft
ZDMG	Zeitschrift der deutschen morgenländischen Gesellschaft
ZDPV	Zeitschrift des deutschen Palästina-Vereins
ZTK	Zeitschrift für Theologie und Kirche

LIST OF CONTRIBUTORS

Walter Brueggemann, Columbia Theological Seminary, USA

J. Andrew Dearman, Austin Presbyterian Theological Seminary, USA

Philip R. Davies, University of Sheffield

Roy F. Melugin, Austin College, USA

Martin J. Buss, Emory University, USA

Thomas W. Overholt, University of Wisconsin-Stevens Point, USA

Guillermo Ramírez, Puerto Rico

Ehud Ben Zvi, University of Alberta, Canada

Norman K. Gottwald, New York Theological Seminary, USA

Burke O. Long, Bowdoin College, USA

Frank H. Gorman, Jr, Bethany College, USA

Suzanne Boorer, Murdoch University, Australia

Yehoshua Gitay, University of Cape Town, South Africa

Stephen Breck Reid, Austin Presbyterian Theological Seminary, USA

Part I
PROPHETS

A 'CHARACTERISTIC' REFLECTION ON WHAT COMES NEXT
(JEREMIAH 32.16-44)

Walter Brueggemann

It is a delight to offer an essay in acknowledgment of Gene Tucker's major contribution to our common life of teaching and scholarship. For me, as for many others, he has been a reliable and generous source of support and encouragement.

In his Yale dissertation and in derivative studies, Tucker paid attention to 'contracts', including the contractual arrangement of Jeremiah in his purchase of his family's patrimony (Jer. 32.1-15).[1] Tucker's investigation concerned the form of the contract itself and therefore he did not venture into 32.16-44, which I now propose to take up. Whereas his interest was primarily form-critical, my own study is concerned with this 'supplement' to the narrative of contract as a piece of characteristic theological reflection in the faith of ancient Israel.

A possible way to organize a theology of the Old Testament/Hebrew Bible is to pay attention to the most 'characteristic' speech of Israel about God.[2] By such rhetoric, I refer to frequently recurring phrases, words, and themes which Israel regularly employed in what appear to be situations of urgency, when Israel is forced back to its most reliable rhetorical resources.[3] To be sure, a judgment about what is 'characteristic'

---

1. G.M. Tucker, 'The Legal Background of Genesis 23', *JBL* 85 (1966), pp. 77-84, and 'Covenant Forms and Contract Forms', *VT* 15 (1965), pp. 487-503. In the latter article Tucker mentions the narrative of Jer. 32.1-15.

2. W. Brueggemann, 'Crisis-Evoked, Crisis-Resolving Speech', *BTB* 24 (1994), pp. 95-105. For such characteristic speech, H. Fisch (*Poetry with a Purpose: Biblical Poetics and Interpretation* [Bloomington: Indiana University Press, 1988], p. 188) uses the happy term 'covenantal discourse'. In such characteristic speech, we may identify the modes of the 'grammar' of Israel's faith.

3. I have recently explored the ways in which rhetoric is decisive for the faith and theological work of Israel, that is, a speech practice not dependent upon any 'essentialism'; W. Brueggemann, 'Texts that Linger, Not Yet Overcome', forthcoming in *Festschrift for James L. Crenshaw*.

is to some extent subjective. I believe, nonetheless, that such a procedure would have served von Rad well in his credo hypothesis.[4] Instead of arguing, as he unsuccessfully did, that the credo recitals are very early, he might have argued only that they are 'characteristic', thus avoiding the insoluble problems of historicity. Here I focus on Jer. 32.16-44, in order to examine the ways in which it articulates what is characteristic in the faith-rhetoric of Israel.

I

The literature upon these verses is not very extensive nor very helpful.[5] It is largely preoccupied with two questions: (1) a determination of what is 'authentic' and what is 'expansion' from the words of the prophet, and (2) what allusions to preceding literature can be identified as the 'sources' of the present phrasing.[6]

On the first question, scholars are largely predictable in their conclusions. William Holladay seeks to match text to occasion with some precision, and Robert Carroll regards the text as an exercise in late scribal activity.[7] Christopher Seitz is surely in broader sweep correct that

4.   G. von Rad, *The Problem of the Hexateuch and Other Essays* (New York: McGraw-Hill, 1966), pp. 1-78. There are now many well-established critiques of von Rad's program. Among the earliest of these was J.P. Hyatt, 'Were there an Ancient Historical Credo in Israel and an Independent Sinai Tradition?', in H.T. Frank and W.L. Reed (eds.), *Translating and Understanding the Old Testament* (Nashville: Abingdon Press, 1970), pp. 152-70. P.D. Miller, *The Divine Warrior in Early Israel* (Cambridge, MA: Harvard University Press, 1973), pp. 166-70, facing von Rad's problem on the credo, has alternatively suggested Exod. 15 as a candidate for model credo; but he still seeks 'early' and not 'characteristic' speech.

5.   In addition to the influential commentaries of W.L. Holladay and R.P. Carroll, studies pertinent to our text include P. Diepold, *Israel's Land* (BWANT, 5; Berlin: Kohlhammer, 1972), E.W. Nicholson, *Preaching to the Exiles: A Study of the Prose Tradition in the Book of Jeremiah* (Oxford: Basil Blackwell, 1970), C.R. Seitz, *Theology in Conflict: Reactions to the Exile in the Book of Jeremiah* (BZAW, 176; Berlin: de Gruyter, 1989), G. Wanke, *Untersuchungen zur sogenannten Baruchschrift* (BZAW, 122; Berlin: de Gruyter, 1971), and H. Weippert, *Die Prosareden des Jeremiabuches* (BZAW, 132; Berlin: de Gruyter, 1973). None of these studies, however, deals with this text in any extensive way at all.

6.   These issues are carefully and thoroughly reviewed by W.L. Holladay, *Jeremiah 2: A Commentary on the Book of the Prophet Jeremiah Chapters 26–52* (Hermeneia; Minneapolis: Fortress Press, 1989), pp. 202-20.

7.   R.P. Carroll, *Jeremiah: A Commentary* (OTL; Philadelphia: Westminster Press, 1986), p. 625 and *passim*.

the whole is a 'concluding supplement', whereby a specific reference to the land has been transposed into a general statement about Israel's future.[8] For our purposes, the delegitimation of what is not 'authentic' is inappropriate and unhelpful, for we are concerned with the rhetorical-theological shape and intention of the whole.

A like answer to the second question, identification of allusions to extant sources, may be given.[9] It is beyond doubt that these verses are a veritable collage of antecedent usages. It is, however, their present configuration and function that interest us. Thus on neither question need issues of 'excavative' criticism long detain us.[10]

II

It is of course recognized that these verses, which no doubt had a complex literary history, are divided into two forms, a prayer of Jeremiah (vv. 16-25) and an oracular response by Yahweh (vv. 26-44). Scholars have of course recognized that the opening verse of the prayer (v. 17) and the opening verse of the oracle (v. 27) are paralleled in their common use of the term *pela'*, which in the NRSV is rendered 'too hard'.[11] It is curious, and perhaps worth noting, that the use of *pela'* in the prayer is an indicative assertion, and in the response, it is a question. These two uses are perhaps inverted from what we might expect. The form of prayer and oracular response might have led us to expect a question in the prayer and an assertion in the oracle, but the text has it otherwise. It will be my plan to take up in turn the prayer and the oracle, and then to consider the function of the whole, after the narrative of contract in vv. 9-14 and after the remarkable oracle of promise in v. 15.

8.   Seitz, *Theology in Conflict*, p. 212 n. 13.

9.   On these allusions, which may take a variety of forms, see R.B. Hayes, *Echoes of Scripture in the Letters of Paul* (New Haven: Yale University Press, 1989), pp. 18-20 and *passim*. Hayes takes over the notion of literary 'echoes' from J. Hollander.

10.   R. Alter (*The World of Biblical Literature* [New York: Basic Books, 1992], p. 133) uses the term 'excavative' to refer to reading methods which approach the biblical text by way of philology, archaeology and comparative ancient religions.

11.   Holladay (*Jeremiah 2*, p. 206) suggests that Gen. 18.14 is the source for both vv. 17 and 27. On the Genesis text, see W. Brueggemann, '"Impossibility" and Epistemology in the Faith Traditions of Abraham and Sarah (Genesis 18.1-15)', *ZAW* 94 (1982), pp. 615-34.

III

The first part of our text is cast as a prayer of Jeremiah (vv. 16-25). While the casting of the prayer is not unimportant, it is important to recognize, with Samuel Balentine, that prayers in prose texts of the Old Testament/Hebrew Bible can serve 'as a means of conveying ideological and theological perspectives'.[12] At that level this prayer, in the mouth of the prophet, is an exercise of Israel's recurring issue of theodicy. The issue of theodicy, in the world of ancient Israel, is not, as it has become in the modern world, a speculative problem. It is rather a concrete pastoral theological crisis, because Israel, with Job-like determination, clings passionately and relentlessly to the conviction that coherent moral sense can be made of its lived experience by reference to the will, purpose and commands of Yahweh. Were Israel to give up that conviction, the practical problem of theodicy would evaporate: but of course Israel cannot and will not give it up.

Following Greenberg, Balentine rightly insists that such prayers must be understood in their narrative context.[13] Thus, even if vv. 16-25 are 'late' and 'expansionist', in context they are evoked by the preceding narrative which jarringly articulates Israel's sense of incongruity between lived reality and Yahweh's voiced purpose. The incongruity concerns the lived experience of destruction and displacement and the voiced purpose of rehabilitation and resettlement. Israel, moreover, has no way to process this incongruity except to reuse its classic modes of rhetoric in daring and venturesome ways.

The intention of the prayer is to enter faithfully and unflinchingly into that profound incongruity, and to see what sense can be made. One can characterize the mood of the prayer as one of trustful incredulity, that is, the praying voice takes the command and promise of v. 15 as 'absurd',[14] but at the same time obeys and does not doubt. In coping with this deep incongruity, which is context-specific to 32.1-15 but which is also paradigmatic for Israel's faith, the prayer must mobilize Israel's rich resources of rhetoric that here are brought together in a remarkable

12. S. Balentine, *Prayer in the Hebrew Bible: The Drama of Divine–Human Dialogue* (OBT; Minneapolis: Fortress Press, 1993), p. 12.

13. *Prayer in the Hebrew Bible*, p. 27. See M. Greenberg, *Biblical Prose Prayer as a Window to the Popular Religion of Ancient Israel* (Berkeley: University of California Press, 1983), p. 8.

14. See Carroll, *Jeremiah*, p. 625.

theological statement.[15] Thus it may be that there is 'literary growth' here, but in the final form of the text, one must ask how these several rhetorical strategies together serve Israel's faith in the face of Yahweh's staggering reversal of intention.

We may identify five rhetorical strategies, that is, characteristic modes of speech, which together constitute the prayer.[16]

1. After the narrative introduction of v. 16, the prayer is set in the context of *doxology* (vv. 17, 18b-19a). The opening ejaculation, *'ahah*, is a cry which characteristically responds to an unexpected divine announcement, most often negative.[17] The doxology focuses upon Yahweh's strength and power, as evidenced in the creation of heaven and earth. (As we shall see, there is a dimension of creation theology here, used to enhance Yahweh's splendor. That accent is not nearly as prominent in the oracle which follows.) It is the doxology about the wonder of creation that leads to the affirmation that Yahweh is *pela'*! Creation itself is confirming evidence that Yahweh is capable of anything, anything regarded by humankind as 'impossible' (*kol-dabar*).[18] The doxology continues in vv. 18b-19a with the assertion:

> O great and mighty God whose name is the Lord of hosts,
> great in counsel and mighty in deed; whose eyes are
> open to all the ways of mortals...

Yahweh is extolled for power and for watchful monitoring of the whole of creation. The language here appears to be influenced by sapiential

---

15. Carroll (*Jeremiah*, p. 621) regards the entire narrative about the purchase of the land as a 'paradigmatic account'. Because of that, Carroll regards the historical character of the event as being undermined. For my purpose, I am content to disregard the question of historicity and work with what is the ostensive history of the text.

16. I choose here to speak of 'rhetorical strategies'. In a paper honoring Gene Tucker, it is important to recognize that what have come to be called rhetorical strategies are in fact closely related to literary forms, on which see G. Tucker, *Form Criticism of the Old Testament* (Guides to Biblical Scholarship; Philadelphia: Fortress Press, 1971). I prefer the much more dynamic nomenclature of 'strategy', because we are enquiring about what the text intends to accomplish.

17. See the other texts in *BDB*, p. 13.

18. The phrase 'Lord of Hosts' is missing from the LXX. Here and in a number of places the MT of our chapter is longer. None of these differences, however, distract from my argument. On the comparison of texts, see J.G. Janzen, *Studies in the Text of Jeremiah* (Cambridge, MA: Harvard University Press, 1973).

traditions, for Yahweh is thus the guarantor and orderer of all of creation.[19]

2. The doxology of vv. 17, 18b-19a is intertwined in vv. 18a, 19b with a different, though not unrelated, pattern of rhetoric. In these two half verses, reference is made to the ancient formula of Exod. 34.6-7 which articulates a *structure of 'deed–consequence'* concerning God's commands.[20] This formulation, deeply rooted in the tradition of Moses, voices a two-sidedness if not contradiction in Israel's faith. God does ḥesed (cf. Exod. 34.6a). This text, however, does not linger over that positive affirmation. Its intent, rather, is in the two verbs, *šlm* and *pqd*, which seem to pick up themes from Exod. 34.7b, concerning tight moral accountability.[21] Thus right into the next generation, just deserts are assured, especially negative ones. The provision for ḥesed is not negated, but ḥesed is clearly marked by a requirement of reciprocity. The prayer thus far has set in close juxtaposition a *doxology* and a statement of *rigorous covenantal accountability*. It has, however, exhibited no interest in the relation between the two statements.

3. In the long middle section of this passage (vv. 20-23a), the prayer makes use of the elements of a *well-established* credo.[22] The key elements in the recital, of course are deliverance from Egypt and entry into the land. The latter point is grounded in the promise to the ancestors.[23] It is worth noting here the language of 'sign and wonder',

---

19. It is not unproblematic to identify something as 'sapiential', as J.L. Crenshaw has made clear. I refer to the theological claim that Yahweh is the upholder and guarantor of an order that is both cosmic and moral, and not one who intrudes with concrete acts. The contrast has been well articulated by C. Westermann, *Elements of Old Testament Theology* (Atlanta: John Knox Press, 1978), Part III. It is not clear that this is necessarily 'sapiential'. See H.H. Schmid, *Gerechtigkeit als Weltordnung* (BHT, 40: Tübingen: Mohr [Paul Siebeck], 1968).

20. The classic presentation of this construct is that of K. Koch, 'Gibt es ein Vergeltungsdogma im Alten Testament?', *ZTK* 52 (1955), pp. 1-22. An abridged version in English is 'Is there a Doctrine of Retribution in the Old Testament?', in J.L. Crenshaw (ed.), *Theodicy in the Old Testament* (Philadelphia: Fortress Press, 1983), pp. 57-87.

21. Koch ('Is there a Doctrine of Retribution', pp. 60-61, 75-78) pays attention to both of these verbs. In n. 40, Koch acknowledges his debt to K. Fahlgren, *Sedaka, nahestehende und entgegengesetzte Begriffe im Alten Testament* (Uppsala: Almquist & Wiksell, 1932).

22. See n. 4. Von Rad's credo hypothesis has been reiterated in many places, and has now been critiqued as well in many places.

23. On the crucial nature of the ancestral narratives for the 'Mosaic events' of the

terms not unrelated to *pela'* in v. 17. In this usage, the rhetoric is completely confined to Israel's communal experience. It includes nothing of a more comprehensive (creation) horizon, as is found both in the doxology and in the derivative use of the deeds–consequence formulation of Exod. 34.6-7, which in this text speaks of 'all the ways of the sons of *'adam*' (v. 19). Here the rhetoric is drawn much closer to the specific content of Israel's glorious past, which concretely attests to Yahweh's capacity to do 'hard things'.

4.   As might be expected in the tradition of Jeremiah–Deuteronomy, the unreservedly positive recital of vv. 20-23a is quickly broken off.[24] It is followed in vv. 23b-24 with an abrupt adversative *waw*, which introduces a *law-suit form*. The indictment is filled out with three negatives, 'not listen, not walk in, not do'. Israel is completely recalcitrant and unresponsive to Yahweh's actions.

The indictment is matched by a sentence, also introduced with an abrupt *waw* (v. 23b), rendered in NRSV by 'therefore'. Oddly enough, the sentence stays in the voice of the prayer and addresses the punishing God in the third person, 'you summoned'. After the general announcement of 'evils' (disasters) (v. 23b), the sentence consists in the specificity of the siege-ramps of the Babylonians, and then is generalized by the stylized formulary, 'sword, famine, pestilence'. In a quite brief statement, the covenant curses have been voiced in three distinct ways, 'disasters, siege-ramps, and sword/famine/pestilence'.

We have seen that the prayer does not trouble over the tension between doxology and the assertion of tight moral accountability as deeds–consequence. Now, in parallel fashion, the prayer does not linger over the devastating juxtaposition of positive recital (vv. 20-23a) and the harsh law-suit (vv. 23b-24) which seems to negate the recital.[25] Such a juxtaposition compels the reader to conclude that Jerusalem has come to its final ending in sword, famine and pestilence, without any sustaining power from those old remembered deeds. Such a sequence of *recital/law-*

credo, see R.W.L. Moberly, *The Old Testament of the Old Testament: Patriarchal Narratives and Mosaic Yahwism* (OBT; Minneapolis: Fortress Press, 1992).

24.   I have chosen simply to speak of the tradition of 'Jeremiah–Deuteronomy'. The complexity of the relation between Jeremiah and the Deuteronomic tradition is yet to be sorted out. Here I simply refer to that entire complex tradition without needing to probe those complexities.

25.   On the negation and inversion of the credo, see the way in which the language of Exodus is turned against Israel in Jer. 21.5-6. See W.L. Moran, 'The End of the Unholy War and the Anti-Exodus', *Bib* 44 (1963), pp. 333-42.

suit presents a complete and coherent theodicy. 'Evil' comes from doing 'evil'. Evil evokes God's response in kind.[26] Such a way of reasoning provides a demonstrable vindication of the tight moral reasoning of vv. 18b-19a, which allude back to Exod. 34.7b. Yahweh

> will by no means clear the guilty,
> but visiting the iniquity of the parents

The two terms 'iniquity' (*'wn*) and 'visit' (*pqd*) in these verses are the same as in Exod. 34.7b. Yahweh is serious and cannot be mocked. Jerusalem has come to its rightful termination, as already forewarned in the oldest Mosaic tradition. The entire tradition of Jeremiah–Deuteronomy has been aimed at such a theodic conclusion.

5. Such a conclusion, however, does not yet reckon with the context in which the prayer is set. In v. 25, we encounter yet another abrupt *waw* which turns the cogent theodicy of vv. 18b, 19b-24 on its head by a reiteration of the earlier divine oracle of v. 15.[27] Verse 25 seems to jump over the carefully wrought theodic statement of the main body of the prayer, back to the initial doxology of v. 17. Here again is the foundational address, '*adonai* YHWH', we heard in v. 17. And here again is the full pronoun *'attah*, addressed to Yahweh as in v. 17. And here again is a reference back to Yahweh's magisterial performance. In v. 17, it is 'you made', here it is 'you said'. The two assertions form an envelope around the more conventional theodicy and appeal to the creating, asserting God who is capable of anything *(kol-dabar)*, even an 'impossibility'. The primal impossibility of v. 17 is 'the heavens and the earth'.

Now the impossibility is 'Buy the field...though' (v. 25).[28] In truth, Yahweh did not utter the imperative 'buy' in this verse, as is here claimed. It was Jeremiah's cousin Hanamel who spoke the word as an imperative (vv. 7-8), but his utterance is taken as 'the word of the Lord' (v. 8). The instruction to buy contradicts everything on the horizon, the

---

26. P.D. Miller, Jr, *Sin and Judgment in the Prophets* (Chicago: Scholars Press, 1982) has explored this understanding of covenantal curse and prophetic sentence. Miller has also included a close critique of Koch's notion of 'deed–consequence'.

27. It is worth noting that while v. 25 alludes back to the oracle of v. 15, in fact it is not strictly a reiteration. In v. 15, the key verb 'buy' (*qnh*) is in the *niph'al*, but in v. 25 it has become a *qal* imperative. The form in v. 25 is consistent with the narrative use of the verb in vv. 7-8, in the mouth of Hanamel.

28. The term rendered 'though' in the NRSV helps to make sense of the adversative force in the verse, but in fact the Hebrew is yet again a powerful *waw*.

current reality of Babylonian occupation as well as Israel's carefully reasoned theodicy which justifies a harsh ending wrought by Yahweh.

The carefully framed structure of the prayer in five elements is:

doxology (vv. 17, 18b-19a)

theodicy (vv. 18a, 19b-24)
— statement of *deeds–consequences*
— *recital* of saving deeds
— *law-suit*

reiteration of *divine oracle* (v. 25).

The completed prayer takes into full account Israel's normal covenantal reasoning which squares completely with the current situation of Jerusalem. The whole makes coherent sense of faith and experience, both of which now face an exhausted, drastic ending. The purpose of the prayer, however, is to confront both experience and tradition by a new disclosure that is rooted in doxology and eventuates in a coming possibility, authorizing a present human act of daring obedience. This divine oracle of command and promise is not rooted either in the old tradition of covenant or in the present circumstance of defeat, but is a new utterance.

The prayer thus makes use of Israel's most trusted, characteristic theological rhetoric in order to utter a newness that violates all trusted rhetoric. The arrangement of the theodicy in the main body of the prayer (vv. 18a, 19b-24) had permitted the law-suit to veto the recital. The law-suit had won. Except for the God of *pela'*! The wonder of all creation in v. 17 comes down to a specific transaction that the context defines as nonsensical. In the end, this explosive rhetoric pushed Israel out of its perceived context into a world grounded only in the speech of the God for whom nothing is too hard.

IV

The oracle of Yahweh (vv. 26-44) is positioned to be a response to the prayer of vv. 16-25.[29] No indication is given in the text, however, that the oracle is a response. But if my reading is correct, that the affirmation of Yahweh's *pela'* in v. 17 leads to the command of v. 25 which over-

29. For purposes of convenience, I shall refer to all of vv. 26-44 as 'an oracle'. While all its parts belong to that form of speech, the several 'messenger formulae' indicate that it is no single speech. Treatment of it in the singular is convenient for contrasting it with the preceding prayer, but my analysis will consider each element separately.

rides the conventional rhetoric of vv. 19b-24, then a response from Yahweh is not inappropriate. Verse 25 converts the promise of v. 15 into an imperative. But the prayer appears to end in v. 25 with a puzzlement. The speaker cannot fathom that in the face of the theodicy of vv. 19b-24, the command of v. 25 is uttered. What can it mean? How shall it be understood? Is it serious? Is it possible? Shall it be acted upon? In the present arrangement of the text, we may take the two large units as prayer and response, even if the oracle was originally independent, or added only later to this expanded text.

As prayer and response, we may notice, the structural arrangement is not unlike that of the book of Job. In the book of Job, there are three primary voices, the explanatory friends, the unaccepting Job, and the lordly resolution.[30] Here the explanatory element of faith is voiced in vv. 19b-24, and the voice beyond convention is in vv. 17, 25. And now comes the lordly resolution.

The oracle is marked by four messenger formulae in vv. 26, 27, 36 and 42, perhaps signs of ongoing supplementation and expansion. I will consider each of these units separately, even though they are not proportionate in length to each other.

1. The first messenger formula in v. 26 introduces only the brief, freighted statement of v. 27. This initial and abrupt statement of Yahweh consists in three parts. First, there is the ejaculatory particle, *hinneh*. Secondly, there is the self-assertion of Yahweh as 'the God of all flesh'. And thirdly, there is a rhetorical question (in the same form as Gen. 18.14), enquiries about Yahweh's capacity to do *pela'*. The three elements function in the present setting in ways that correspond to the three elements of v. 17 in the prayer: (1) the ejaculatory particle is matched in v. 17 by *'ahah*, (2) there is a doxology about creation, and (3) an assertion of *pela'*. Thus the oracle, like the prayer, begins with a sweeping assertion, rooted in the wonder of creation, here signified by 'all flesh'. This doxological claim is then extended to any and all *pela'*. The God who governs 'all flesh' can indeed do 'all things' (*kol-dabar* in v. 17). The sentence in v. 27 concerning *pela'*, unlike the parallel

---

30. On these voices, see Walter Brueggemann, 'The Third World of Evangelical Imagination', *HBT* 8.2 (1986), pp. 61-84. J.A. Wharton ('The Unanswerable Answer: An Interpretation of Job', in W.E. March [ed.], *Texts and Testaments* (San Antonio: Trinity University Press, 1980], pp. 37-70) has seen that even though the response of Yahweh in Job 38.1ff. is severe and uncompromising, it is a response, which is what Job most wanted and sought.

statement in v. 17, is not an assertion but a question. It may be that this is simply a rhetorical question. Or it may be a serious probing question which intends to evoke an answer and a commitment from the one who prays.[31] In either case, the subject is again surfaced, but with much less of a conclusive statement.

2. The much longer speech, introduced by the second messenger formula of v. 28, concerns a *law-suit speech* (vv. 28-35). As one might expect, the sentence concerning the fate of the city at the hands of the Babylonians is interwoven with a series of massive indictments. The sentence is confined to vv. 28-29a and 31b and concerns the sure destruction of the city. The indictment is much more extensive (vv. 29b-31a, 32-35). The indictment remains general through v. 33, even though there is specificity about the list of perpetrators in v. 32. The governing language of the Deuteronomic tradition concerns 'evil, provoke, arouses, evil, provoke'. The only specificity is found in vv. 34-35 concerning the abomination and high places, offering to Molech, but even that statement is stylized.[32] The only other element is the characteristic exceptionalism that Yahweh did make special efforts concerning Judah but these also were resisted (cf. 2 Kgs 17.18-20).

The outcome and intent of this second 'message' is that Judah is locked with Yahweh into a hopeless process of disobedience and commensurate punishment. The oracle does not indicate that the destruction of Jerusalem is itself a *pela'* but we may infer that this event is an unthinkable wonder which was judged to be 'impossible'. It is unthinkable, but surely credible in Yahweh's world of *šlm* and *pqd*, given us in the prayer (vv. 18-19). Thus again, we have a self-contained, all-encompassing theodicy which leaves no element unaccounted for.

3. The third messenger formula (v. 36) is clearly the decisive one in this long oracle. Unlike the other three formulae, it is introduced with *we'attah* and marks a decisive discontinuity from the preceding utter-

---

31. On the possibility of this intention for rhetorical questions on the lips of Yahweh, see J.G. Janzen, 'Metaphor and Reality in Hosea 11', *Semeia* 24 (1982), pp. 7-44. Holladay (*Jeremiah 2*, p. 212) suggests that the question is ironic.

32. For a possible historical-theological understanding of the offering of children to Molech, see J.D. Levenson, *The Death and Resurrection of the Beloved Son: The Transformation of Child Sacrifice in Judaism and Christianity* (New Haven: Yale University Press, 1993), pp. 3-52. We can see in these indictments a move from the general and stylized to the concrete, just as we have seen in the sentences in vv. 23b-24.

ances.[33] The MT has *lakēn* (lacking in LXX) which is a curious use given the *non sequitur* which follows. What comes now is not 'therefore'. It comes from nowhere, except out of the unfettered mouth of Yahweh.

The subject of this third message is again the city, the one just under massive nullification in vv. 28-31. The city is the one under the formulaic abuse of 'sword, famine, pestilence' (cf. v. 24). Verse 36, however, treats all of this negativity only as a dependent clause. The main clause begins in v. 37 with a marker, *hinnî* (cf. v. 27). The utterance now introduces three new and powerful verbs:

> I will gather,
> I will return,
> I will settle.

These verses do not deny what has previously been said (and experienced), for they are voiced in an immediate context of 'anger, wrath, and indignation'.[34] But now, the culminating point is *lbṭḥ* ('in safety'). Because of these three verbs, all will be well. There is no explanation given, no linkage to the rightful punishment just announced, but a new announcement, preceded only by a magisterial messenger formula.

This startling assertion, surely a *pela'* as wondrous as anything in the old recital, is reinforced by a series of assertions in vv. 38-41 which bespeak the making of new covenant. In v. 38, the standard 'covenant formula' is uttered which figures so prominently in the exilic hope of the books of Jeremiah and Ezekiel.[35] This formula is followed by the promise of 'one heart' and 'one way', whereby Israel (Judah, Jerusalem) will be gladly committed to obedience, with a positive inclination and without any resentful grudge or resistance.[36] That new obedience, moreover, will

33. J. Muilenburg, 'The Form and Structure of the Covenantal Formulation', *VT* 9 (1959), pp. 347-65 has, in passing, pertinent observations on the particle *we'attah*.

34. In speaking of what Jerusalem 'experienced', I refer to the ostensible experience reflected in the text. Such an 'experience' may indeed be fictive, and it may be that the notion of 'exile' is primarily an ideological concept. I do not claim more than what is in the text itself for 'experience', which may indeed be ideology-generated.

35. On the formula, see R. Smend, *Die Bundesformel* (Theologische Studien, 68; Zürich: EVA Verlag, 1963).

36. The modifier 'one' for heart and way is rendered variously in the versions. It is possible that instead of *'ḥd* a Hebrew text had *'ḥr* or *ḥds*, thus to read 'other' or 'new'. Clearly such variants give the phrase a very different nuance, though the intent in any case is clear.

yield 'good', that is, covenant blessings.[37]

The rhetoric of new covenant and its blessing is intensified in vv. 40-41, so that the 'new heart' and 'new way' and the covenant formula are now heightened with the adjective *ôlam*—'everlasting covenant'—in which Yahweh will never turn from doing 'good' and Israel will never depart from 'fear of me'. Both parties are revived to a new and glad mutual fidelity that will not again be disrupted. This remarkable promise, surely a *pela'*, is reinforced in two ways. First, the term *b'emth* (v. 41) corresponds to *lbth* in v. 37. Israel will rest *in security*, Yahweh will plant *in fidelity*. Secondly, the final phrase of v. 41 is typically the phrasing of the tradition of Deuteronomy, 'with all my heart and all my soul'. Except that here the terms pertain to Yahweh's own intense and unreserved resolve for fidelity toward Israel. This is a most extreme and singular commitment on the part of Yahweh. It is not clear that the 'everlasting covenant'[38] is 'unconditional'.[39] Perhaps, in good Deuteronomic fashion, it is conditional upon obedience to torah. But Israel's 'one heart' and 'one way' affirm that Israel will never depart from the torah, and therefore the conditions are assuredly met and the covenant will not and need not be disrupted. That is, the conditions are not abrogated, but guaranteed.

4.   The fourth messenger formula (v. 42) introduces one more assurance which becomes fully concrete after the more relational, covenantal language of vv. 36-41. In v. 24, Yahweh's resolve for 'good' will overcome the 'evil' asserted in vv. 28-35.[40] The term 'good' is continued from vv. 39-41 where it is used three times. The term in the foregoing is undifferentiated, but now 'good' is made quite specific. The reference to 'field' in v. 43 refers back to the promise of v. 15 and the imperative of v. 25.[41] That singular promise in the *niph'al* of v. 15 (unlike the *qal*

37. On the term 'good' as 'covenant blessing', see D.R. Hillers, 'A Note on Some Treaty Terminology in the Old Testament', *BASOR* 176 (1964), pp. 46-47; W.L. Moran, 'A Note on the Treaty Terminology of the Sefire Stetas', *JNES* 22 (1963), pp. 173-76.

38. See n. 36 for this possible rendering.

39. On the problem of the 'unconditional', see S.G. Post, 'Conditional and Unconditional Love', *Modern Theology* 7 (1991), pp. 435-46, and D.H. Wrong, *The Problem of Order: What Unites and Divides Society* (New York: The Free Press, 1994), pp. 42-54.

40. On the displacement of 'evil' by 'good' in the tradition of Jeremiah, see 29.11; 42.6.

41. The term 'field' is singular as it is in v. 25, whereas it is plural in v. 15. The singular seems to stay much closer to the initial command in vv. 7-8 which did refer

imperative in v. 25) is then fully expanded in v. 44, so that 'field' becomes the several geographic regions of Judah and Benjamin, that is, David's patrimony. Finally the whole is tied to ch. 31 (v. 23) and to ch. 33 (vv. 7, 11, 26) by the key phrase 'restore their fortunes'.[42]

In light of my more detailed comments on vv. 16-25, we may now summarize the rhetorical strategies employed in this complex and multifaceted oracle:

1. Verse 27 is a self-announcement of Yahweh which we may take as self-praise, that is, *doxology* in Yahweh's own mouth. The tone is not unlike the whirlwind speeches of the book of Job.

2. The long second message is a *law-suit speech*, an intermingling of indictment and sentence, with primary emphasis upon the former (vv. 28-35).

3. The decisive turn in the passage, with a series of strong verbs, is an anticipatory *recital* of God's transformative, rescuing action which is to come.

4. The tight covenant formulation of vv. 38-41 is not easy to categorize, because the rhetoric is quite complex. For our purposes, I suggest it is a revisitation of the old *deed–consequence* construct of covenantal obedience. This time, however, it is altogether positive. Thus the old assumptions about Israel's recalcitrance which caused the construct to be used primarily for threat and open-ended uncertainty are now overcome by an assurance, in which both parties are sure to do the right deeds and yield the best consequences.

5. The final message of vv. 42-44 is a *promissory oracle* of impossibility.

V

The analysis of rhetorical strategies I have presented makes it clear in some detail that the intention and construction of the prayer and the oracle are closely paralleled. Scholars have of course noted the parallelism concerning *pela'* in vv. 17 and 27. We may observe the following, fuller parallelism which is reasonably comprehensive of both passages:

to a particular field. The plural moves beyond this particular reference in a paradigmatic direction. The versions make adjustment in the term.

42. On this formula and its intention for Israel's hope, see J.M. Bracke, 'The Coherence and Theology of Jeremiah 30–31' (PhD dissertation, Union Theological Seminary, Richmond, 1983), pp. 148-55.

prayer	*oracle*
vv. 17, 18b-19a *doxology*	v. 27 self-praise as *doxology*
vv. 18a, 19b formula of	vv. 38-41 formula of *'deeds–consequence'*
'deeds–consequence'	is now made positive
vv. 20-23 a *recital* of memory	vv. 36-37 a *recital* of anticipation
vv. 23b-24 *law-suit speech*	vv. 28-35 *law-suit speech*
v. 25 *oracle* of impossibility	vv. 42-44 *oracle* of impossibility.

It is not my intention to suggest that these two texts are completely
parallel in either form or substance, nor to force parallels in an excessively rigorous way. Two qualifying comments are especially important.

First, the second element which I have entitled 'formula of deed–
consequence' may be the least compelling parallel. In the prayer this
element is governed by the verbs *šlm* and *pqd*, which together make a
clear case. Such language is absent in vv. 38-41. I suggest a parallel
because vv. 38-41 clearly envision complete obedience and its contingent,
unmitigated 'good'. These verses do not suggest that torah obedience is
any less urgent now or in time to come than it was under the aegis of
Moses, but only that such obedience is now assured. The important
difference between the old economy of obedience and the new is that
vv. 38-41 leave no uncertainty or option, as is reflected in v. 18a, 19b
and in the formula more generally. But that difference makes all the
difference in the envisioned time of well-being which is to come.

Secondly, the recital in vv. 20-23a is conventional and standard. I am
not sure that it is correct to term vv. 36-37 a recital, but it does depend
upon Yahweh's active verbs, as does the old recital. The difference of
course is that what is there stated is all promised and anticipated, not yet
in hand and therefore not remembered. This recital anticipates that
Yahweh's verbs will create *bth*, well-being not unlike the circumstance
of 'milk and honey' wrought in the events of Moses and Joshua.

VI

It is not my purpose to do a form-critical analysis, but to observe complex rhetorical strategies which permit theological reflection and
affirmation in ancient Israel.[43] This rich array of quite distinct forms and

43. The volume of FOTL (Eerdmans) for Jeremiah has not yet appeared, so we
await that detailed analysis. In the meantime I am in fundamental agreement with
J.J. Collins, 'Is a Critical Biblical Theology Possible?', in W.H. Proff *et al.* (eds.),
The Hebrew Bible and its Interpreters (Winona Lake: Eisenbrauns, 1990), pp. 1-17,

rhetorical maneuvers may suggest a process of expansion in this extended text. My impression, however, is that the use of such rhetorical strategies is necessary, not merely to extend the statement, but in order to express exactly the delicate point to be made among exiles concerning the present state of Judah and its future potential intended by Yahweh.

The text does not want to depart from the heavy claims of Israel's old convictions concerning the moral shape and moral accountability of the historical process. This is evident in the prayer, in the formula of deeds and consequences, in the nullification of the old recital and in the law-suit speech, that is, in all those elements I have termed 'theodicy'. In the oracle, the law-suit of vv. 28-35 makes the same point at great length.

This extended reassertion of and insistence upon the moral shape and accountability of Israel's public life, however, does not say everything that here wants to be said. There is in ancient Israel a deep sense of the tension between Yahweh's free capability and Yahweh's steady system of sanctions. The theological intention of both prayer and oracle is to affirm that system of sanctions, but then to give voice to the odd ('impossible') capacity of Yahweh to break out beyond Yahweh's own system of sanctions. The categories for that 'breaking beyond' are, in terms of rhetoric, *doxology, promise, oracle*, and substantively, *pela'*.

By juxtaposing this rich arrangement of available rhetorical strategies, the text evidences how much depends upon utterance, and how diverse and dense are Israel's rhetorical possibilities, in order to bear witness to Yahweh's *fragile order* (creation, moral coherence) in which Israel lives and to the *delicate possibilities* that constitute Israel's world of faith. The abrupt shifts of rhetoric, for example in vv. 25, 36, leave Israel staggered, perhaps breathless (but not speechless). We subsequent readers are left to ponder: what if some scribe (or whoever) had not hosted such profound rhetorical incongruity...what then? But of course, someone did.

VII

In its final form, ch. 32, ostensibly a comment on land purchase, is in truth a mediation upon Yahweh's *pela'*. This peculiar chapter of narrative and prose speech is odd amidst a series of poetic promises in chs. 30-31 and 33. Chapter 32 is odd because it is partly narrative and

that biblical theology must begin with and pay close attention to genre analysis. That is what I have sought to do in this essay.

all prose, and because it concerns such a specific act as the purchase of land. Its purpose is to move Israel to the edge of 'covenantal nomism', and then to plunge beyond it into newness, as Israel had to do in exile.[44] Such breaks beyond the conventional system of covenantal sanctions are not easy or assured. They are hard fought and hard won, partly growing out of Yahweh's resolve and partly out of Israel's daring speech. The chapter moves exiled Israel along to a possibility as wondrous as the creation of 'heaven and earth', 'for all flesh', as concrete as a field signed, sealed and witnessed.

This carefully shaped theological mediation takes on larger canonical power, as subsequent readers are not concerned with Jeremiah's specific patrimony. In adjudicating the odd interface between wondrous creator and beloved creation, this theological reflection asserts the inexplicable chance for newness. That odd interface concerns system and sanction, and perhaps more. The 'more' so readily mocked, yet so greatly treasured by synagogue and church, is the 'more' which Israel still bespeaks to a fated, shut-down world.

It is my impression and urging that in this text we encounter much of Israel's 'characteristic speech'. Of course the old recital, the formulation of deeds and consequences, and the law-suit speech are characteristic. That characteristic speech is broken by a more deeply required speech about *pela'*. This speech, because of the Utterer, also becomes characteristic in Israel. In speech about *pela'*, however, it is Israel's rhetorical work to insist that what seems to be characteristic, *pela'*, is in fact every time inscrutable, inexplicable and uncharacteristic. Israel's rhetorical imagination serves to employ its characteristic ways of speech about this Holy Uncharacteristic Possibility.

Professor Tucker knows all this. I hope he will find my move from *form* to *faith* a credible one, for the legitimacy of our discipline as a public enterprise depends upon some such maneuver.

---

44. The term 'covenantal nomism' is taken from E.P. Sanders, *Paul and Palestinian Judaism* (Philadelphia: Fortress Press, 1977), pp. 511-15 and *passim*. The term is of course an anachronism with reference to Jer. 32, but I believe it accurately connotes what must be affirmed about the requirement of the commandments in emerging Judaism.

THE SON OF TABEEL (ISAIAH 7.6)

J. Andrew Dearman

The name 'Son of Ṭab^e'al' (MT: *ben ṭāb^e'al*; hereafter BT) exists in a single verse (Isa. 7.6). According to the narrative report of Isaiah 7, an Aramean king named Rezin and Pekah, the king of Israel, initiated a campaign against Ahaz, the Judean king and descendant of David, whose seat of rule was Jerusalem. One goal of the campaign was to replace Ahaz with BT. Perusal of the proposals for the identity of BT suggest that even in his obscurity there is something to be learned about the nature of biblical interpretation. Additionally, I have some modest proposals to offer concerning BT in the hope that they will stimulate further discussion. It is a pleasure to dedicate this essay to Gene M. Tucker, scholar, teacher and friend.

Until the exploration of the Middle East by Western scholars, which coincided with a flowering of critical, historical analysis of the biblical text, the obscure reference to BT did not receive much attention. Calvin's comment from the sixteenth century is typical: 'Who this Tabeal was cannot easily be learned from history'.[1] He went on briefly to surmise that BT was an Israelite and an enemy of the Davidic dynasty. The alternative identity of BT espoused by some interpreters was that of an otherwise unknown Aramean (or 'Syrian' in the parlance of other commentators), a conclusion based on the form of the name.[2]

The Late Nineteenth and Early Twentieth Centuries

In the last quarter of the nineteenth century, scholars offered additional suggestions for the identity of BT, based on critical, historical methods of

1. *Commentary on the Prophet Isaiah* (trans. W. Pringle; Grand Rapids: Eerdmans, 1953), p. 235.
2. See the brief comments by H. Ewald, The *History of Israel* (4 vols.; London: Longmans, Green & Co., 1871), pp. 158-59. Ewald also believed that Rezin was the dominant personality in the assault on Jerusalem.

analysis and on the accumulating textual material derived from exploration and archaeology. The analyses of T.K. Cheyne are a good illustration of scholarly trends in this period, although the claims he made at the end of his career are more eccentric than mainstream. In 1870 he published a commentary on the book of Isaiah. His brief comments on Isa. 7.6 came in a section entitled 'Immanuel and the Syrian Invasion', where, following generations of previous commentators, he noted simply that BT was 'evidently a Syrian'.[3] In a separate commentary published in 1889 he was somewhat more expansive, describing BT as 'an obscure adventurer like Pekah' and a 'pretender to the throne'. He also commented that in the first readings of recently discovered and edited Assyrian texts, some (such as J. Oppert and E. Schrader) had discerned a reference to a place called Tabeel; further examination, however, demonstrated that the references to *Idiba'ilu* actually referred to biblical Adbeel.[4] This is apparently the first case of an extra-biblical text used to identify BT and it illustrates the eager use of recently discovered textual data to interpret biblical texts. It indicates particularly a trend in the discussion of the identity of BT; the majority of subsequent proposals will also take their cue from extra-biblical texts. In 1902 Cheyne proposed that accumulating extra-biblical evidence pointed to a possible North Arabian origin for both BT and Pekah. His conclusion meant that the editors of the biblical text had made errors in judgment while passing on traditions already distorted.[5] This illustrates yet another trend of the

3. *The Book of Isaiah Chronologically Arranged* (London: MacMillan, 1870), p. 30.

4. For references see *The Prophecies of Isaiah* (London: Kegan, Paul, Trench & Co., 1889), pp. 42, 44. For a recent treatment of *Idiba'ilu*/Adbeel with references to the annals of Tiglath Pileser III, see I. Eph'al, *The Ancient Arabs* (Jerusalem: Magnes Press, 1982), pp. 215-16.

5. See his entries on 'Rezin', Tabeel' and 'Tubal' in the *Encyclopedia Biblica* (ed. T.K. Cheyne; 4 vols.; London: A. & C. Black, 1902), pp. 4097, 4860-61, 5220-21. He proposed, for example, that all the passages dealing with Tubal (= Tab'el) in the Old Testament 'were manipulated by editors, who approached the already corrupt texts with most inaccurate preconceived opinion' (p. 5221). BT, therefore, was really the son of 'Tubal', a place located in North Arabia and not north of Cilicia; and Pekah was really an Arab confederate ('Pir'am, the Ishmaelite'). During this period of scholarship there were intense debates about 'pan-Babylonian' methods of interpreting the Old Testament. Cheyne's proposal finally became an eccentric illustration of a 'pan-Arabian' interpretation. In 1913 he published a work in which he claimed that King David was also a North Arabian. See his *The Veil of Hebrew History* (London: A. & C. Black, 1913), pp. 25-46.

period. Not only were scholars quick to use extra-biblical material in interpreting biblical texts, but some—like Cheyne—in their eagerness to use this material proposed widespread textual emendations and drew historical conclusions.

The late nineteenth century produced versions of most of the reconstructions still discussed today regarding the identity of BT and the form of his name. H. Winckler, for example, proposed that BT was none other than Rezin himself, probably the dominant party in the Aramean alliance with Pekah.[6] If Pekah was referred to contemptuously as the 'son of Remaliah', then BT was a contemptuous term for Rezin. His proposal was accepted by E. Kraeling, among others, in his influential study of the Arameans.[7] Assyrian texts note that Rezin's homeland was Hadara and not Damascus, but unfortunately they do not preserve his patronym.[8] Thus it is possible that he (or his father Ṭab'el?) was a usurper like Pekah and, like Pekah, deserving of the contemptuous reference 'son of Ṭab'el' rather than 'king'. A problem with this reconstruction is Isa. 7.6 itself, which presents Rezin and Pekah as the speakers who intend to set BT on the Judean throne. It is awkward literarily to have Rezin refer to himself in the third person.

In his widely read commentary on Isaiah, Duhm identified BT as an 'upstart' (*Emporkömmling*); and he offered doubts on the widespread assumption that BT was an Aramean, suggesting instead that he was a Judean rival to Ahaz now supported by Pekah and Rezin.[9] In the fourth

---

6. *Alttestamentliche Untersuchungen* (Leipzig: Pfeiffer, 1892), pp. 74-75. A number of scholars have continued to maintain that Rezin was the dominant party in the campaign against Ahaz and Jerusalem; cf. S. Irvine, *Isaiah, Ahaz, and the Syro-Ephraimitic Crisis* (SBLDS, 123; Atlanta: Scholars Press, 1990), pp. 69-72, 83-85, 101-07; and J.H. Hayes and M. Miller, A *History of Ancient Israel and Judah* (Philadelphia: Westminster Press, 1986), pp. 323-37. The discovery of ND 4301 + 4305 , which in line 5 alludes to an alliance between the Tyrian king Hiram and Rezin (below), would support this conclusion.

7. *Aram and Israel* (New York: Columbia University Press, 1918), pp. 102, 115.

8. For the texts concerning Rezin (ra-qi-a-nu, ra-hi-a-ni; probably Aramaic רקין) and discussion see W. Pitard, *Ancient Damascus: A Historical Study of the Syrian City-State from Earliest Times until its Fall to the Assyrians in 732 BCE* (Winona Lake: Eisenbrauns, 1987), pp. 179-89. The last known king of Damascus before Rezin was Hadianu, who was on the throne in 773. See Pitard's discussion, pp. 106-107, 175.

9. *Das Buch Jesaia* (Göttingen: Vandenhoeck & Ruprecht, 1892), p. 51.

edition of 1922, he offered additional support for the Judean identity of BT, claiming that the name Ṭabʾel (which he regarded as the original patronym of BT) could be Judean as well as Aramean, and that there was organized opposition to Ahaz in Jerusalem (Isa. 8.12) which may also have supported BT. Duhm accepted the view that in place of the actual patronym (*Ṭabʾel* = 'God is good'; cf. the LXX) the MT preserved a pejorative punctuation (*Ṭabʾal* = 'good for nothing'). [10]

The interpretation of Duhm raises a significant question concerning the original form of the patronym, although he himself regarded the answer as almost self-evident and he did not pursue the matter in any detail. Whether BT was Judean or Aramean, if the rendering of the MT is a slur, then one must face the possibility that the 'original' form of the name is not quite so self-evident to later readers as Duhm assumed, and that it is not clearly indicated by the consonantal text (see below). This is an issue to be kept separate from the question of the nationality of BT.

In 1929 J. Begrich published a major study of the motives behind the assault on Jerusalem by Rezin and Pekah, a study with possible implications for the identity and function of BT.[11] In brief, Begrich combined an analysis of Tiglath Pileser III's annals with the relevant section of his reconstructed chronology for Israelite and Judean kings. He proposed a sequence of events in which Rezin and Pekah assaulted Jerusalem and Ahaz in order to force Judah into supporting their anti-Assyrian coalition. Surprisingly he offered no discussion of the place of BT in the coalition's objectives, despite the fact that Isa. 7.6, which is formulated as the stated intention of Rezin and Pekah, indicates that the replacement of Ahaz with BT is their goal. Either of the two 'classical' suggestions for the identity of BT (an Aramean or Judean/Israelite) would fit with Begrich's reconstruction, but the implication is that BT also had anti-Assyrian proclivities. Although Begrich was not the first scholar to discuss the so-called 'Syro-Ephraimite War' in the context of Assyrian

10. Duhm believed that Tabʾel was as appropriate in Judean circles as was Tobiah, since *ʾel* and *iah(u)* were interchangable. For evidence he cited the example of the change of name from ʿEliakim to Jehoiakim in 2 Kgs 23.34. That Ṭabeʾal of the MT preserves a pejorative twist ('good for nothing') on the actual patronym Tabʾel ('God is good') became popular among late nineteenth-century commentators and it remains common among contemporary scholars. I have been unable to trace the origin of this proposal. The expected vocalization of the name, *ṭabeʾel*, appears in Ezra 4.7 in a Samarian name.

11. 'Der Syrische-Ephraimitische Krieg und seine weltpolitischen Zusammenhänge', *ZDMG* 83 (1929), pp. 213-37.

designs on the region, his proposals have been widely discussed and accepted, wholly or in part, by the majority of scholars in the last half of the twentieth century.[12]

Possible Transjordanian Connections

Two studies in the 1950s made use of new, extra-biblical material in offering an identity for BT. W.F. Albright proposed that a letter recently discovered in the Nimrud archives (ND 2773, lines 4-5), which contained a reference to an Ayanûr the Ṭabelite (*ṭa-ab-i-la-aya*),[13] 'clears up the mystery' of BT.[14] The letter provides notice of a report to the Assyrian court of a slaughter which took place in Moab. Albright interprets the gentilic 'Ṭabelite' as a reference to a location north of Ammon and Gilead, since the name Ayanûr is Aramaic and 'typical of the desert fringes of Palestine and Syria'. The BT of Isa. 7.6, therefore, was probably a son of Uzziah or Jotham by an Aramean princess from the land/tribe of Ṭab'el. As analogies, he points to Absalom and Rehoboam, whose mothers were from Geshur and Ammon respectively, and to the names of persons whose 'patronym' is also a geographic name (for instance, Hadadezer son of Rehob = son of Beth Rehob).

Albright's insightful proposal has been accepted by a number of scholars and it remains widely noted in secondary literature. It is not without problems, however. S. Mittmann has proposed that since 'we know nothing about a land of Ṭab'el', BT is better understood as a personal name rather than that of a land. Secondly, he concluded that the form of the name BT (i.e. 'son of X' where X is a personal name) represents 'the official form of designation for family members who occupy an inherited position in the royal administration...but [the form of name] does not characterize a family member of a ruling house'.[15]

---

12. For the history of discussion concerning the 'war', see the well-documented studies by Irvine, *Isaiah, Ahaz*, and R. Tomes, 'The Reason for the Syro-Ephraimite War', *JSOT* 59 (1993), pp. 55-71. Tomes does not discuss the role or identity of BT in his own proposals, where he argues that the 'war' was the result of local concerns rather than efforts to form an anti-Assyrian coalition.

13. H.F.W. Saggs, 'Nimrud Letters, 1952: Part II', *Iraq* 17 (1955), pp. 131-33, and plate XXXII.

14. 'The Son of Tabeel (Isaiah 7:6)', *BASOR* 140 (1955), pp. 34-35.

15. 'Das südliche Ostjordanland im Lichte eines neuassyrischen Keilschriftbriefes aus Nimrūd', *ZDPV* 89 (1973), pp. 15-25. Quotes taken from p. 17. For his interpretation of 'son of X' as a reference to an official holding an inherited office in

Mittmann is likely correct in his claim that BT is a personal name; whether 'Ṭabelite' is also an indication of an Aramean region is a separate issue. Contextually the evidence is strong for this interpretation of the name. Four times Pekah is described as the 'son of Remaliah' (7.1, 4-5, 9), and the implied elaboration of 7.9a is 'and the head of Jerusalem is Ahaz, the son of David' (cf. the 'House of David' in 7.13). In his criticism of Albright's view, however, Mittmann seems to have missed Albright's acknowledgment that Ṭab'el is *also* 'properly a personal name'.[16] Secondly, the context in Isaiah 7 does not necessarily support the claim by Mittmann that 'son of X' refers to people in the state administration rather than royalty. Pekah, even if a usurper (2 Kgs 15.25), was the ruler of Samaria (so Isa. 7.1, 9). If the designation 'son of X' is used atypically and derogatorily in Isaiah 7, it still designates a ruling figure when used of Pekah. Thus the enigmatic BT also may be a royal figure or a prince (Rezin the usurper?).

Albright's identifications of an Aramean land of Ṭab'el and of BT remain possible, but they seem unlikely for yet another reason. What Albright fails to show is why a *Judean* prince would be called by his mother's homeland. He cites no examples of this phenomenon, and his appeal to Absalom and Rehoboam as analogies to BT do not really explain the name itself.[17] All the examples that Albright cites to illustrate his point are *personal names* (such as Hadadezer, Mesha) *with* a geographic name (such as 'son of Rehob', 'the Dibonite'). The BT of Isa. 7.6 does not fit this pattern either.

In 1957 B. Mazar published a study of the Jewish Tobiad family which drew in some measure on the interpretation of Albright.[18] He proposed that BT was an ancestor of the Tobiads. According to him,

the state administration, Mittmann depends on the study by A. Alt, 'Menschen Ohne Namen', *ArOr* 18 (1950), pp. 9-24.

16. 'Son of Tabeel', n. 6, p. 35.

17. In defense of Albright's view, one might explain the name BT in Isa. 7.6 as a derogatory reference to a Judean prince who wished to cooperate with Rezin and Pekah. In effect, BT would be supporting the Aramean side and would qualify as its 'son'. There are possible analogies to this phenomenon in the Old Testament; for example, the people of the land made Jehoahaz king after the death of Josiah, apparently supplanting an older prince (Eliakim). This older son was perhaps more amenable to Egyptian influence. After three months, the Egyptians removed Jehoahaz and installed Eliakim as king. As a sign of Egyptian hegemony, the name of Eliakim was changed to Jehoiakim. Cf. 2 Kgs 23.29-37.

18. 'The Tobiads', *IEJ* 7 (1957), pp. 137-45, 229-38.

Ṭōb'el[19] was originally the family name, but that the theophoric ending *'el* was changed to *iah(u)* under the influence of Josiah's reform. He interpreted the reference to Ayanûr the Ṭabelite in the Nimrud correspondence as confirmation of the earlier name Ṭab'el (in Aramaic form) and also that BT had a Transjordanian homeland. BT was likely a 'descendant of a noble Judean family, perhaps even a relation of the house of David, who had many supporters among Ahaz's enemies in Jerusalem'.[20] The well-known connection of the later Tobiads with Ammon[21] was explained by him as the result of estates given to the family as 'a pledge of loyalty towards Pekah, the king of Israel'. Mazar would locate the land of Ṭab'el in the region of Ammon and Gilead, closer to Jerusalem than the locale proposed by Albright.

The most serious weakness in Mazar's reconstruction is the claim that the original name of the Tobiad family was Ṭob'el, but that it was later changed to Tobiah as a result of the Josianic reformation. Without this change of name, there is no reason at all to link the enigmatic BT with the Tobiads (Persian period and later).[22] And while the evidence is clear that Yahwistic names dominate the epigraphic corpus of Judean names in the seventh/early sixth centuries BCE, there is no compelling evidence of widespread name changes and no evidence at all that the Second Temple Tobiad family underwent a name change in the late seventh century BCE.[23] When one considers the scope of Mazar's interpretation

19. Mazar accepted the common view that the MT rendering Ṭabe'al is pejorative. Tob'el is his reconstruction of the original family name.

20. Mazar, 'The Tobiads', p. 236.

21. Cf. Neh. 2.19 and the reference to Tobiah the Ammonite. On the Hellenistic/Roman estate of the Tobiad family at 'Araq el Amir, west of Amman, see N. Lapp (ed.), *The Excavations at Araq el Amir* (Cambridge: ASOR, 1983).

22. Among the First Temple Tobiads Mazar would include a prominent Tobiah mentioned in the Lachish letters (3.19-21; 5.7-10) and another in Zech. 6.14. The persistence of the name Tobiah through several centuries is explained as an example of naming sons after their grandfather. Although an appealing theory and one argued with great erudition, Mazar's reconstruction of the First Temple Tobiad genealogy is not compelling. Even a link between Tobiah the Ammonite of Nehemiah's time with the Hellenistic Tobiads of the third century BCE and later, though probable, is not certain. For a thorough study of the Tobiads in the Hellenistic period, see J.A. Goldstein, 'The Tales of the Tobiads', in J. Neusner (ed.), *Christianity, Judaism, and Other Greco-Roman Cults: Studies for Morton Smith at Sixty* (Leiden: Brill, 1975), pp. 91-121.

23. Since Mazar wrote his study, two references to the name Tobiah have appeared in extra-biblical texts. See N. Avigad, *Hebrew Bullae from the Time of*

of BT as a member of the Tobiad family, and the range of biblical and extra-biblical material brought to bear on the question, his theory represents the the best example of attempts to solve the puzzle of BT in the broader context of the ancient Near East.

In 1972 B. Oded proposed a new occasion for the Syro-Ephraimite war, taking issue with the dominant interpretation of Begrich and others.[24] He suggested that struggles for the control of Transjordan led to the conflict. Rezin, the dominant party in the alliance with Pekah, encouraged BT, the governor of Judah's holdings in Transjordan, to become independent. And in return, Rezin promised to place him on the throne in Jerusalem.[25] BT must have been related either to the line of David or to a noble family in Judah, since Judah was supportive of the Davidic dynasty, and Rezin sought a candidate well known in Jerusalem as a replacement for Ahaz.

Oded's thesis is intriguing, and his interpretation of the role of Transjordan in the tensions between Rezin, Pekah and Ahaz merits serious consideration. In particular, his insistence on the leadership of Rezin and on the Gilead connections of Pekah echo conclusions also drawn by others.[26] And regarding BT, Oded makes a plausible case that he was well known, perhaps even supported by factions in Judah, and that he was integral to the designs of Rezin and Pekah. His identification of BT as the governor of Judean holdings in Transjordan, however, depends almost entirely on the unconvincing reconstruction of Mazar (i.e. a noble Judean family in Transjordan who changed its name) and is thus implausible in the form in which he presents it.[27]

Jeremiah (Jerusalem: Israelite Exploration Society, 1986) no. 14, p. 65. There is only one extant example of the name Tab'el in pre-exilic Hebrew. A seal with the reading 'belonging to Tab'el [son of] Padi' has been dated to a late eighth century context. See P. Bordreuil and A. Lemaire, 'Nouveaux sceaux hébreax, araméens et ammonites', *Sem* 26 (1976), p. 52 (no. 18).

24. 'The Historical Background of the Syro-Ephraimite War Reconsidered', *CBQ* 34 (1972), pp. 153-65.

25. 'The *purpose* [my italics] of the siege laid by the allies to Jerusalem was plainly to place Ben Tobeal on the throne there' (Oded, 'Historical Background', p. 161).

26. See the discussion of these points in Irvine, *Isaiah, Ahaz*, pp. 69-74.

27. His thesis also depends to some degree on a powerful Uzziah/Azariah in Judah, who had been involved previously in coalition-building in Syria-Palestine and who had acquired extensive control in Transjordan. See the discussion and critique of this view in Irvine, *Isaiah, Ahaz*, pp. 101-102.

Possible Phoenician Connections

In 1972 L. Levine published two stelae discovered in Iran and dated to the reign of Tiglath Pileser III.[28] The first stele inscription contains a list of tributaries to Tiglath Pileser III, although unfortunately no date is recorded for the reception of tribute. The Syro-Palestinian tributary list is very much like that of others from the reign of Tiglath Pileser III[29] with one significant exception. Whereas the Tyrian kings who paid tribute are listed as Hiram[30] and once Mitinni[31] in the previously known tributary lists, line six of the Iranian stele has Tubail (tu-ba-ìlu), a new name for the period in question. This has led to discussion over the sequence and dating of Tyrian kings in the period 740–727 BCE. The best reconstruction seems to be that of M. Cogan, who proposes that the Iranian stele list must date from 738 or slightly earlier when Tubail was the Tyrian ruler, and that Hiram paid tribute in the campaigns of 734 and following.[32] The dates for Mitinni are uncertain. Hiram may have been Tubail's son, but this is also uncertain.

Levine raised the possibility of an identification of BT as a son of the Tyrian king Tubail, but without discussion. The identification was

---

28. *Two Neo-Assyrian Stelae from Iran* (Toronto: Royal Ontario Museum, 1972); 'Menahem and Tiglath-Pileser: A New Synchronism', *BASOR* 206 (1972), pp. 40-42.

29. For the complete list of texts related to Tiglath Pileser III's campaigns in Syria-Palestine, see Irvine, *Isaiah, Ahaz*, pp. 23-72. For those with the list of tributaries see conveniently *ANET*, pp. 282-83.

30. See especially ND 4301 + 4305, published by D.J. Wiseman, 'A Fragmentary Inscription of Tiglath Pileser III from Nimrud', *Iraq* 18 (1956), pp. 117-29. Line 5 lists Hiram in league with Rezin.

31. See the Nimrud tablet K 3751 and the discussion among scholars in the following note.

32. 'Tyre and Tiglathpileser III: Chronological Notes', *JCS* 25 (1973), pp. 96-99. See also M. Weippert, 'Menahem von Israel und seine Zeitgenossen in einer Steleninschrift des assyrischen Königs Tiglathpileser III. aus dem Iran', *ZDPV* 89 (1973), pp. 26-53, esp. 46-48; A. Vanel, 'Tabeˤel en Is. vii 6 et le roi Tubail de Tyr', in *Studies on Prophecy* (VTSup, 26; Leiden: Brill, 1974), pp. 16-24; W.H. Shea, 'Menahem and Tiglath-Pileser III', *JNES* 37 (1978), pp. 43-49; F. Briquel-Chatonnet, *Les relations entre les cités de la côte phénicienne et les royaumes d'Israël et de Juda* (Orientalia Loveniensia Analecta, 46; Studia Phoenicia, 12; Leuven: Peeters, 1992), pp. 141-44.

proposed and discussed by Vanel and has been accepted by others.[33] Initially there is much to commend it. From the Assyrian text 4301 + 4305 a plausible case can be made for the cooperation of Tyre (under Hiram) with Rezin. Perhaps this is additional evidence for an 'alliance' (including others such as Pekah) which would be analogous to that of the previous century when Israel, Damascus and others worked in concert against Shalmaneser III.[34] If an anti-Assyrian alliance in the 730s is denied, then some form of cooperation for regional gain between Tyre, Israel and Damascus, with Rezin as the ringleader, is probable. Such cooperation makes good economic sense: the strong maritime enterprises of Tyre and Sidon, coupled with Israelite and Aramean control of the inland trading routes, offered benefit to each of the partners. From the biblical texts concerned with the ninth century, we learn that both the Israelite and Judean ruling houses had marriage alliances with the Phoenicians. There are references in the Old Testament to the marriages of Davidic princes to foreign princesses. Although extant texts are silent on the matter, one naturally assumes that Judean and Israelite princesses were occasionally married to foreign princes. According to this scenario, BT may have been a son of the Phoenician king Tubail and a princess from the Davidic House. Indeed, BT may have been Hiram himself, quite apart from any speculation on his mother's ancestral home.

That BT was a Phoenician king or prince in league with the anti-Assyrian coalition of Rezin and Pekah is a theory which is limited by the silence of Tiglath Pileser III's fragmentary annals. The theory is supported by the plausibility of historical reconstruction and analogy in conjunction with suggestive biblical evidence. In light of the stele inscription published by Levine, there is at least limited extra-biblical evidence to compare with the enigmatic reference in Isa. 7.6, whether or not BT should be linked with an anti-Assyrian movement. The primary question, therefore, concerns the philological equation of Ṭabe'al (MT) with the

33. For instance Irvine, *Isaiah, Ahaz*, pp. 153-55; H. Cazelles, 'La guerre syro-ephráimite dans le contexte de la politique internationale', in D. Garrone and F. Israel (eds.), *Storia e tradizioni di Israele: Scritti in onore di J. Alberto Soggin* (Brescia: Paideia, 1991), pp. 31-48 (p. 42); J.M. Asurmendi, *La Guerra Siro-Efraimita: Historia y Profetas* (Valencia: Institutión San Jerónimo, 1982), pp. 51-54.

34. The ninth-century alliance was based primarily on shared economic concerns vis-à-vis Assyrian intentions. See H. Tadmor, 'Assyria and the West: The Ninth Century and its Aftermath', in H. Goedicke and J.J.M. Roberts (eds.), *Unity and Diversity: Essays in the History, Literature, and Religion of the Ancient Near East* (Baltimore: Johns Hopkins University Press, 1975), pp. 36-48.

Tu-ba-ìl of Levine 1.6 (and its Phoenician equivalent). Pitard concluded that the equation is 'impossible',[35] and Briquel-Chatonnet rendered a negative verdict as well.[36] It is widely agreed, however, that the Phoenician equivalent of Tu-ba-ìl is most probably 'Ittoba'l/Toba'l, a well-attested proper name and royal name.[37] This equation is conceded even by those who would not equate Tubail and Ṭāb'el.[38] The issue turns on the equation of Ṭāb'el with 'Ittoba'l.[39] If Ṭāb'el is understood as an Aramaic or Hebrew pausal form of *ṭob'el* (טובאל = 'God is good'), then plainly it is no rendering of *'ittoba'l/toba'l* (אתבעל = 'Ba'al is with him'), and the identification of BT with a son of the Phoenician king 'Ittoba'l/Tubail must be given up.

The key to a more satisfactory interpretation lies in Vanel's undeveloped remark that the name Ṭabe'al is 'deformed'. For over a hundred years most scholars have held that the MT is a deliberate distortion (see above), but the implication of this has not played the role it should in addressing the concerns of those who deny that Ṭab'el is the equivalent of Tubail. Ṭabe'al does not mean 'God is good'. Ṭabe'al means 'good for nothing', and it distorts a patronym whose corrected form may be irretrievably lost to modern readers. It is, therefore, an *assumption* on the part of scholars that the proper name Ṭob'el (or Tobiah) stands behind the pejorative form of the MT. One might still be inclined to see the name Ṭob'el behind the present form of the Hebrew text, but this should not simply be assumed. There are other possibilities to consider: Ben Ṭabe'al might be formed as an allusive adaptation of the common term *ben(ê) beliya'al* (= 'no profit', 'wickedness', 'destruction'), or as another polemic against a name with the theophoric element *ba'al*.[40] In this last case, Ṭabe'al would make a delightfully

35. *Ancient Damascus*, pp. 184-85, n. 104.

36. *Les relations*, pp. 141-44, 153-54.

37. See the documentation provided by Weippert, 'Menahem von Israel', pp. 47-48, and Vanel, 'Tabe'el en Is. vii 6', pp. 23-24.

38. Pitard (*Ancient Damascus*, p. 185) describes the equation (Tu-ba-ìl = 'Ittoba'l) as 'certain', and Briquel-Chatonnet (*Les relations*, p. 142) concurs that it is 'the most probable' solution.

39. Or Toba'l with *aleph* elided, as with Hiram derived from 'Ahiram.

40. There are several examples of pejorative paronomasia among names in the Old Testament; for example, Cushan Rishathaim (Judg. 3.8), the 'evil' Aramean king, Ishbosheth and Mephibosheth (2 Sam. 3–4), the 'shameful' sons of Saul; Nabal, the 'foolish' husband of Abigail (1 Sam. 25.3-4); the 'Tower of Confusion' (Gen. 11.9); the 'Mount of Corruption' (2 Kgs 23.13); the 'Abomination of

polemical counterpart to Ṭobaʻl.[41] And if BT is a reference to Rezin, then 'good for nothing' reverses the sense of 'pleasure/goodness' associated with Hebrew *raṣōn*.[42]

One might explain the pejorative form Ṭabe'al as a late intrusion in the transmission of the text, since it depends on the punctuation of the MT and not the consonantal text. Moreover, since the LXX does not pre-suppose the MT punctuation, it possibly preserves the more original pronunciation.[43] One can, however, make the counterargument with equal facility: the LXX simply reflects an interpretation which had lost the sense of the pejorative wordplay in Hebrew.

Cazelles offers an intriguing suggestion in his support of equating BT with a son of Tubail.[44] He thinks that Tabe'al is an Aramaic form of Phoenician 'Ittobaʻl. Furthermore, he proposes that the announcement of a 'dynastic heir',[45] named Immanuel (= 'God with us') in 7.14 is Isaiah's use of a 'parallel name' in response to the attempt by Rezin and Pekah to place 'Ittobaʻl ('Baʻal with him') on the throne in Jerusalem.

Desolation' (Dan. 9.25-27; 12.11). And there are examples like Abed Nego, widely recognized as an avoidance of the name 'servant of [the Babylonian deity] Nebo', where the name Nego is without clear meaning.

41. Ṭabe'al would also make a polemical counterpart to Ṭobbaʻl, should that be the name behind the distortion of the MT.

42. On this interpretation of the name, see L.G. Rignell, 'Das Immanuelzeichen: Einige Gesichtspunkte zu Jes 7', *ST* 11 (1957), p. 104.

43. The LXX form (Ταβεηλ) does not reflect the distorting pronunciation and it apparently presupposes *ṭab'el* as the patronym. Briquel-Chatonnet (*Les relations*, p. 154) argues that the LXX form is 'without doubt the more ancient' reading.

44. Cazelles, 'La guerre syro-ephraimite', p. 42.

45. The identity of Immanuel is, of course, a discussion with a long history and a huge bibliography. It is not certain that Immanuel was a name predicted for the Davidic House. Some, for example, have argued that Immanuel is a child of the prophet Isaiah like Shear Yashub and Maher Shalal Hash Baz. See J.J.M. Roberts, 'Isaiah and his Children', in A. Kort and S. Morschauser (eds.), *Biblical and Related Studies Presented to Samuel Iwry* (Winona Lake: Eisenbrauns, 1985), pp. 193-203; R.E. Clements, 'The Immanuel Prophecy of Isa. 7.10-17 and its Messianic Interpretation', in E. Blum, C. Macholz and E. Stegemann (eds.), *Die Hebraische Bibel und ihre zweifache Nachgeschichte. Festschrift für Rolf Rendtorff zum 65. Geburtstag* (Neukirchen–Vluyn: Neukirchener Verlag, 1990), pp. 225-40. Whether Immanuel is the son of Isaiah or of the Davidic House, he would still bear a 'parallel name' to that of BT. Clements admits that the interpretation of Immanuel as the son of the Davidic House is the intention of the canonical compiler(s) of the book of Isaiah.

Although the interpretation of Ṭabe'al as the Aramaic form of 'Ittoba'l is more difficult to maintain, Cazelles' proposal is attractive in other respects. It illumines the address of the prophet to Ahaz and it undergirds the significance of the symbolic names so prominent in the context, particularly the prediction of the birth of Immanuel (the 'parallel name') as a sign to the Davidic House. His starting point can be strengthened by adopting the suggestion above, namely that Ṭabe'al (MT) is a polemical wordplay on Phoenician Toba'l (with initial *aleph* elided). The assonance of Ṭāb^e'al/Toba'l effects a double wordplay, first as a slur on the Phoenician patronym and secondly as a foil for the announced birth of Immanuel. BT also takes its place as another 'prophetic' name, along with Shear Yashub, Maher Shalal Hash Baz, the contemptuous 'Ben Remaliah' and the implied 'Ben David' of Isa. 7.9a.

Conclusions

Perusal of the suggestions for the identity of BT should caution one in drawing dogmatic conclusions. Of the proposals, however, the strongest one appears to be the connection with the Phoenician king 'Ittoba'l (whether BT is Hiram or a prince cannot be determined). Should new material make this connection untenable, then it is impossible to determine whether BT is Aramean, Israelite or Judean. The old suggestion of Winckler, that BT is none other than Rezin, would make good sense were it not for the literary awkwardness of having Rezin speak about himself in Isa. 7.6. Since, however, Rezin and Pekah are (in literary terms) at the mercy of the narrator, perhaps their combined speaking of Rezin in the third person is understandable. After all, it is the narrator (literally, the final form of the MT) who describes the pretender to the Judean throne as 'good for nothing', hardly a term that Rezin and Pekah themselves would employ.

As noted above, it is possible that the Ṭabe'al of the MT is a late, polemical distortion and that the form of name is unhelpful in seeking a historical identity for the figure in league with Rezin and Pekah. That the form of the name is late is less likely than that it was a phonetic polemical alteration in the earliest forms of the Isaianic *Denkschrift* (Isa. 6.1–9.6[8.18?]),[46] but lost to the LXX translator. In either case, the name still

---

46. In spite of the arguments of S. Irvine, 'The Isaianic *Denkschrift:* Reconsidering an Old Hypothesis', *ZAW* 104 (1992), pp. 216-31, once it is granted that elements of 'proto' Isaiah continued to undergo development into the post-exilic period, one may

plays an interesting role in a 'canonical' or a sequential reading of the book,[47] where the symbolic functions of the name and of the role of BT are more prominent.

K.P. Darr has pointed out that the book of Isaiah is particularly rich in language about family and siblings.[48] It begins with a reference to Israel as God's recalcitrant sons (Isa. 1.2-3; cf 30.1; 57.4), symbolic names are given to children (cf. 8.18), the future hope associated with the Davidic House is expressed in sonship language (for example, 9.5[6E]), and Jerusalem/Zion is God's daughter (cf. 52.2; 62.11). Regarding imagery for the divine, Yahweh is 'father' (63.16) and 'husband' (54.5), and metaphorically 'nursing mother' (49.15) and 'forsaken wife' (54.6). The contemptuous references to the son of Remaliah and BT, as opposed to dignifying their status with the title 'king', places them in the category of rebellious children opposed to the purposes of YHWH. Additionally, readers have already been informed that YHWH requires the removal of evil and the learning of good (*tōb*, 1.17), and also that there is recompense for those who call evil good and good evil (*tōb*, 5.20). That the puppet of Rezin and Pekah is called 'good for nothing' would tell faithful readers that he would not prevail against either YHWH's anointed son or Jerusalem, the daughter of YHWH. And even if Ahaz should fail to respond to the prophet, Hezekiah would respond to the divinely sent sign.[49]

Despite surviving in a single reference, the person of BT has an interesting place in the history of biblical interpretation, illuminating its

still see remnants of a memoir behind 6.1–9.6.

47. The literature on this approach to the book of Isaiah is already substantial. For examples and further bibliography, see R.E. Clements, 'The Unity of the Book of Isaiah', *Int* 36 (1982), pp. 117-29; R. Rendtorff, 'Zur Komposition des Buches Jesaja', *VT* 34 (1984), pp. 295-320; J. Vermeylen (ed.), *Le livre d'Isaie: Les oracles et leurs relectures, unité et complexité de l'ouvrage* (BETL, 8.1; Leuven: Leuven University Press, 1989); E. Conrad, *Reading Isaiah* (Minneapolis: Augsburg Fortress, 1991); C.R. Seitz, *Zion's Final Destiny: The Development of the Book of Isaiah* (Minneapolis: Augsburg Fortress, 1991); H.G.M. Williamson, *The Book Called Isaiah: Deutero-Isaiah's Role in Composition and Redaction* (Oxford: Clarendon Press, 1994); R.H. O'Connell, *Concentricity and Continuity: The Literary Structure of Isaiah* (JSOTSup, 188; Sheffield; JSOT Press, 1994).

48. *Isaiah and the Family of God* (Louisville, KY: Westminster/John Knox Press, 1994).

49. As Seitz (*Zion's Final Destiny*, p. 195) has pointed out, there are a number of parallels between Isa. 7 and Isa. 36–39 in the final canonical shaping of Isaiah.

twists and turns. And in his continuing obscurity, he is a testimony not only to the provisional nature of the 'assured results of biblical criticism' but to the enduring faith of the prophetic movement, whose distortion of his real name serves as a reminder that God alone ultimately defines what is good.

THE AUDIENCES OF PROPHETIC SCROLLS:
SOME SUGGESTIONS*

Philip R. Davies

I

Research into biblical prophecy has been advancing on two fronts throughout this century. One front is the historical/anthropological study of individuals and social types (whether ecstatics, messengers or inter-mediaries) who functioned in ancient Near Eastern societies and other contemporary pre-state societies.[1] This first front is relevant to an under-standing of the figures whose names adorn various biblical books or whose activities are described in them, mainly in Judges–Kings. The second front is the literary analysis of the literary books that are called 'prophetic'. The literature here is too vast to be listed, for this constitutes the main bulk of scholarly writing on 'prophets'.

These two lines of research should be strictly independent, because they are studying different things, and indeed employing different methodologies. The anthropological line concerns itself with intermedia-tion in ancient Israel, whatever that means, and the literary approach is concerned with 'biblical prophecy', whatever *that* means: one addresses a social function, one a literary corpus. These two separate programmes of research may be expected to enter into each other's territory from time to time, but one would not wish to confuse them. Unfortunately,

*   This paper is a developed version of a contribution to a panel discussion at the 1994 Annual SBL Meeting in Chicago. I am delighted to be able to offer it to Gene Tucker, whose influence both on the development of the SBL and on scholarly discussion of biblical prophecy is considerable and well known.
1.   R.R. Wilson, *Prophecy and Society in Ancient Israel* (Philadelphia: Fortress Press, 1980); D.L. Petersen, *The Roles of Israel's Prophets* (Sheffield: JSOT Press, 1981); T.W. Overholt, *Prophecy in Cross-Cultural Perspective: A Sourcebook for Biblical Researchers* (Atlanta: Scholars Press, 1986); *idem, Channels of Prophecy: The Social Dynamics of Prophetic Activity* (Minneapolis: Fortress Press, 1989).

that is precisely what does happen in a great deal of biblical research. The relationship between the literature and the social practices ought to be a fundamental problematic of the whole question of 'prophecy' but it is for the most part taken for granted. The complacent confusion of the two may arise partly from the fact that the Hebrew Bible has a division called 'Prophets' but also speaks of 'the prophets' as a sequence of individuals bearing the divine message to Israel (see for example 2 Kgs 17.13, 23; 21.10; 24.2; Jer. 7.25; 25.4; Amos 3.7). But what is understandable as part of biblical ideology does not warrant the assumption on the part of the critic that a book designated as 'prophetic' must thereby necessarily have a connection with social intermediation, or that social intermediation would assume the form of scrolls.[2]

The truth is that the more we learn from anthropology about intermediation the *less* we understand the 'prophetic' literature, while the more we examine the books carefully, the murkier becomes the profile of an individual intermediary. Studying intermediation is not the way to investigate the books, nor is literary analysis of the books the way to understand social intermediation. Jonah and Second Isaiah, for instance, are conventionally called works of prophecy, but few scholars would regard either as the work of people we could define realistically as intermediaries. Are the 'prose sermons' of Jeremiah the work of intermediaries, in the anthropological definition of that term?

What, then, is the connection, or what are the connections, between social intermediation and the production of the prophetic literature—if any? More precisely, how, if at all, does the activity of intermediation bring about artifacts like the scrolls of Isaiah, Jeremiah or Ezekiel? The majority of biblical scholars appear content to suppose that the biblical prophets were mostly real figures whose words were recast and added to by successors. This process is given the name of 'tradition', which serves the dual function of declaring a kind of continuity to the process and endowing that assumed continuity with a label that is theologically fruitful. But this concept of 'prophetic tradition' is devoid of any anthropological value and equally unhelpful for the study of so-called 'prophetic' scrolls. The notion of prophetic redactors faithfully preserving treasured words from God to an inspired individual for the benefit of successive

---

2. See the excellent analysis and discussion of this and several other issues raised in this essay in R.P. Carroll, 'Prophecy and Society', in R.E. Clements (ed.), *The World of Ancient Israel* (Cambridge: Cambridge Univeristy Press, 1989), pp. 203-25.

generations is romantic, but how far is it supported by anthropological studies? The hypothesis seems to me more a way of avoiding a problem than of solving it, and it is based on no *evidence* at all, but on an assumption that intermediation and the production of prophetic books are part of a continuous process. It is true, of course, that some of the prophetic books open with phrases like 'The words of X' or 'The word of YHWH that came to X'. But that heading is no basis for assuming that the book of, say, Amos derives from a continuous chain of transmission between a prophet Amos and the book. That assumption goes beyond the anthropological models of intermediation by proposing a meta-intermediary literary activity on the part of persons who are often dubbed 'disciples' of the intermediaries, and sometimes just called 'Deuteronomists', but once we get to redaction criticism and tradition history, the treatment has passed over from being anthropological to being literary. These 'redactors' are not themselves 'prophets'.

If our focus of interest aims to embrace both literary and anthropological aspects of 'prophecy' a better procedure is to begin with the artifacts we have, the often lengthy texts, and investigate the social function they exercised, working back towards the social function of their producers and—finally—back to the individuals whom these scrolls invoke as their eponyms. If we can get as far back, that is. In the case of several books, we have no information about such persons: Joel, Obadiah, Nahum, Habakkuk and Malachi are names only. This is strange if there is a continuous tradition of preserving their words. Even in the case of Amos, Micah and Zephaniah, we have superscriptions, assigning them to the reigns of certain kings, which give the impression of being formulaic and probably rather late, raising a doubt about whether much was actually transmitted about these individuals and prompting the question: how was this information transmitted, if not within the body of the words assigned to them? Why was the information so scant? And why has it not been preserved elsewhere in the Hebrew Bible? For of the fifteen 'canonical prophets' only Isaiah and Jonah, Haggai and Zechariah are mentioned outside the books that bear their names.[3] Here surely are

---

3.   Isaiah: 2 Kgs 19 and 20, 2 Chron. 26 and 32; Jonah: 2 Kgs 14.25, which if the majority of commentators are right, is a source for the story, and so hardly counts for anything in this list. Haggai and Zechariah are in Ezra 5.1 and 6.14 (there are many Zechariahs in the Old Testament, mostly in Chronicles; but the association with Haggai seems crucial). The Obadiah of 1 Kgs 18 could be the Obadiah of the book (*b. Sanh.* 39b) and the book's contents linked to the reports of 2 Kgs 8.20, but

factors to weigh in adopting the assumption of continuous prophetic 'traditions'.

Another way of addressing the same agenda would be from the anthropological end, beginning with an investigation into the literary activity of intermediaries in ancient agrarian societies. How commonly, according to data available, do they write long books, or even short ones, or even individual oracles? How common is it for them to have scribes or disciples (as opposed to 'followers') who transcribe their sayings?[4] From this sort of evidence (or lack) we might be able to proceed towards a discussion of whether or how such activity might develop from intermediation.

The problem of relating the biblical prophetic books to types of intermediation is complicated by the fact that it is the producers of the 'prophetic' scrolls and other biblical literature who may have been responsible for inventing an institution whose members they called *'nabi'*.[5] If that view is even partly true, we must beware of imposing this artificial institution upon the undoubtedly complex intermediary functions of Iron Age (and later) Palestinian society. That is why I insist, following Wilson, in using the more neutral and anthropologically defined term 'intermediary'. What the Bible calls 'prophecy' and those it terms 'prophets' are no basis at all for a study of social mediation until and unless we have extracted from this motley crew a set of clear criteria to denote their social activity and categorize them correctly.

II

The real topic of this paper, however, is not the authors but the readers of the prophetic scrolls. Who *read* them, or who was supposed to? We do not have to start our answer with any general theory, because we

I have been unable to find this view supported in any recent critical commentary.

4.   The reference to disciples 'binding up the scroll' in Isa. 8.16 does not point to the existence of written transcripts of his sayings. Here I follow, for instance, R.E. Clements, *Isaiah 1–39* (NCB; London: Marshall, Morgan & Scott; Grand Rapids: Eerdmans, 1980), pp. 100-101.

5.   See A.G. Auld, 'Prophets Through the Looking Glass: Between Writings and Moses', *JSOT* 27 (1983), pp. 3-23, with the responses by R.P. Carroll and H.G.M. Williamson (pp. 25-31 and 33-39) and Auld's reply (pp. 3-23); a strong challenge to Auld's view by H. Barstad, 'No Prophets? Recent Developments in Biblical Prophetic Research and Ancient Near Eastern Prophecy', appeared in *JSOT* 57 (1993), pp. 39-60.

have direct evidence. After describing various occupations, ben Sira
(39.1) turns to his own, that of the scholar:

> How different it is with the man who devotes himself to studying the law
> of Elyon, who investigates all the wisdom of the past and spends his time
> studying the prophecies.

Ben Sira is one of a class that reads the prophecies as part of his educa-
tion and/or part of his profession, just as he reads proverbs and studies
the law of Elyon. The audience of the prophetic books in the second
century BCE includes the scholar. Indeed, in the context of his remark,
ben Sira implies (38.24) that *only* the scholar has time to read books.

In Daniel 9, also from the second century BCE, we find another wise
man reading a prophetic scroll:

> In the first year of Darius the son of Ahasuerus, by birth a Mede, who
> became king over the realm of the Chaldeans—in the first year of his
> reign, I, Daniel, perceived in the books the number of years which,
> according to the word of the LORD to Jeremiah the prophet, must pass
> before the end of the desolations of Jerusalem, namely, seventy years.

But is the scholar a secondary audience? Were prophetic books originally
produced for other audiences? Here the end of Hosea (14.9) may give
us a clue:

> Whoever is wise, let him understand these things; whoever is discerning,
> let him know them; for the ways of the LORD are right, and the upright
> walk in them, but transgressors stumble in them.

This is admittedly the only clear allusion in a prophetic book to a
scholarly audience. But it is unfortunately the only allusion to the reader-
ship of a biblical prophetic book. We must nevertheless bear in mind
Jeremiah 36, which tells of a scroll written at Jeremiah's dictation. The
actual audience of the scroll is the king and his entourage, and the reader
of the scroll one of his officials. But the *intended* audience mentioned in
the story itself is otherwise (v. 6):

> so you are to go, and on a fast day in the hearing of all the people in the
> LORD's house you shall read the words of the LORD from the scroll
> which you have written at my dictation. You shall read them also in the
> hearing of all the men of Judah who come out of their cities.

So the writer of this story presents Baruch reading out to all the people
in the sanctuary a scroll on which are all the words dictated to him by
the prophet Jeremiah. We frequently find oracles in this book which are

ordered to be proclaimed to the 'inhabitants of Jerusalem'[6] or 'people of Judah'.[7] But before we accept that this reflects the actual practice of certain intermediaries, we need to reconstruct how such a scroll might have been read out in any authorized way during a cultic occasion, while it is hard to imagine anyone voluntarily listening to it for very long. The picture of a prophet, or rather his scribe, reading out in the sanctuary court anything like the book of Jeremiah to any kind of alert or attentive audience requires some critical reflection. Other considerations need also to be borne in mind, such as whether this chapter is written so as to convey accurate information about the practice of intermediation, or to endorse the authority of such a scroll. But these can be left aside for present purposes. For there are simpler objections: if Jeremiah had already cried out these words, why did he need to have them repeated? But if it was regular practice for such people to declare their words more than once, and Jeremiah was simply following this practice, the story itself explains that he was obliged to have his words written only because he was unable to go and say them in person. This story would describe an exception to the rule, and offer no explanation of why any *other* prophetic scrolls should ever have come into existence.

We might suggest, alternatively, that during the Second Temple period excerpts from prophetic scrolls were recited on public occasions, and that the author of Jeremiah 36 has retrojected this practice into the time of the eponymous hero. But this is pure speculation, without supporting evidence. We know that sections of the prophetic books (*haftorahs*) were read in synagogues much later, but we cannot show, and have no reason to assume, that this developed from practices in the Jerusalem sanctuary centuries earlier.

In any event, the larger biblical books of prophecy hardly fulfil what is required by a theory that prophets might use written texts or have words subsequently taken down. Such a process does not account for Isaiah, Jeremiah or Ezekiel, and hardly for Hosea or Amos. These are not transcripts for use by prophets. They contain stories about prophets. And even if we wish to present biblical prophets as indulging in 'street theatre'[8] the prophetic books do not look, on the whole, like scripts for

---

6. Jer. 4.3, 4; 8.1; 11.2, 9, 12; 13.13; 17.20, 25; 18.11; 19.3; 25.2; 32.32; 35.13, 17; 36.31; 42.18.

7. Jer. 4.3, 4; 7.2; 11.2, 9; 17.25; 18.11; 32.32; 35.13; 36.6, 31; 43.9; 44.27

8. See B. Lang, 'Street Theater, Raising the Dead and the Zoroastrian Connection in Ezekiel's Prophecy', in J. Lust (ed.), *Ezekiel and his Book* (BETL, 74; Leuven:

such performances, even if short episodes might fit the bill.[9]

Of course, we are already in danger of falling into a simple trap: that of assuming that because books have been traditionally lumped together as 'prophets' they must have something intrinsic in common. Jonah is a didactic narrative, perhaps to be loosely compared with the Aramaic fables of Ahiqar and Tobit or with Susannah or Esther or Ruth or Judith. Isaiah and Jeremiah contain sections that seem to have been independent at some time; Ezekiel is largely prose. Malachi is very likely an artificial book, carved out of Zechariah to make a total of twelve little books in a single scroll. Just because a book falls into a canonical section called 'Prophets' we cannot connect it automatically with intermediation. Indeed, the Hebrew Bible has Former Prophets, which we do not nowadays treat in our critical work as being 'prophetic'. Even proceeding in a strictly literary manner, abandoning anthropology, we have to be careful not to fall into a 'canonical' trap when it comes to classification.

Despite the widespread application of form criticism to this literature, it is also clear that we cannot by this method deliver reliable portraits of intermediation. We are confronted with assorted collections of similar genres: laments, oracles against other nations, oracles of hope and of doom, denunciations, visions of a transformed future, victory songs, messages from the deity. It is possible that these genres belong to intermediaries of various kinds; there are slight parallels outside Palestine for some of them (such as messenger formulae), and plausible contexts for 'fear not' oracles, 'woe' oracles and judgment speeches can be offered. Others, though, may be genres not used by intermediaries. Some may even be scribally developed forms, like the extended parables or the stories of weird behaviour presented as divine commands to the prophet we find in Ezekiel. Literary forms can utilize real-life situations without deriving from them. Consider a well-known modern genre: the country house murder. Such murders are a literary and not a social cliché, as is the aristocratic sleuth. We shall learn little either about murders or

Peeters Press, 1986), pp. 297-316; 'Prophetie, prophetische Zeichenhandlung und Politik in Israel', *TQ* 161 (1981), pp. 273-80.

9.   B. Peckham, *History and Prophecy: The Development of Late Judean Literary Tradition* (ABRL; Garden City, NY: Doubleday, 1993), makes much of the prophetic books as performance texts. But his extremely long book contains absolutely no comparative data; it is entirely a set of inferences from the biblical literature and although it makes some interesting suggestions has no kind of scientific methodology.

detective work from this genre, even though people do get murdered and country houses exist. Any enterprising writer can draw on the social genres of the day in constructing fiction. You do not need to be a pulpit preacher to be able to write or describe a sermon. The form-critical approach to prophetic literature does not allow us to invoke real intermediaries. It may, at best, suggest that the authors are reflecting the behaviour and speech of intermediation. But most people could do that, and certainly those able enough to write scrolls.

III

So far I have shown that prophetic literature was read by the 'wise'; I have, working from the other end, found it problematic to assume that prophetic literature was produced by intermediaries for their listeners or by disciples. Finally, I have suggested that even the use of possibly intermediary forms does not prove that the writers were actually intermediaries as opposed to observant and literate members of a society in which intermediation was well known.

Between these two ends of the argument, can we fasten onto any *pieces of writing* in the prophetic books (as distinct from complete scrolls) that suggest either authorship or audience? Jeremiah 13 may be a useful example:

> [1]Thus said the LORD to me, 'Go and buy a linen waistcloth, and put it on your loins, and do not dip it in water.' [2]So I bought a waistcloth according to the word of the LORD, and put it on my loins. [3]And the word of the LORD came to me a second time, [4]'Take the waistcloth which you have bought, which is upon your loins, and arise, go to the Euphrates, and hide it there in a cleft of the rock.' [5]So I went, and hid it by the Euphrates, as the LORD commanded me. [6]And after many days the LORD said to me, 'Arise, go to the Euphrates, and take from there the waistcloth which I commanded you to hide there.' [7]Then I went to the Euphrates, and dug, and I took the waistcloth from the place where I had hidden it. And behold, the waistcloth was spoiled; it was good for nothing. [8]Then the word of the LORD came to me: [9]'Thus says the LORD: Even so will I spoil the pride of Judah and the great pride of Jerusalem. [10]This evil people, who refuse to hear my words, who stubbornly follow their own heart and have gone after other gods to serve them and worship them, shall be like this waistcloth, which is good for nothing. [11]For as the waistcloth clings to the loins of a man, so I made the whole house of Israel and the whole house of Judah cling to me,' says the LORD, 'that they might be for me a people, a name, a praise, and a glory, but they

would not listen. [12]You shall speak to them this word: "Thus says the LORD, the God of Israel, 'Every jar shall be filled with wine'." And they will say to you, "Do we not indeed know that every jar will be filled with wine?" [13]Then you shall say to them, "Thus says the LORD: Behold, I will fill with drunkenness all the inhabitants of this land: the kings who sit on David's throne, the priests, the prophets, and all the inhabitants of Jerusalem. [14]And I will dash them one against another, fathers and sons together," says the LORD. "I will not pity or spare or have compassion, that I should not destroy them."' [15]Hear and give ear; be not proud, for the LORD has spoken. [16]Give glory to the LORD your God before he brings darkness, before your feet stumble on the twilight mountains, and while you look for light he turns it into gloom and makes it deep darkness. [17]But if you will not listen, my soul will weep in secret for your pride; my eyes will weep bitterly and run down with tears, because the LORD's flock has been taken captive. [18]Say to the king and the queen mother: 'Take a lowly seat, for your beautiful crown has come down from your head. [19]The cities of the Negeb are shut up, with none to open them; all Judah is taken into exile, wholly taken into exile. [20]Lift up your eyes and see those who come from the north. Where is the flock that was given you, your beautiful flock? [21]What will you say when they set as head over you those whom you yourself have taught to be friends to you? Will not pangs take hold of you, like those of a woman in travail?' [22]And if you say in your heart, 'Why have these things come upon me?' it is for the greatness of your iniquity that your skirts are lifted up, and you suffer violence. [23]Can the Ethiopian change his skin or the leopard his spots? Then also you can do good who are accustomed to do evil. [24]'I will scatter you like chaff driven by the wind from the desert. [25]This is your lot, the portion I have measured out to you', says the LORD, 'because you have forgotten me and trusted in lies. [26]I myself will lift up your skirts over your face, and your shame will be seen. [27]I have seen your abominations, your adulteries and neighings, your lewd harlotries, on the hills in the field. Woe to you, O Jerusalem! How long will it be before you are made clean?'

Although some scholars think this describes a real action,[10] a significant number regard it as a 'visionary experience'.[11] But as has also been

10. For instance, W.L. Holladay, *Jeremiah* (Hermeneia; Philadelphia: Fortress Press, 1986), I, pp. 394-95, who places it 'in the period of Carchemish'; W. Thiel, who places the entire action in the vicinity of Anathoth (*Die deuteronomistische Redaktion von Jeremia 1–25* [WMANT; Neukirchen–Vluyn: Neukirchener Verlag, 1973], p. 174).

11. For instance, A. Weiser, *Das Buch des Propheten Jeremia* (Göttingen: Vandenhoeck & Ruprecht, 1960), p. 112; W. Rudolph, *Jeremia* (HAT; Tübingen: Mohr, 1968), pp. 85-86. According to W. McKane (*Jeremiah* [ICC; Edinburgh:

pointed out, this performance as a whole cannot have been witnessed: the report given here does not rely on the evidence of the people's eyes—would anyone have followed Jeremiah to the Euphrates to see Jeremiah's undergarment under a rock? Attempts to meet the objection by speculating that פרת refers to the present-day ʿAin Farah in the vicinity of Anathoth[12] are rather implausible because they require that the audience recognized *in the action* a *verbal* play on the name of the place and thus linked it with the Euphrates. But surely such wordplay presupposes a verbal account, and if the action has just been witnessed, it can only be weakened in its dramatic impact by following it with a verbal account, because symbolic actions are supposed to *replace* words. The logic suggests that we do not have here a piece of realism, of street theatre. One does not imagine an intermediary *telling people the story of what he has just done.*

We can also suggest that, if the meaning of this episode requires a written (or spoken) *account*, then the hypothesis of an earlier vision is irrelevant. Visions, in any case, cannot be verified, and this story does not claim to originate with one. It is surely the most likely view that Jeremiah 13 is, and always was, a written or possibly oral text, by which I mean that whether or not any such deed was done is irrelevant to writer or audience. In any case, most of the 'action' that takes place is a conversation between the deity and the prophet, and the only audience for this kind of action is the reader or listener, not the observer of a series of gestures without the inner dialogue that gives it its meaning. It goes without saying that the hearer or reader of the report is not supposed to have witnessed the 'event' (or else why the report?), and thus cannot know whether it took place. Indeed, no one can know whether it took place, and so its facticity does not matter. The unlikelihood of a round journey of several hundred miles tends to prompt us to incredulity, but in principle there is no reason why Jeremiah (if he is the author of this report) should not feel morally obliged to make the trip rather than make it up to an audience who would not be any the wiser unless they too had trekked to the Euphrates and back.

This story is one example of hundreds of reports of things that were *apparently* said or done to and by prophets, and where it is the report

T. & T. Clark, 1986], I, pp. 285, 287), this view goes back to Maimonides (*Guide of the Perplexed*), while the 'symbolic action' view was supported by Kimchi.

12. The possibility is discussed by most of the major commentaries, including Holladay (*Jeremiah*, p. 396) and McKane (*Jeremiah*, pp. 285-88).

that carries the message. Prophetic scrolls are a literary phenomenon, but so, I think, are many of their contents. Whether or not all the material in the prophetic books originated in a literary form, I believe that enough of it did to force us to regard 'biblical prophecy' as a literary phenomenon not just in its final stages, but also to a very large extent in its creation as well. Between on the one hand a story such as Jeremiah 13 and on the other hand a scroll of Isaiah or Jeremiah or even of Zechariah there is a gap to be filled. But if it can be accepted that much of the material originated in literary form and was not necessarily connected to any piece of historical intermediation, the production of such large-scale written texts becomes slightly less of a problem. The significant gap is not between individual literary unit and redacted literary whole but between individual literary unit and social action.

IV

We need, perhaps, a further motivation and some elaboration. Why write in the style of intermediaries? Why cultivate eponymous 'prophets'? The answer is not easy. But prophetic forms do allow a pretext for political and social critique. By preserving criticisms of ostensibly dead 'prophets' on ostensibly past monarchs and societies, a writer could permit his own frustrations, ideas and sentiments safe expression, if he wanted, as well as (more safely) have another go at writing a poem condemning or threatening Egypt or Edom. The development of a historiographical corpus within these same scribal schools (though without any knowledge of their existence, as noted earlier) permitted the past reference of such 'prophetic' compositions, and indeed, of their eponymous authors, to acquire a more definite and specific context: we have the fall of the Northern Kingdom, the law book of Josiah, the siege of Jerusalem by Sennacherib, the rebuilding (or lack) of the 'Second Temple'. This emerging historiographical picture enabled the 'prophetic' books to develop various kinds of contextualizing. The insertions of Isaiah 36–39 or Jeremiah 52 into the 'prophetic' scrolls' are striking, but Jeremiah himself is absent from the latter. The superscriptions, which do not provide historical references in every case, are slim in respect of historical detail concerning the eponyms. But many of the materials have relatively clear contexts: a story in Amos 7 puts him under Jeroboam; Ezekiel flits between Tel Abib and Jerusalem in the aftermath of the first deportation; the poems of 'Isaiah' and 'Jeremiah' are integrated with stories that put them under specific rulers and political situations.[13] Other collections acquired eponyms rather late, to bring them into line and enable a classification of such scrolls to be made.

In other words, we have evidence of various processes of 'historicization' within these 'prophetic' collections; such evidence needs careful examining from the perspective not of a tradition history which places the historical context at the *beginning* of the process but of a redaction history that accumulated 'historical' context by various means (though sometimes not at all). The prophetic books in any case must be understood as having come into existence in several different ways (we must remember again that the category 'prophetic' is a purely canonical one) and as the result of a number of processes: learning to write in various styles, producing one's own examples and copying them into the growing collection, and creating a historical context for the collections. Within the habits and motives of the scribes of Jerusalem in the Second Temple period we can find a context for such processes, but hardly earlier, where much greater historical contextualization would be found overall. Since we do not know in detail about these schools (any more than we know about literary activity in monarchic Judah or Israel) we have to proceed by induction. We need to investigate the social and ideological climate of scribal schools and the scribal class in Second Temple Jerusalem. How did they relate to the ruling class—Persian administrators, Judean aristocracy, the priestly families? Did these writers typically adopt any particular religious opinions or practices? Were they underemployed, giving them time for composing in their leisure? Were they relatively homogeneous in their political, social or religious affiliations? Research into the highly intriguing problem of the genesis of 'prophetic' literature needs to clarify the motivations of these groups, for it is only among them, I suggest, that we can find any plausible explanation of why there are such things as the scrolls of Isaiah and Jeremiah and Zechariah and Hosea. I have suggested earlier that their efforts were being read and studied by their own kind in the mid Second Temple period. But were they developed for such purposes?

13. I leave out of account here the vexed question of the growth of the book of Isaiah by the addition of chs. 40–66 (if that is what happened). The opinions are as varied as they are hypothetical.

V

Let me now return to the question of audiences, real and intended. The large scrolls of 'prophecy' were studied by the learned like ben Sira. But was this audience in the mind of their authors? Had they been creating literature for such study, they would presumably have provided more of a shape, by which I do not mean the kind of shape that ingenious modern literary and canonical critics and theologians can invent *post factum*. If someone intended any version of the book of Jeremiah to be consumed *as a whole*, as a single literary text, it would have been furnished with a structure and a point. But it has neither: it is rather the result of compilation, of a process of compositional accretion done without any intention of being 'read' except by another copyist. My answer to the question 'who were the audience of the prophetic books' is, therefore, that there was not necessarily any audience at all, either in the mind of the producers of these scrolls or in the subsequent owners of them. I am not saying that the contents were not intended to be read; only that they were not intended to be read as one reads a modern book, that is, as a whole, with the expectation of some overall shape, plot or purpose. The obvious contrast with Hosea or Micah is Jonah; there is a text to be read as a whole.

For the *creators* of the literary units of the larger prophetic scrolls and the scrolls themselves we might think for a moment about scribal schools again and what they did. A scribe might learn to copy texts in a range of styles and genres and to learn how to write in them—not in order to use them but so as to demonstrate a competence in his language. The large number of pieces in the 'major prophets' that exhibit the same style, and recur to the point of tedium, suggests that they were composed as exercises rather than for particular occasions. The obvious candidate is the 'oracle against the foreign nation', though oracles of assurance and salvation (as they are conventionally called) may also be susceptible to this explanation. Thus, many of the literary units of the prophetic books are exercises in composing in traditional styles. Scribes might practise these either as individual compositions or add them in the course of copying existing collections. By 'traditional styles' I mean not exclusively the styles used by intermediaries, though these will obviously have predominated. Indeed, it seems reasonable to suppose that some remnants of written prophetic oracles, such as the famed Mari examples, in the form of letters to the king, might have provided the initial inspiration. Did the Temple archives yield a sherd inscribed with 'Amos of Tekoa' or did a lost Lachish letter contain a reference to a 'Jeremiah'? Possibly; but we must remember that a letter is not a book and a sherd is not a scroll. The relationship between such possible origins and the final shape of the literature is hardly a simple one.

But it is not necessary to suppose that this kind of literature grew largely from frivolous motives. If there is a serious message to some components of this literature, it lies in the area of social criticism and political theory. But is social criticism necessarily condemnatory of the contemporary scene or may it also be reassurance? Past political leadership was corrupt, the God of the Judeans did not want it this way and punished them in the past. The converse is that lack of punishment suggests lack of corruption. Past contexts might either be literal/contrastive or allegorical/comparative. They might thus be palatable or unwelcome to contemporary rulers. In some cases we may be in little doubt. It needs very little decoding to transfer past rulers into present ones; nor is much of the social criticism of Micah or Malachi or Isaiah necessarily to be thought of as relating to the monarchic period. There is hardly any abuse that cannot be assigned just as fittingly to later times.

It is also frequently remarked that many of the prophetic books seem to follow different orbits around the theme of world order: is Israel to have final victory over its enemies? Or will all come to Zion? Will the world-ruling Yahweh finally vanquish them all, or forgive them all? The debate between the 'prophetic' word and wise counsel, which may or may not have been a reality in the monarchic state, becomes sterile under a world-empire. But the claims of a monotheistic cult whose local deity is also identified as the high God provoke questions such as whether or not a foreign king may not be Yahweh's anointed, the descendant of David, Temple-builder even. In much of the 'prophetic' literature can be detected the kind of interest in the political implications of such a colonial monotheism that fit as well if not better with the scribes employed by the administrative centre, be that the colonial governor's or the high priest's, than with intermediaries.

According to the suggestion I am making, the material that was being added with each new copying of a collection of 'words of Isaiah' or 'sayings of Zephaniah' was the voice of social and political philosophy, for which there was otherwise little place within the political economy. It can be conceded—indeed, it follows from the logic of the suggestion— that such activity replicates closely what the 'prophetic' eponyms are

now held by scholarship to have been doing: reflecting on the interaction of social justice and political fortune. The truth, I think, is that the
position is reversed and that the 'prophetic' figures are made to replicate
the function of their literary creators.

It may seem a futile exercise preserving words, composed only for a
present generation, for a future one. But what authors wants their best
poems, their most eloquent rhetoric, their stinging social critique to be
lost? The hope that it will be read, even if by the next copyist, is sufficient
motivation. We do not *need* any stronger explanation. The simple wish
to preserve one's words is adequate to explain the form of many of the
prophetic scrolls.

In the end, though, I have allowed myself too often to generalize
about what I have said is a canonical category: 'prophecy'. Not all these
books are confused compilations: Obadiah and Nahum for some reason
stayed separate; Zechariah (at least the first chapters) is an extended and
brilliant piece of *bricolage* from a gifted individual. Amos exhibits some
signs of chiastic shaping; and so on. Each scroll (and in the case of the
Minor Prophets, each composition within the scroll) needs its own
account. But perhaps we could start without assuming either intermediaries or audiences and think instead of the compulsive neurosis that
is called 'writing'. My guess is that the scribal class wrote for their own
interest, not for consumption by the illiterate masses, not for oral proclamation, liturgical use or any such motive. And whether or not they
were ever inspired by the discovery of scraps of written prophetic oracles
in Temple archives (which is possible, since intermediaries doubtless
existed in monarchic and post-monarchic Judah, but so far entirely
speculative), their productions do not require the hypothesis of an
institution called 'prophecy' or of any of the individuals that some of
these scrolls present as eponyms.

PROPHETIC BOOKS AND THE PROBLEM
OF HISTORICAL RECONSTRUCTION

Roy F. Melugin

I am delighted to be invited to write an essay honoring Gene Tucker, whom I have known since we studied together as undergraduates. We also share a common background in form criticism which we learned from our teachers Brevard Childs and Erhard Gerstenberger and in dialogue with our colleague Rolf Knierim. Professor Tucker has always been dedicated to high standards of historical analysis; thus I consider it appropriate to contribute an essay about historical criticism.

Every biblical scholar knows that historical criticism has been the reigning paradigm in biblical scholarship for a considerable period of time. Its impact on the study of prophetic books is abundantly evident. Every prophetic book has been the object of many inquiries about authorship and historical setting. Historical investigators have usually concluded that most prophetic books are composite works consisting of materials originating from various historical periods. Form criticism has been a particularly valuable tool for separating units of speech from one another, and redaction criticism has been widely employed to reconstruct stages in the growth of prophetic books.

As far as I can see, few scholars are prepared to challenge the widespread belief that most prophetic books underwent a complex history of growth. But there appears to be a growing skepticism in the scholarly community about the reliability of the results of historical-critical inquiries. In some cases, scholars choose to employ other paradigms (for example, new criticism, structuralism, certain forms of canonical criticism, deconstruction), not because they reject the accomplishments of historical criticism, but because they have decided to pursue goals for which they consider other methods to be more suitable. In other cases, however, the doubt is directed more at historical criticism itself. There seems to be increasing doubt concerning the ability of historical criticism to deliver on its promises.

I see at least three forms of doubt about the capacity of historical criticism to fulfill what it promises. (1) A relatively mild form of this kind of doubt worries that historical reconstructions too often run unacceptably far beyond the available evidence. A proposed dating of a prophetic speech may be deemed unpersuasive, not because the method of historical analysis is inherently faulty, but rather because in a particular instance there is insufficient evidence to render the hypothesis probable as opposed to merely plausible. (2) A harsher form of skepticism argues that the language of the text itself is sometimes fundamentally resistant to the historian's probes. It is one thing to contend that in particular cases there happens to be insufficient evidence to support a methodologically acceptable line of argument and quite another to claim that the very language of the text itself blocks the way to successful historical reconstruction. (3) Still another line of argument challenges the very epistemic foundations of any claim to be able actually to recover the past. The decisions made by the historian, according to this line of reasoning, are so decisive in giving shape to any given process of historical inquiry that one may question whether the result of a historian's research is more a picture painted by the historian than a reproduction of the past as it really was.

I do not believe that historical criticism of prophetic books can move ahead without dealing with questions such as these. Thus I hope that, by discussing each of these three lines of argumentation in turn, I can make a modest contribution to an ongoing discussion.

I

For a considerable period of time it has been widely accepted that differences in literary form or style can be used to reconstruct different sources within a prophetic book and assign these sources to different historical settings. The community of scholars has generally agreed, for example, that basic stylistic differences between some of the passages in Isaiah 1–39 and the texts in Isaiah 40–66, together with apparent differences in historical referents, are convincing criteria for assigning them to different historical situations. Many other historical reconstructions, however, have not enjoyed such widespread acceptance, despite the fact that the *methods* move in a similar direction.

Why have some literary-historical reconstructions met with general approval while others have not? Some have obviously been more skillfully constructed than others. Yet some exceptionally sophisticated literary-historical analyses have failed to attract a large following, not because their approach would generally be considered to be basically faulty, but because of insufficient evidence.

The reconstruction of the history of redaction of the book of Amos by Hans Walter Wolff is a good example of a proposal not widely accepted, despite its brilliant use of stylistic differences for the purpose of distinguishing layers of redaction.[1] He argued that the book of Amos came to its completed form through six stages of redaction over a period lasting between the time of Amos himself and the post-exilic period: (1) 'the Words of Amos from Tekoa', (2) 'the Literary Fixation of the Cycles', (3) 'the Old School of Amos', (4) 'the Bethel-Exposition of the Josianic Age', (5) 'the Deuteronomistic Redaction', and (6) 'the Post-Exilic Eschatology of Salvation'.[2]

1. The earliest layer of redaction, according to Wolff, was the original kernel of speeches collected together in chs. 3–6. Since the speeches in Amos 1.3–2.16 are in their entirety formulated as words of *Yahweh*, Wolff thought that the phrase 'words of Amos' in the earliest form of the superscription referred to words placed in the prophet's mouth rather than in the mouth of God. Many of the utterances in Amos 3–6 are formulated as words of the prophet, while others begin as word of Amos and become Yahweh-speech only as the speech proceeds. Wolff believed that this collection of sayings was put together by Amos himself.[3]

2. A second layer of redaction, 'the Literary Fixation of the Cycles', was also organized by Amos himself. It consists of the oracles against the nations (1.3–2.16) and the vision reports (7.1-8; 8.1-2; 9.1-4), both of which are 'cyclical' in that considerable repetition takes place within each of the two groups. Each of them originally contained five parts. Each concludes with the portrayal of an earthquake (2.13-16; 9.1-4).[4]

3. Disciples who knew Amos personally also generated a layer of redaction ('the Old School of Amos').[5] Wolff thought this redactional school could be isolated because its style is similar enough to Amos's speech to indicate disciples' closeness to Amos himself yet exhibits

---

1.　H.W. Wolff, *Joel and Amos* (trans. W. Janzen, S.D. McBride, C.A. McBride, and C.A. Muenchow; Philadelphia: Fortress Press, 1977), pp. 89ff.

2.　Wolff, *Joel and Amos*, pp. 106-13.

3.　Wolff, *Joel and Amos*, p. 107.

4.　Wolff, *Joel and Amos*, p. 107.

5.　Wolff, *Joel and Amos*, pp. 108-11.

sufficient differences from the master's style to suggest different
authorship. This layer of redaction is especially visible in the narrative of
the conflict between Amos and Amaziah (7.10-17). Since it is a narrative *about* Amos rather than a report expressed in the first person,
someone other than Amos appears to be the author. Because the narrative reports the style and themes of Amos quite accurately, we may
conclude, Wolff contended, that its composer(s) had actually seen and
heard Amos in the flesh. At that same time, *Amos* never said 'Hear the
word of Yahweh' (7.16) but rather 'Hear this word' (3.1; 4.1; 5.1).[6]

Other examples of closeness to Amos's style along with subtle differences can be seen, for example, in Amos 8.4-14 and 9.7-10. Amos 8.4-7,
8 is a prophetic oracle of judgment which reminds us of those formed
by Amos himself (for example, 4.1-3). But the introductory 'Hear this'
is the sign of a disciple, for Amos said 'Hear this word'. Moreover, the
disciple introduces the citation with *lē'mōr* (8.5) instead of with participles, as is characteristic of Amos himself (4.2; 6.13).[7] Indeed, the
reason for judgment uses a chain of infinitives (8.5-6) instead of the
participles generally used by Amos.[8] The *announcement of judgment* in
8.7b is quite general when compared with concrete pictures found in
announcements of judgments thought to be from Amos himself (such as
2.13-16; 4.2-3; 6.14).[9] And the rhetorical questions in 8.8 are not characteristic of Amos's announcements of judgment.[10] Amos 9.7-10 also
employs rhetorical questions in a speech in Yahweh's mouth (9.7),
whereas Amos himself (according to Wolff's reconstruction) did not use
rhetorical questions in Yahweh-speech (see 3.3-8; 5.20).[11] Amos 8.9-14
differs also from Amos himself in that a *reason for judgment* does not
accompany an *announcement of judgment* (8.9-10, 12) or that the *reason*
(v. 14a) is both preceded and followed by *announcement* (8.13, 14b).[12]

Amos's 'seek me and live' (5.4) is reformulated by disciples' 'seek
good and not bad *in order that* you may live'/'hate bad and love
good...' (5.14, 15). The substitution of *lᵉma'an* and imperfect for the
original imperative indicates the work of disciples, as do the generalities

6.   Wolff, *Joel and Amos*, p. 108 n. 101.
7.   Wolff, *Joel and Amos*, p. 108 n. 103.
8.   Wolff, *Joel and Amos*, p. 325.
9.   Wolff, *Joel and Amos*, p. 328.
10. Wolff, *Joel and Amos*, p. 108.
11. Wolff, *Joel and Amos*, pp. 109, 346.
12. Wolff, *Joel and Amos*, p. 324.

'seek good and not bad', as reformulations of 'seek me...but do not seek Bethel'.[13]

4. The 'Bethel-Exposition of the Josianic Age', Wolff argued, is a layer of redaction which reflects Josiah's reform.[14] The fate of the sanctuary at Bethel was its special concern. In Amos 5.6, the preceding exhortation against Bethel and Gilgal (5.4-5) has been supplemented by an exhortation which focuses on Bethel alone. The Yahweh-speech of 5.4-5 has become prophetic speech (5.6). Moreover, the language of 5.6 is prosaic and awkward in contrast with the poetic parallelism of 5.4-5.[15] Amos 3.14b, 'and I will visit upon the altars of Bethel', appears to be an insertion which reinterprets vv. 13-15 as an announcement of the destruction of the altar(s) at Bethel.[16]

Three hymn fragments (4.13; 5.8-9; 9.5-6) were inserted into the text as doxologies responding to utterances concerning Bethel.[17] The hymn fragment in 5.8-9 clearly follows the exhortation about Bethel in v. 6. The hymn fragment in 4.13 follows a litany about refusal to repent (vv. 6-12) which in turn follows an ironic invitation in vv. 4-5 to visit the sanctuary of Bethel.[18] Verse 12, like 5.6, is prosaic and awkward. Thus Wolff considered 4.6-12 + 13 in its entirety to reflect the 'Bethel' layer of redaction. Finally, the hymn fragment in 9.5-6 follows a vision report involving the destruction of an altar (9.1-4), an altar which the Bethel-redactor understood to be at Bethel. The hymnic narration of Yahweh's roaring from Zion (1.2) also originated as part of the 'Bethel' layer of redaction. The Deuteronomistic redactors, argued Wolff, did not speak so positively about Jerusalem.

5. A 'Deuteronomistic' redaction is evident in the Tyre, Edom and Judah oracles in Amos 1.3–2.16.[19] 2.10-12 should also be seen as a Deuteronomistic addition. Following a third-person narration of Yahweh's destruction of the Amorites (v. 9), the Deuteronomistic redactors added a second-person narration of Yahweh's deliverance of Israel from Egypt, divine leadership in the wilderness during 'forty years', and Israel's

---

13. Wolff, *Joel and Amos*, p. 104.
14. Wolff, *Joel and Amos*, pp. 111-12.
15. Wolff, *Joel and Amos*, p. 232.
16. Wolff, *Joel and Amos*, pp. 111, 199.
17. Wolff, *Joel and Amos*, pp. 111-12.
18. Verses 4-5 speak of Bethel and Gilgal, but Wolff argues that the redactor responsible for v. 13 was interested only in Bethel.
19. Wolff, *Joel and Amos*, pp. 112, 139-40.

abuse of the prophets and Nazarites whom Yahweh 'raised up'. The clause, 'I made you walk in the wilderness forty years' is almost identical with Deut. 29.4a, and language about a forty-year sojourn in the wilderness is characteristically Deuteronomistic (see Deut. 1.3; 2.7; 8.4; Jos. 5.6).[20]

Deuteronomistic language is also visible in 5.25-26, with the mention of forty years in the wilderness.[21] Amos 3.1b is also Deuteronomistic; the Deuteronomistic phraseology of 2.10a appears also in 3.1b.[22] Finally, Wolff considered 3.7 and 8.11-12 to be Deuteronomistic.[23]

6. A post-exilic layer of redaction is evident especially in Amos 9.11-15, according to Wolff.[24] As opposed to the remainder of the book of Amos, these verses exhibit no polemic against the northern kingdom. Moreover, they are concerned with the restoration of the Davidic monarchy. Would not such a text have originated after the fall of the Davidic monarchy at the time of the Babylonian exile rather than in the eighth century?

A critique of Wolff need not seriously question the belief that Amos is a composite book with a long and complex history of growth. Indeed, few would question that 9.11-15 is post-exilic. Moreover, Wolff has made a strong case for a Deuteronomistic layer of redaction. But what about the rest of Wolff's hypothesis? Can it be said to be probable? Or merely an intriguing possibility?

Undoubtedly the post-exilic and Deuteronomistic layers of redaction postulated by Wolff do not exhaust the body of traditions in the book which originated later than Amos himself. The Amos–Amaziah narrative (7.10-17) must have come from someone other than Amos. Whether Wolff has successfully reconstructed its origin in a school of Amos's personal disciples is quite another question. Whether indeed Wolff has succeeded in arguing persuasively the outlines of a layer of redaction from such a school of disciples must be considered.

The credibility of Wolff's reconstruction of an 'Old School of Amos' depends upon an ability to show that differences in speech can most probably be accounted for as indicators of different authors or schools. Such a line of argumentation would not generally be considered

20. Wolff, *Joel and Amos*, pp. 112, 169-71.
21. Wolff, *Joel and Amos*, pp. 264-65.
22. Wolff, *Joel and Amos*, p. 175.
23. Wolff, *Joel and Amos*, pp. 188, 330-31.
24. Wolff, *Joel and Amos*, p. 113.

methodologically unsound in most circles of biblical scholarship; many widely accepted theories of differences in authorship have used similar methods. But is the supporting evidence persuasive in this particular case? Is the distinction between 'hear this word' on the one hand and 'hear this' and 'hear the word of Yahweh' on the other sufficient to distinguish between Amos himself and a school of early disciples? Is the fact that disputation style occurs sometimes only in prophetic speech and sometimes in Yahweh-speech sufficient grounds for distinguishing between Amos and the speech of disciples? Or could these differences just as well reflect a single author who sometimes varied the style? My intent is not to argue in favor of a single author; Wolff's hypothesis indeed has *plausibility*. My purpose is rather to contend that, in this case, the evidence is not strong enough to create a scholarly consensus in favor of the *probability* of his proposal.

Similar arguments could be made with regard to Wolff's hypothesized 'Bethel-Exposition of the Josianic Age'. Is the prophecy of the destruction of the altar(s) at Bethel in 3.13-15 *clearly* secondary? Is it abundantly clear that the speech originally contained no reference to the sanctuary at Bethel? Does it make sense to retain the clause, 'and the horns of the altar shall be cut off', while deleting 'I will visit upon the altars of Bethel' as secondary to the original text? It appears to me that the statement about cutting off the horns of the altar needs the preceding announcement of Yahweh's visitation upon the altar at Bethel.

There is admittedly much to be said for Wolff's contention that Amos 5.6 is a reinterpretation of earlier material (vv. 4-5) for the purpose of focusing singularly on Bethel. Verses 4-5 are concerned with both Bethel and Gilgal (also Beersheba); they are formulated in Yahweh-speech; and they announce the annihilation of Bethel and Gilgal. Verse 6, by contrast, speaks only of Bethel; it takes the form of prophetic speech; and it *warns* about the fate of the sanctuary instead of prophesying its destruction. To connect this apparent reinterpretation with the time of Josiah's reform, however, is highly speculative. To be sure, Josiah did destroy the sanctuary at Bethel. But is it not plausible that other threats to Bethel might have taken place in other historical circumstances? Is there sufficient evidence to construe Wolff's hypothesis about the setting for Amos 5.6 as highly probable? I think not.

Wolff's conclusions about the hymn fragments is equally problematic. Although the doxology in Amos 5.8 follows an exhortation concerning Bethel (5.6), it is by no means clear that the doxologies in 4.13 and 9.5-6 are responses focused primarily on Bethel and its fate. Why should one assume that the doxology in 4.13 was precipitated more by interest in Bethel (vv. 4-5) than in Gilgal, since the reference to Bethel in 4.4 features Gilgal as well? Moreover, Wolff's claim that the doxology in 9.5-6 responds to a vision report about the destruction of the altar at *Bethel* is open to question, for the altar described in 9.1 is not given a place name. To be sure, one might possibly reason that the sanctuary at Bethel where Amaziah confronted Amos (7.10-17) is the sanctuary which 9.1 presupposes; since no name of another sanctuary appears in the text subsequent to the Amos–Amaziah narrative, one might decide that this narrative provides the context for interpreting all subsequent language about a sanctuary. Such a construal is by no means unreasonable, but it is not the only possibility worthy of serious consideration.

To sum up: Wolff's proposed reconstruction of the layers of growth in Amos employs methods which have been widely accepted in the community of scholars who study prophetic literature. Skepticism about Wolff's conclusions is not rooted in Wolff's methods, at least for the rather large community of scholars who accept the paradigm within which Wolff worked; the doubts about Wolff's reconstruction would be focused primarily upon the strength of the evidence brought forth rather than upon the methodology itself. An approach which seemed to be so persuasive for distinguishing, for instance, Second Isaiah from earlier Isaianic tradition, appears less successful when stylistic differences are relatively minor.

Based on this line of argumentation, strong doubts as to the ability of historical criticism to deliver on its promises would have to ground its critique in a belief that persuasive evidence is very often unavailable. An increasing reliance on synchronic over diachronic analysis might seem unavoidable, from the perspective of this paradigm, because the evidence needed for convincing historical reconstruction can actually be obtained only in a limited number of instances.

II

What if the difficulty of achieving satisfactory historical conclusions is not simply scarcity of evidence, but rather that the very language of the text itself prevents successful historical reconstruction? The metaphorical character of many prophetic texts is often the reason why historians cannot discover the historical situations which lie behind these texts. Highly figurative texts portray certain pictures of reality, but the pictures are often fictive. Just as a novel's portrayal of things may resemble circumstances in actual history, so many figurative texts seem to portray a 'world' which looks much like actual situations in historical reality. But dissimilarity can occur also: figurative texts can depict a 'world' which differs markedly from the kind of circumstances normally experienced in the ordinary world, for instance, invading armies described as threshing sledges (Amos 1.3), defeated Israel depicted as a dead virgin (Amos 5.2), or Jerusalemite leaders called 'rulers of Sodom and Gomorrah' (Isa. 1.10).

Poetic language creates its own world. Like a self-contained work of sculpture, poetic discourse seems to shape a world of its own which can be strikingly independent in its referential function. Let me illustrate: Isa. 1.21-26 is an artistically formulated text which, though it emerged in a real historical context to which it was quite intentionally originally addressed, depicts a 'world' which has been created by poetic imagination—a fictive 'world' markedly different from the situation in the 'real' world which the poet sought to address. The text opens with language about a faithful bride turned harlot:

> How the faithful city has become a harlot,
> She that was full of justice.
> Righteousness lodged in her, but now murderers.
>
> (Isa. 1.21)

The word 'how' signals a well-known genre in ancient Israel—the genre of the funeral lament.[25] The prophet imitates the conventional speech of the funeral dirge, here sung over a city metaphorically depicted as a once faithful wife. But it is an unusual funeral dirge indeed, for it is sung, not over a woman who has literally died, but over a once-faithful wife who turned to a life of harlotry.

The text is clearly a prophecy of judgment against Jerusalem and its corrupt leaders. Without doubt the prophet was speaking of actual conditions in his historical experience; there *was* corrupt behavior which Isaiah sought to condemn. But the text converts that historical experience into a fictive scene. The *text* leads us to imagine a funeral dirge sung over a once-faithful bride turned harlot.

We can clearly say quite a bit about the 'world' which we construct in the reading of this text, but we can say much less about the actual historical situation in Jerusalem as experienced by the prophet. We can

25. H. Wildberger, *Isaiah 1:12: A Commentary* (trans. T.H. Trapp; Minneapolis: Fortress Press, 1991), pp. 62-64.

readily see only the fictive world which we construe by reading the text. We can know the actual historical context only in the vaguest of terms, for we must apprehend the historical reality through the fictive portrayal.

Let us explore these observations in more detail. When we read the book of Isaiah, we can readily see that the book is concerned with a real history which lay behind the text's portrayal of reality. The super-scription (1.1) locates Isaiah's prophetic activity within a certain period of time. The explicitly described events of the Syro-Ephraimite war (7.1–8.15) and of Sennacherib's attack on Jerusalem (chs. 36–37) help us to see that various passages seem to be concerned with the Assyrian threat of the last half of the eighth century. And the explicit references to Cyrus (44.28; 45.1) lead us to understand that the poems in Isaiah 40–66 appear to be concerned with Israel in exile in the time of Cyrus. We can have no doubt that this prophetic book manifests profound concern for the actual history which lay behind the text.

Most of what the book of Isaiah portrays, however, is difficult to correlate precisely with actual historical events. We read about 'daughters of Zion' whose stylish glitter will be replaced by the worst ready-to-wear imaginable (3.16–4.1), but we know almost nothing about the particular historical events which might have occasioned this utterance. We hear a song about Israelites and Judahites who judge Yahweh's vineyard because of the failure to produce justice (5.1-7), but we know virtually nothing of the specific circumstances which may have occasioned this song. Because these portrayals are metaphorical, we do not know whether specific events generated them or whether they are metaphorically formulated descriptions of *characteristic* behavior. The very language of the text is indeed a barrier to precise resolution of such uncertainties.

The debate about the portrayals of events in Amos's oracles against the nations is especially suitable for illustrating the problem of reconstructing history because the language of the text itself renders historical reconstruction virtually impossible. James Luther Mays, for example, dates the events mentioned in the oracle against Damascus (Amos 1.3-5) in the period shortly before 800.[26] The military campaign against Israel in which Syria 'threshes Gilead with iron threshing sledges' is to be equated with the battle in 2 Kgs 13.3-7, when Syria attacked the army of Jehoahaz and 'made them like dust from threshing'. The similarity in metaphor between the Damascus oracle in Amos and the report in

---

26. J.L. Mays, *Amos* (Philadelphia: Westminster Press, 1969), pp. 29-30.

2 Kings 13 leads Mays to believe that both texts refer to the same event. Moreover, Mays argues, the war must have occurred shortly before 800, for in that year the Assyrian king Adadnirari III drastically reduced Assyrian power. After 800, however, and for half a century thereafter, Assyria undertook no invasions of Syria-Palestine. The oracles against Philistia and Ammon may also be dated around the same period, Mays argues. He thinks that Gaza might have had an opportunity to deport a large population (Amos 1.6) in the period when Jehoahaz was under severe pressure by Syria.[27] The reference to ripping open pregnant women (Amos 1.13), according to Mays, seems to refer to a convention of warfare during the last third of the ninth century (see 2 Kgs 8.12; 15.16).[28]

Hans Walter Wolff, by contrast, dates the events to which these particular oracles refer much later. He considers it unlikely that Amos would have referred to events which occurred 'at least two generations earlier'.[29] And *no* text, he says, shows evidence of a military campaign against Gilead during the last part of the ninth century.[30] So he argues that Amos refers to events much closer to his own time. After the battle between Shalmaneser IV and Damascus in 773, Wolff contends, the succeeding kings Asshur-Dan III (772–754) and Asshur-nirari V (754–745) were weakened so much that Syria had an opportunity to regroup and carry out military campaigns against its neighbors.[31] Moreover, he argues, there exists no textual evidence to militate against an assumption that the Ammonites might also have attacked Gilead during this same period.[32]

In my judgment, both Mays and Wolff draw conclusions far beyond what the text will support. Amos 1.3-5 uses the metaphor of threshing sledge to describe what Damascus did to Gilead, and Amos 1.13-15 uses the image of pregnant women ripped open to portray Ammon's treatment of Gilead. The prophet may well be rehearsing certain well-known traditions about atrocities committed against Gilead. But how can we know whether Amos was referring to particular historical events or whether these were conventional ways of speaking about what Syria

27. Mays, *Amos*, p. 32.
28. Mays, *Amos*, pp. 36-37.
29. Wolff, *Joel and Amos*, pp. 150-51.
30. Wolff, *Joel and Amos*, p. 150.
31. Wolff, *Joel and Amos*, p. 150.
32. Wolff, *Joel and Amos*, p. 150.

and Ammon did *whenever* they attacked Gilead, however many times such military incursions took place? Or how can we know whether Gaza's crime of delivering up an entire population to Edom referred to a particular event or was instead something which could depict typical Philistine behavior? I doubt whether these word-pictures can carry us very far in the process of historical reconstruction. The imagery itself resists the historian's attempts to find referents outside the fictive 'world' which the reader constructs by reading the *text*.

III

The metaphorical character of many texts exhibits the common difficulty of distinguishing between the fictive and the real. As I discussed it in Part II of this essay, the problem of distinguishing the fictive from the real was limited to texts whose particular linguistic form erects a barrier against the recovery of the historical situations which occasioned them and to which they may originally have been directed. But what if we can never count on language to replicate the past and reproduce it as it actually was? What if all portrayals of the past are in no small measure creative portraits painted by the historian rather than reproductions of the past? What if all depictions of the past are in a significant way *constructs* created by the historian?

Hayden White contends that no one can simply describe the past. There is always more in the record than a reporter of the past can include in his or her report. One must choose what to include and what to exclude. But the record is also too sparse. The historian will necessarily have to bring into consideration things which are not in the 'record' of the past in order to make a story of the past comprehensible. The historian must fill in gaps through inference or speculation.[33] Indeed, the historian must 'emplot' the past, that is, must not only choose which parts of the record to include but must also decide how to interrelate these individual parts into a connected narrative whole.[34]

Let me illustrate rather simply. Recently my wife returned from a church meeting in which the report of a study committee exploring a possible merger between two congregations was the subject of discussion. She narrated at some length the events of the meeting, starting

---

33. H. White, *Tropics of Discourse: Essays in Cultural Criticism* (Baltimore and London: Johns Hopkins University Press, 1978), p. 51.

34. White, *Tropics of Discourse*, pp. 61-75.

at the meeting's beginning and describing how the events unfolded until the meeting reached its end. Obviously she had to choose what to narrate and what to leave out. She chose, of course, what she considered of importance to tell. In so doing, she constructed a plot by which to narrate the course of the meeting; another participant might have emplotted the meeting in a different way. She had to choose whether to emplot the meeting as a tragedy, as a comedy, or in some other way. And her choice might not have been conscious; she might have unconsciously employed a genre widely used in the world of her experience.

Amos 7.10-17 narrates an encounter which purportedly took place between Amos the prophet and Amaziah, priest of Bethel. We do not know what the 'record' to which the composer had access actually contained. Was it a set of traditions which already focused primarily on the conflict between the priest and the prophet? Or did the storyteller take a rather differently formulated set of traditions and re-emplot them to construct a story featuring a conflict between prophet and priest? Obviously we do not know. But we do know that someone chose to formulate the event as such a conflict. Indeed, it is told not only as a conflict between priest and prophet, but as a conflict about prophetic authority. Moreover, it is emplotted as a narrative in which prophetic *speech* is central to the narration of events. The occasion of the conflict— the report of Amaziah to Jeroboam about Amos's 'conspiring' against the king—is narrated briefly (v. 10). What is emphasized is what Amos *said* (v. 11). The narrator does not tell us what the king's reaction was to Amaziah's message; what Amaziah *said* to Amos becomes the focus of attention. And what Amaziah says to Amos is important because it precipitates speech by the prophet (vv. 14-17)—surely the most important outcome of the entire narrative. A modern historian who seeks to reconstruct the ministry of Amos obviously has no direct access to the past; the historian who examines the Amos–Amaziah narrative should be well aware that someone has shaped its plot. An attempt to penetrate behind the story requires an act of 're-emplotment' by the modern historian. J.L. Mays, for example, emplots it as a 'prophetic biography' composed by a contemporary of Amos. The direct quotations from Amos and Amaziah and the supposedly well-informed nature of the report lead Mays to believe that this narrative is a fundamentally accurate account composed either by an eyewitness or someone who was informed by an eyewitness.[35]

35. Mays, *Amos*, p. 134.

The construal by Mays is certainly plausible, but it is by no means the only possibility. It also seems reasonable to imagine that the 'directness' of quotations could be the way the composer of a prophetic legend chose to emplot the course of events, even if that composer had a rather imprecise set of traditions. Even if the 'record' available to the author did not include the precise content of what was said by Amos and Amaziah, it is by no means unimaginable that the composer might have invented a detailed account of what was said by Amaziah and Amos for the purpose of supporting a claim of the supremacy of the prophetic word over royal (and priestly) authority. Such an author might have employed well-known conventions of prophetic speech to lend verisimilitude to the plot which the composer chose.

The difficulty for those who would be historians is clear. Any proposed historical reconstruction is in no small degree the *historian's* story. Whenever we inquire concerning the intent of a text's author or how a text was originally used, it is *we* who *imagine* what the author intended or how the text was employed. *We* decide what questions to ask; we decide which aspects of the 'record' are important; we decide which 'facts' in the 'record' to connect with other 'facts' and how to connect them; we assess questions of probability and improbability from the vantage point of our worldviews.[36]

Our scholarly activity is admittedly not arbitrary. Historians participate in interpretive communities whose 'rules' are widely shared.[37] Differences about 'rules' of interpretation are quite often differences between communities rather than individuals. But rules change as communities of interpretation evolve over time; future generations will undoubtedly consider our methods and conclusions quaint. Questions about reliability are to a considerable extent 'settled' on the basis of community-produced standards.

It is not my intent to declare dogmatically that under no circumstances can the past ever be recovered. If one were to interview several participants in the church meeting which my wife attended, one might find enough similarity in the different stories told by the various participants to believe that 'what happened' can to some degree be discovered. Even so, the line between discovery and invention would remain somewhat unclear. Historical evaluation of prophetic books, however, is a

---

36. See S. Fish, *Is There a Text in This Class?* (Cambridge, MA and London: Harvard University Press, 1980), pp. 1-17, especially p. 13.

37. Fish, *Is There a Text in This Class?*, pp. 13-15, 320-21.

quite different matter. We do not have a large number of sources from our own society whose testimonies we may compare. Instead, we possess a small number of sources from a culture quite different from ours. The gaps we must fill are usually rather large. Furthermore, we must construct ways of looking at another culture through scholarly approaches developed in *our* culture. Under such circumstances, how can we possibly know to what extent our constructions of the past are accurate recapturings of past reality?

IV

The intent of this essay is not to proclaim historical study of prophetic books to be an illegitimate enterprise. Indeed, I consider it useful, as long as the limitations described above are clearly recognized. Because conclusions of the historian must, however, be rather modest, it does seem appropriate to me to consider carefully when primary reliance on a historical paradigm remains useful and when it does not.

If one's primary purposes have to do with the reconstruction of redactors' use of literary traditions in the history of the shaping of a prophetic book, approaches such as that of Marvin Sweeney's excellent monograph about Isaiah 1–4 in the context of the post-exilic Isaiah 1–66 remain valuable.[38] Even though many of his redaction-historical proposals are highly speculative, his analyses of structure, genre and setting are well worth emulating—as long as we do not forget that his portrayal of historical development is a construct inspired by conventions of the interpretive community to which he belongs.[39] But if one's primary concerns were instead with the use of Scripture for the shaping of life in today's communities of faith, I doubt whether Sweeney's approach would be useful as the *primary* paradigm for interpretation. Even if one were oriented to the kind of theology of salvation history which considers historical reconstruction to be *theologically* of great importance, the fragility of historical reconstruction as outlined above threatens the viability of such a theological program.

38. M.A. Sweeney, *Isaiah 1–4 and the Post-Exilic Understanding of the Isaianic Tradition* (BZAW, 171; Berlin and New York: de Gruyter, 1988).

39. Sweeney, as a student of Rolf Knierim, has become a participant in a particular interpretive community of form critics, many of whom are producing volumes in the FOTL series. This interpretive community has a definite approach to interpretation which distinguishes it from other interpretive communities.

In my judgment, use of Scripture for shaping today's communities of faith can generally proceed more fruitfully by focusing more on Israel's 'story' than on attempting to get behind the story through historical reconstruction. In Judaism and Christianity, it is primarily Israel's 'story', rather than the history which may lie behind the 'story', which functions as revealing word. Although historical research can sometimes contribute to insightful retelling of the 'story', the recovery of that history is less important than interpretation which facilitates an understanding of the 'story' itself. And prophetic books contribute to the 'story' of Israel's past, present and future.

In sum: I believe that historical criticism should play a more modest role in the study of historical books than most of us were taught in graduate school. It remains a valuable tool, but one whose place in the larger scheme of things must be very carefully evaluated.

HOSEA AS A CANONICAL PROBLEM:
WITH ATTENTION TO THE SONG OF SONGS

Martin J. Buss

The role of the Jewish/Christian Bible as a 'canon' has received fresh attention recently. The topic as such is, of course, not new. For instance, a major beginning of historical criticism in Germany lay in a work by J.S. Semler with the title 'Treatise of Free Investigation of the Canon' (1771). What was important in this title was the word 'free', for it meant that the canon—which had been treated prior to this time primarily as an authoritative structure—would be investigated without obedience to an external authority. This process reflected a major shift in the intellectual character of a good part of Europe, one that was connected with a rejection of aristocratic authority in society.

A little more than a century later, this shift, which included a heightened individualism, was challenged by a perspective that gave renewed attention to commonality, in part in order to express a concern for the more vulnerable members of society who are trampled upon in a 'free' reign of competition. Within biblical scholarship a greater sense of community brought about a renewal of respect for the canon, especially in the middle of the twentieth century.

In contrast to the historical preoccupation of the preceding period, the new concern with the canon focused less on its history—how it came to be—than on its structure. That was true in the work of H.W. Robinson (1946), W. Zimmerli (1956), C. Westermann (1957, etc.), G. von Rad (1957–60),[1] the present writer (1969, etc.),[2] J. Sanders (1972), B. Childs

---

1. Further data about studies by these four scholars, including their background in a Jewish tradition that includes Buber's *I and Thou*, are to appear elsewhere.
2. In 1956–57 (perhaps stimulated by Zimmerli 1956), I chose an analysis of Hosea as a window into prophecy and thereby into the canon. (This was completed as a dissertation in 1958, revised in 1964–65, published in 1969.) Canonical analysis was central for my article in *JBR* (1961) as well as in subsequent, as yet uncompleted, essays. The present essay represents another step in this line.

(1979, etc.), and W. Brueggemann (1982). They related the structure of the canon closely to the nature of the genres contained in each of its parts.

This discussion, to be sure, did not settle the issue of the nature of the canon. It is useful to approach it both from a structural and from a historical point of view.

On the structural side, one can point to a differentiation within the canon. The first part of the Jewish canon contains largely foundational narratives and laws, the second largely prophecies, and the third primarily literary forms that are styled as human rather than as divine speech. It is fairly clear that each of these represents a specialization within Israelite culture, associated with priests, prophets, and wise (roughly lay) people, respectively. This brief sketch is a vast oversimplification, for there are many overlaps between these three major categories. We shall, however, here ignore this fact and move to a theoretical question.

This question asks whether the specializations acted as functional complements to each other, as one would expect in a 'harmony' model of society. On one level, undoubtedly, they were complementary in that each aspect is needed. Perhaps no society can operate without orientations and laws, which together form a foundation. Furthermore, every society—in fact, every individual—requires some means for assessing actuality: evaluating the recent past and estimating future prospects. In a society that holds to a superhuman order, such considerations are related to that greater reality and are embodied in a sacred tradition that constitutes a foundation and in divination that assesses actuality (including 'prophecy').[3] At the same time, societies of this kind do not expect all insight to come to human beings receptively, but they give room to the active engagements of their minds, which in Israel found its expression especially in what it called 'wisdom', which came to form a major part of the third division of the canon.

Theoretically, perhaps, there should be no conflict between these specialized approaches. In practice, however, tensions develop. These are, in part, due to the fact that views from different angles lead to different

---

3.　In an ancient view such as that of the Israelites, there is a distinction between revelation generally applicable, at least within a given group—which needs to be given only once or only a few times, precisely since it is general—and specific insight that is needed for particular situations. The former could be handed down by priests, who are not themselves revelatory persons, but the latter required a procession of persons especially close to deity ('prophets').

perspectives that at least appear to contradict each other. Furthermore, it is a human phenomenon that every profession tends to exaggerate the importance of its own role. Thus, a priest may very well stress the ability of ritual (which calls on foundational powers) to cleanse, while a prophet may believe that a situation is so bad that it cannot be rescued by ritual and requires a more drastic step. In other words, roles that are in principle complementary can enter into conflict with one another. The prophet Hosea presents a good example of such a conflict. He rejects the offering of sacrifices and related forms of ritual (4.15, 19; 6.6; 8.11, 13; 10.1, 2; 12.12; etc.).

The ancient collectors of the Tanakh can hardly have been unaware of a conflict between Hosea and Pentateuchal directions about sacrifices. Yet they placed both into the canon. That their doing so represents not simply an oversight can be seen from Jewish discussions about the canonical status of the book of Ezekiel, which contains instructions for ritual that are different from those of the Pentateuch. A solution to this real or apparent conflict was stated by Maimonides (*Code of Maimonides*, 8, 5, 2.14) thus: the prophecy of Ezekiel presents not a general law but an 'exhortation' relevant for a future situation.[4] Perhaps the editors of the canon similarly took Hosea as one who speaks to a particular situation, one in which sacrifices are inappropriate.

A question that arises with such a 'solution', however, is, 'Was the situation in Hosea's day worse than that of other times?' If the answer is 'No', then there would never be a proper time for carrying out the Pentateuchal regulations about sacrifices. Indeed, Jewish tradition, as found in the Babylonian Talmud and later, has criticized Israelite prophets for voicing excessively sharp condemnations (see Buss 1969: 138) and thus has left room for a legitimate exercise of ritual.

There is another problem. Hosea appears to conflict not merely with the priestly tradition but also with the Song of Songs, which at the same time stands in some tension with Pentateuchal law. Admittedly, this question involves quite a few uncertainties, especially since it is not clear to what extent there were sexual rituals in Israel, to which Hosea might object and in which the Song might be involved. It should be noted, however, that sexual experience in the Song is one of union, in contrast

---

4.   An earlier rabbinic solution (was it the same?) is mentioned but not expressly described in the Babylonian Talmud (*b. Šab.* 13b). That Maimonides has prophecy in mind as a genre is clear from the fact that he refers to Ezekiel as 'exhorting'.

to the alienation expressed by Hosea for the present.[5] An ancient way of
dealing with the tension between the Song and other biblical writings
has been to interpret the Song allegorically. (In a similar way, Confucian
tradition, which was sexually strict, interpreted ancient love songs non-
erotically.) A more recent possibility of harmonization lies in viewing all
or part of the Song as a dream or series of dreams; indeed, the Song
seems dreamlike in many ways.[6] Specifically, the Song may represent
the wishful fantasy of Israelites (Lohfink 1983: 241; van Dijk-Hemmes
1989: 86). It would then furnish entertainment[7] comparable to that
obtained by moderns from literary works (including films) more licentious
than their actual lives.

Interpreted either as realistic love poetry or as imaginative literature,
the Song of Songs certainly presents a genre less heavy-handed than law
or prophecy. That is appropriate for a book located in the third division
of the Jewish canon with no, or virtually no, express reference to deity.

An important difference between Hosea and the Song, highlighted
recently, is that Hosea is male-oriented, while the Song represents to a
large extent a female perspective.[8] Although female voices are not
absent from the first two divisions of the Hebrew Bible, they are, in fact,
especially well represented in its third division, perhaps because women

---

5.   The book of Hosea uses a term for sexual misbehavior (*zanah*) figuratively
for false worship; this may or may not involve sexual congress, but at least 4.14
seems to indicate a sexual ritual. Although Hosea does not expressly condemn
premarital relations and even excuses women's involvement in pre- and extramarital
relations since the men engage in sexual rites (4.13-14), it is likely from the overall
tenor of the words that nonmarital sex is disapproved of, especially in a cultic context
(see Yee 1992, with references to discussions). The judgment that the Song of Songs
goes beyond marital relations—largely, although perhaps not entirely, premaritally—
has been expressed repeatedly (from Jacob 1902: 26, to Brenner 1993: 282), but
there have also been contrary voices (see for instance Phipps 1974).

6.   Versions of this interpretation have appeared, for instance, in Bentzen 1948:
132, and Freehof 1948–49. (See, further, Pope 1977: 132-34.) Falk (1982: 78) has
noted 'dream-like modes of wishing, anticipating, and day-dreaming...in several
places'. Fisch (1988: 98-99) thinks of the Song as having a dream-like quality but as
also going beyond this.

7.   Fox 1985: 244-49. Not necessarily at a ritual banquet (Pope 1977: 210-29).

8.   A duality of male and female perspectives have been discussed with regard to
Hosea by Balz-Cochois (1982), Setel (1985) and Weems (1989), among others, and
in some detail by Brenner and van Dijk-Hemmes (1993; cf. Brenner 1993: 273, for a
relevant observation as early as 1861, and Brenner [ed.] 1993, reprinting a number of
recent discussions).

were placed in a marginal position in a primarily patriarchal culture.[9] Related to the presence of a woman's voice—although not without potential controversy—is the widely observed phenomenon that limitations on sexuality tend to be heavier in patriarchal than in egalitarian societies.[10] In the Song, non-exclusive involvements are accepted not only for the man (1.3-4; 6.1-3, with the woman retaining confidence) but also for the woman. Specifically, the theme of 1.6(?), 7 and 8.11-14 is that the woman is with men other than the one she primarily loves, but that she (1.7; 8.12, 14) and he (8.13) would like the two primary lovers to be together.[11]

Nevertheless, the difference between Hosea and the Song is not an absolute one. Hos. 4.14 rejects a sexual double standard and is thus in part anti-patriarchal, although patriarchal 'sexual violence' (Weems 1989: 101) is clearly expressed in chs. 1–3 (possibly by a different author). Hosea 11 pictures God as a parent, using the gender-neutral word *'adam*,[12] and 13.8 compares God with a she-bear (Vieira Sampaio 1993:

9. See Ruth, Esther, aspects of Proverbs, and Job 42.15. Perhaps also relevant is psalmody (in Psalms, Lamentations and Chronicles); women are known to have played major roles in that sphere.

10. Restrictions have usually focused most directly on females in order to assure that a woman 'belongs' to a male, who wants to make sure that children born are his.

11. In Song 1.7, the woman is with the man's companions, but would prefer to be with him. The response in 1.8 gives partial encouragement for her hope. In 8.13, the man says: 'You who dwell in the gardens the companions hear your voice; let me hear it' (the LXX version—scandalized by the MT?—has the woman say this to the man); in v. 14 the woman probably replies encouragingly, asking that the two get away together (cf. 2.13, 17 [*pace* Landy 1983: 72, 112]). On the symbolic level of 8.11-12, Solomon has handed over to keepers a vineyard the annual value of which (what 'one will give for it') is a thousand pieces of silver (probably net, after deducting the cost of tending, two hundred pieces of silver). In line with this symbol, the woman directs most of her love ('a thousand') toward one who (by intention or default) leaves her to others, although she grants a small amount ('two hundred') to these. (Cf. Gordis 1974: 101-102 for the relatively small pay for the vintners.) If the Song forms a unity, much of the intervening material must contain a memory or wish (cf. n. 6, above); in fact, within it accounts of union precede descriptions of distance, but a strict unity cannot be assumed. (Statements in 2.15; 4.12 and 8.6 are less than fully clear but may imply a desire for exclusivity. The end of 5.1 ['Friends, eat and drink abundantly of love!'] can be interpreted orgiastically, but probably should not be.)

12. Motherly features have been emphasized by Terrien (1985: 56, 139) and, more fully, by Schüngel-Straumann (1986; cf. Nissinen 1991: 268-71; also, for evidence, Buss 1969: 110, without carrying through with this point).

45). The Song, too, is not univocal but includes among other male voices one that uses an image of conquest (8.9);[13] the woman counters this with an offer of peace (v. 10).[14]

There is a certain similarity between these two conflicts—with priestly tradition and with the Song of Songs—within which Hosea stands. Namely, both ritual and sexuality express less opposition between oneself and ultimate reality than does Hosea's vision.

In short, in a structural view of the canon one can recognize complementarities in the Bible together with tensions that arise in conjunction with the representation of different aspects of life. In addition, however, one must also take a historical view of the canon. This can cover either a relatively short period (less than a thousand years) or a relatively long one. In a short-range, or microhistorical, view one can inquire about the temporal context of specific words within the biblical period. This kind of question has occupied much of biblical scholarship for the last two hundred years. During the nineteenth century, that endeavor was rather clearly justified, since important conclusions were reached. A continued preoccupation with it is, however, of doubtful value, for by the turn of the twentieth century the endeavor appears to have reached and even gone beyond its approximate limits both in terms of what can gain widespread agreement and in its potential for enlightening or challenging human existence.[15] In regard to most of the Pentateuch (including its social and ritual laws), and of Psalms and Proverbs, it may not matter

---

13. 'Insofar as she is a wall, we will build on her a turret of silver; insofar as she is a door, we will besiege her with a plank of cedar.' *Contra* the usual defensive interpretation, *sur ʿal* is a normal idiom for 'laying siege to' something (thus also Meyers 1986: 215). Gordis (1974: 75) thinks of persuasion with the help of gifts; but the plank may well represent the phallus (Winckler 1905: 240), although literal force (rape) may not be implied. 'Wall' probably refers to the woman's torso, which begins flat without breasts; cf. v. 8. (The identity of the 'brothers' speaking in 8.8-9 [cf. 1.6] remains uncertain, but 'sister' in the book means a beloved; in any case, the issue in v. 8 is sexual readiness at a future time.)

14. In this verse, the woman declares that she has a torso with breasts, either actually by the time of her speaking or in anticipation (tense is notoriously unclear in Hebrew); in that situation ('then'), she provides for a peaceful union, in contrast to (probably better than 'after') conquest.

15. Childs (1979) has argued, with some justification, that biblical tradition has toned down the relation of texts to their specific contexts in order to highlight their continuing meaning; by doing so, the tradition has also made the reconstruction of those contexts difficult.

much humanly whether a given text is pre-exilic or post-exilic.[16]

This does not mean that the historical-critical enterprise is unimportant. Its contributions lie, however, more in the area of principle than in that of detail. Two principles are especially important. The first is that historical criticism removes from the Bible an aura of automatic authority. In fact, as we have seen, a 'free' attitude toward the Bible is one of its basic assumptions. This 'free' attitude has included a willingness to disregard its socio-economic injunctions—such as the call to lend without interest and the Tenth Commandment's prohibition of seeking to obtain one's neighbor's belongings[17]—and includes now a rejection of some of its sexual outlook.

The second principle is the recognition that the texts as we have them for the most part do not form strict unities. It is true that this insight is not entirely new. Biblical editors must have been aware of tensions both within and between books, without being extremely bothered by them. To cite one example, it is hard to believe that the biblical editor was not aware of a tension between the accounts of Genesis 1 and Genesis 2; yet the two were set side by side. Freedom from contradiction was not valued in early Jewish interpretation, especially for non-legal materials, as has been mentioned by M. Tsevat.[18] Yet historical criticism has underlined the presence of disunity in the extant form of biblical books.

Indeed, what holds the individual books together is not so much ideational or artistic unity as the fact that each presents one or more genres, or aspects of existence. Form criticism, in the sense of synchronic genre criticism—as in Tucker 1971—should thus be an important aspect of a canonical approach. R. Lowth was probably not far from the truth in his assessment that the book of Job is not unified but is 'a representation of those manners, passions, and sentiments which may actually be expected in such a situation';[19] is that not enough, and indeed profound?

Interestingly, the fact that most of the texts that we have are not

16. The difference between pre-exilic and post-exilic Israel may not, in fact, have been very large. (I concluded [Buss 1969: 82-115] that the book of Hosea presupposes literary forms and themes that are more directly presented in literature usually dated after the exile. Does that make the whole book late?)

17. Although the precise meaning of the Tenth Commandment is controversial, it can hardly be reconciled with an unrestrained market.

18. Tsevat 1986: 37. Barton (1986: 150) argues that ancient *readers* did not treat biblical books as unities.

19. *On the Sacred Poetry of the Hebrews*, lecture 23.

unities shows that the precursors of the texts had already gained a degree
of canonicity or status of 'Scripture'[20] so that the editors were reluctant
to make major changes to them. One can, of course, hypothesize that
editors were simply inattentive or lethargic, but it is more likely that
they, at least in part, venerated the texts.[21] In fact, a quasi-magical
veneration of texts has been especially pronounced during the early
phases of writing, despite a simultaneous presence of distrust toward a
piece of writing if its authenticity is not orally supported.[22]

The fact that early forms of a text can be observed leads to the
possibility—perhaps temptation—of attempting to locate the precursors
precisely in space and time. To some extent, such an attempt is indeed
justified. For instance, Hos. 5.8-15 can be seen to reflect situations in the
Northern Kingdom prior to the fall of Samaria, although opinions
diverge beyond this somewhat general statement.[23]

It is questionable, however, to assume for either the final form or for
its antecedents a well-formed organic whole (Tsevat 1975). Specifically,
the somewhat ragged (not smoothly unified) condition of much of the
book of Hosea does not justify the conclusion that large parts of it come
from quite different times.[24] Still, the dating of the parts is not a crucial
issue, for the human meaning of the book consists in the fact that it contains both criticisms and announcements of renewal—variations of

20. Tucker (1977: 70), like some others, prefers the term 'Scripture' for such
early forms of the canon.

21. Gese, too, has argued that editors consciously accepted texts with tensions
between them (1987: 258).

22. Cf. Nielsen 1954: 64-79 (arguing for that reason against the historicity of the
book mentioned in Jer. 36); Buss 1969: 35.

23. See Davies 1992: 145-46; Arnold 1989: 457-58. I continue to hold the
opinion that Hos. 5.8-15 is better stylistically and historically in that context if 'Israel'
is read for 'Judah', even though the geographical part of the argument in Buss 1969:
37 is less than certain (cf. van der Woude 1989). However, others disagree.

24. A number of recent interpreters (including Yee [1987], Nissinen [1991] and
Mowvley [1991], but not Daniels [1990] and Davies [1992]) have dated quite a few
portions of Hosea (especially those with a promise) to a time later than that of the
prophet, but while such dating is not impossible, it seems speculative and even
doubtful; for instance, announcements of salvation (although these were probably
expanded) go with, rather than counter to, the terrible judgments of Hosea, which
otherwise have no point (Buss 1969: 128-29). The organization of the book—with
catchword connections between units and word repetitions within them, together
with attention to specializations in content—is remarkably like that attributed to the
New Testament book of Hebrews by Vanhoye (1963: 37-49; cf. Guthrie 1994: 14).

prophetic genres, which complement each other. Although microhistorical considerations of changes within a period of a thousand years have limited value, a long-range, macrohistorical perspective is very important.

To begin with an obvious point: the language used—biblical Hebrew—is a historical phenomenon, although it was fairly stable during the biblical period, so that its development during that time rarely affects the meaning of a biblical text. Since no native speakers of that form of Hebrew are available, the meaning of its words and grammatical constructions, including syntax, must be deduced or confirmed by means of reference to the Hebrew Bible. The language of the Bible as a whole, then, serves as an appropriate historical context for a given text.

In addition, social and economic conditions have varied in history. Again, they did not change very much within the biblical period: Israel began in the midst of, and as a part of, empires and had a similar status at the end of that time. The overall situation, however, presented a macrohistorical development. Empires were relatively new when Israel began. The rule of a state (large or small) by a king had become standard and continued to be so for another two thousand years. Only somewhat recently—perhaps because of new developments in communication—has royal organization receded as a predominant political form.

Social conditions have affected not merely the details of biblical religion but its very structure. Religion in a relatively small society deals largely with liberation from sickness and other fairly ordinary evils. In Israelite, Chinese, and other larger-scale cultures a new concern came to be with sociopolitical liberation. A further step—propelled in part by empire formation—envisioned a more drastic liberation from the evils of the world altogether, with a sense both among those oppressed and among the more sensitive human beings among the oppressors that the world is fundamentally out of joint (cf. Buss 1988: 218-19). (Many Eastern mystics went so far as to turn against sexuality.) Both radicalizing and domesticating such a transcendence, Christianity located the eschatological event paradoxically in the present and Mahayana Buddhism found nirvana in samsara. With the rise of more democratic governments, in which citizens have some control over the state, there has been a move again toward a more ordinary social perspective; many now look toward steps more moderate and down to earth than either Hosea or Jesus envisioned. Many of the currently oppressed, to be sure, continue to look for a radical reordering of the world.

In association with the political development described stands the phenomenon that patriarchal organization has been well-nigh universal in cultures that are preserved in writing. A major reason for this fact appears to be the circumstance that males are especially suited biologically (if only because they do not become pregnant) to fight the wars that set up royal organization, which is also aided by writing.[25] Only relatively recently has a patriarchal social structure been extensively challenged. Criticism of the anti-female violence expressed in Hosea is one version of this new challenge. It is, then, appropriate to articulate a theory of Scripture in terms of a long-range view.

The development of writing had an impact on religion in several important ways. One was that it gave to previously oral expression a crystallized form in 'Scripture'.[26] In this respect, Scripture represents continuity with an earlier form of faith. Another was that writing contributed to discontinuity, that is, to changes in social structure, by supporting both hierarchies and challenges to them.

One of the discontinuous aspects of Scripture is the fact that a widespread attitude during relatively early stages of writing attributed potentially magical power to a written text. In Protestantism, this attitude was heightened, as print brought texts into private homes. What is appropriate now is a recognition that a quasi-magical veneration for Scripture belongs to a by-gone stage in history. Nonetheless, one cannot simply replace Scripture but one needs to make sure that the text does not take the place of, but points toward, ultimate reality.

In order to see the long-range significance of Scripture it is necessary to combine a macrohistorical perspective with a structural one. Such a combination finds expression in a comparative view. Indeed, it is difficult to gain a good understanding of a canon as a canon without that broader vision. Perhaps an approach should not be called 'canonical' without it, just as it would be odd to call an approach to the Bible 'social' or 'literary' if a knowledge of non-biblical societies or literatures does not stand in its background.[27]

25. The notion of a pre-patriarchal state is controversial, especially in regard to details, but is nevertheless likely (thus Frymer-Kensky 1992: 80). The use of writing was helpful, although not necessary, for kingship.

26. Although the Hindu canon existed for a long time only in oral form, it is quite possible that the presence of writing in the culture stimulated a precise transmission of word, so that even this oral canon was in a sense 'scriptural'.

27. An older relevant study is a 1927 dissertation by Buck (see his 1969 essay). A number of other biblical scholars, especially non-Europeans recently, have dealt with comparative issues.

A comparative view of a canon can deal not only with the attitude of veneration that is extended towards a sacred writing[28] but, more importantly, with the ways in which scriptures or oral canons deal with basic issues. It is true that similarities or differences discovered by comparison do not by themselves solve the problem of truth or value. It is likely, however, that a better understanding of the Bible and of life more generally is obtained through such a procedure.

Significant similarities between scriptures and between the position of a scripture and a present viewpoint to be adopted are likely to lie not so much in the data of the scriptures themselves—that is, in what is specifically said—as in their relation to a problem to be addressed.[29] For instance, defense of the weak—which is a relation—may occur repeatedly and may have continuing importance, although it may take different specific forms. The human sciences deal with such relations.[30]

Among major comparabilities stands the fact that a receptive relation plays an important role for religious canons.[31] (In fact, receptivity toward the authority of scriptures is often confused with receptivity toward that which scriptures symbolize.) In the Hebrew Scriptures— including Hosea—receptivity is symbolized by the linguistic form of God speaking to human beings. This has ethical implications, for ethics involves an openness to the other.

In part under the influence of Taoism, Buber said that the I–Thou relation (toward another viewed personally) has no specific describable content. In Hosea, threatening words which God is expressly represented as speaking[32] are more figurative, emotional and general than are other words. This correlation supports at least partially Buber's analysis in the work referred to and corresponds to some extent to the lack of

28. This aspect is stressed in a number of fine discussions; lacking, however, in most comparative studies is a consideration of the contents of canon as they are formed in major genres (but see Buss 1983).

29. Saussure, who coined the well-known terms 'synchronic' and 'diachronic', also used the term 'panchronic', applicable in his view only to relations (1916: I/III, vii, 2); would 'transchronic' be better?

30. Important for an understanding of the Bible is thus a thorough involvement in the human sciences. Form criticism has already moved in this direction. It is true that the recognition of a relational issue does not by itself solve the question of one's response, but it clarifies an issue so that one can deal with it.

31. Buddhism, a quasi-atheistic religion, may seem to form an exception, but Buddhism rejects self-assertion by holding that there is no 'self'.

32. According to Buss 1969: 61-62.

detailed content in much of the mysticism that is embodied in several Eastern canons.[33] Hosea pictured the future salvation as a divine gift. Most forms of Hinduism, Buddhism and Taoism similarly emphasize non-assertion or receptivity. Indeed, it is likely that this dimension continues to be important.

Moving into these large issues does not, of course, mean the end of controversy. However, these questions—unlike many microhistorical ones—are interesting in the sense that some of us really want to know answers to them.

Thus, a canonical approach—to be complete—needs to be both structural and historical, especially macrohistorical. A structural perspective indicates that Hosea both complements and stands in some tension with other parts of the Bible, including the Song of Songs. A macrohistorical view observes that the prophet's patriarchy and radical eschatology[34]— missing from the Song—represent a historically circumscribed orientation. Perhaps such a temporal relativity fits well the prophet's task to speak to a particular situation. Nevertheless, a relational, comparative view incorporating attention to both structure and history provides evidence that some aspects of Hosea, such as an openness to the Other/other in love, are still important, so that the book has, despite its problems, a legitimate canonical role.

This conclusion should please the honoree, who has been interested in the canon as well as in prophecy. A broad orientation toward the history of religion, also, is in his purview.

BIBLIOGRAPHY

Arnold, P.M.
    1989   'Hosea and the Sin of Gibeah', *CBQ* 51: 447-60.
Balz-Cochois, H.
    1982   *Gomer* (Frankfurt: Peter Lang).
Barton, J.
    1986   *Oracles of God* (Oxford: Oxford University Press).
Bentzen, A.
    1948   *Introduction to the Old Testament*, I (Copenhagen: Gad).

33. Hosea also presents non-divine speech with significant specific content. This phenomenon supports a view that Buber's early understanding of the I–Thou relation needs to be modified, as was indeed done by Buber subsequently. (An adequate discussion of this point goes beyond the limit of this paper.)
    34. Are these connected (cf. Buss 1969: 140)?

Brenner, A.

1993   'To See is to Assume: Whose Love is Celebrated in the Song of Songs?', *BI* 1: 265-84.

Brenner, A. (ed.)

1993   *A Feminist Companion to the Song of Songs* (The Feminist Companion to the Bible, 1; Sheffield: Sheffield Academic Press).

Brenner, A., and F. van Dijk-Hemmes

1993   *On Gendering Texts: Female and Male Voices in the Hebrew Bible* (Leiden: Brill).

Brueggemann, W.

1982   *The Creative Word* (Philadelphia: Fortress Press).

Buck, H.M.

1969   'Saving Story and Sacred Book', in J.M. Meyers *et al.* (eds.), *Searching the Scriptures* (Leiden: Brill): 79-94.

Buss, M.J.

1961   'Language and the Divine "I"', *JBR* 29: 102-107.

1969   *The Prophetic Word of Hosea* (Berlin: Töpelmann).

1983   'Law and Ethics in Traditional China and India', in K. Richards (ed.), *Society of Biblical Literature 1983 Seminar Papers* (Chico, CA: Scholars Press): 297-300.

1988   'Selfhood and Biblical Eschatology', *ZAW* 100, Supplement: 214-22.

Childs, B.

1979   *Introduction to the Old Testament as Scripture* (Philadelphia: Fortress Press).

Daniels, D.R.

1990   *Hosea and Salvation History* (Berlin: de Gruyter).

Davies, G.I.

1992   *Hosea* (Grand Rapids: Eerdmans).

Dijk-Hemmes, F. van

1989   'The Imagination of Power and the Power of Imagination: An Intertextual Analysis of Two Biblical Love Songs: The Song of Songs and Hosea 2', *JSOT* 44: 75-88.

Falk, M.

1982   *The Song of Songs* (New York: Harcourt Brace Jovanovich).

Fisch, H.

1988   *Poetry with a Purpose* (Bloomington: Indiana University Press).

Fox, M.V.

1985   *The Song of Songs and the Ancient Egyptian Love Songs* (Madison: University of Wisconsin Press).

Freehof, S.B.

1948–49   'The Song of Songs', *JQR* 39: 397-402.

Frymer-Kensky, T.

1992   *In the Wake of the Goddesses* (New York: Free Press).

Gese, H.

1987   'Der auszulegende Text', *TQ* 167: 252-65.

Gordis, R.

1974   *The Song of Songs and Lamentations* (New York: Ktav, 2nd edn).

Guthrie, G.H.
  1994   *The Structure of Hebrews* (Leiden: Brill).
Jacob, G.
  1902   *Das Hohelied* (Berlin: Mayer & Muller).
Landy, F.
  1983   *Paradoxes of Paradise* (Sheffield: Almond Press).
Lohfink, N.
  1983   Review of *The Wisdom Literature*, by R. Murphy, *Theologie und
               Philosophie* 58: 239-41.
Meyers, C.
  1986   'Gender Imagery in the Song of Songs', *HAR* 10: 209-23 (reprinted
               in Brenner [ed.] 1993: 197-212).
Mowvley, H.
  1991   *The Books of Amos and Hosea* (London: Epworth).
Nielsen, E.
  1954   *Oral Tradition* (London: SCM Press).
Nissinen, M.
  1991   *Prophetie, Redaktion und Fortschreibung im Hoseabuch* (Neukirchen–
               Vluyn: Neukirchener Verlag).
Phipps, W.E.
  1974   'The Plight of the Song of Songs', *JAAR* 42: 82-100.
Pope, M.H.
  1977   *Song of Songs* (Garden City, NY: Doubleday).
Rad, G. von
  1957–60   *Theologie des Alten Testaments* (2 vols.; Munich: Chr. Kaiser Verlag).
Robinson, H.W.
  1946   *Inspiration and Revelation in the Old Testament* (Oxford: Clarendon
               Press).
Sanders, J.
  1972   *Torah and Canon* (Philadelphia: Fortress Press).
Saussure, F. de
  1916   *Cours de linguistique générale* (Paris: Payot).
Schüngel-Straumann, H.
  1986   'Gott als Mutter in Hosea', *TQ* 166: 119-34.
Setel, T.D.
  1985   'Prophets and Pornography: Female Sexual Imagery in Hosea', in
               L.M. Russell (ed.), *Feminist Interpretation of the Bible* (Philadelphia:
               Westminster Press): 85-95.
Terrien, S.
  1985   *Till the Heart Sings* (Philadelphia: Fortress Press).
Tsevat, M.
  1975   'Common Sense and Hypothesis in Old Testament Study', in
               L. Alonso-Schöckel (ed.), *Congress Volume: Edinburgh, 1974*
               (VTSup, 28; Leiden: Brill): 217-30.
  1986   'Theology of the Old Testament—A Jewish View', *HBT* 8.2: 33-50.
Tucker, G.M.
  1971   *Form Criticism of the Old Testament* (Philadelphia: Fortress Press).
  1977   'Prophetic Superscriptions and the Growth of a Canon', in G. Coats

and B. Long (eds.), *Canon and Authority* (Philadelphia: Fortress Press): 56-70.

1988   'Hosea', in J.L. Mays (ed.), *Harper's Bible Commentary* (San Francisco: Harper & Row): 707-14.

Vanhoye, A.
1963   *La structure littéraire de l'Epitre aux Hébreux* (Paris: Desclée de Brouwer).

Vieira Sampaio, T.M.
1993   'Die Entmilitarisierung und die Befreiung zu einem Leben in Würde bei Hosea', *Texte und Kontexte* 16.1: 44-56 (Portuguese original, 1991).

Weems, R.J.
1989   'Gomer: Victim of Violence or Victim of Metaphor', *Semeia* 47: 87-104.

Westermann, C.
1957   *Tausend Jahre und ein Tag* (Stuttgart: Kreuz-Verlag [ET in *A Thousand Years and a Day: Our Time in the Old Testament* (trans. Stanley Rudman; Philadelphia: Fortress Press, 1982)]).

Winckler, H.
1905   *Altorientalische Forschungen*, III/II (Leipzig: Pfeiffer).

Woude, A.S. van der
1989   'Bemerkungen zum historischen Hintergrund von Hosea 5.8–6.6', in D. Garrone *et al.* (eds.), *Storia e traditioni di Israele: Scritti in onore di J. Alberto Soggin* (Brescia: Paideia): 299-318.

Yee, G.A.
1987   *Composition and Tradition in the Book of Hosea* (Atlanta: Scholars Press).

1992   'Hosea', in C.A. Newsom and S.H. Ringe (eds.), *The Women's Bible Commentary* (Louisville, KY: Westminster/John Knox Press): 195-202.

Zimmerli, W.
1956   *Das Alte Testament als Anrede* (Munich: Chr. Kaiser Verlag).

ELIJAH AND ELISHA IN THE CONTEXT OF ISRAELITE RELIGION

Thomas W. Overholt

By 1 Kings 17, readers making their way through the books of Samuel and Kings will have encountered several narratives telling of the involvement of prophets in the affairs of state, among them Nathan (2 Sam. 7), Ahijah (1 Kgs 11.29-40), and the anonymous 'man of God' at Bethel (1 Kgs 13). The beginning of the Elijah cycle will therefore seem familiar—a prophet confronts a king with a word from Yahweh (1 Kgs 17.1). But nothing that has gone before quite prepares one for what follows.

Having addressed the king, Yahweh orders Elijah into hiding east of the Jordan, where ravens feed him. He then moves on to the Phoenician coast, where he miraculously extends a widow's supply of food and eventually brings her dead son back to life. Returning to Israel, he champions Yahweh's cause in a dramatic contest on Mount Carmel with prophets of Baal and Asherah, then flees for his life into the southern desert and an eventual encounter with Yahweh at Sinai. On his return from the desert, Elijah anoints a successor (Elisha; 1 Kgs 19.19-21) and twice more appears to defend Yahwism against the social (Naboth's vineyard; 1 Kgs 21) and religious (Ahaziah's attempt to consult Baal-zebub; 2 Kgs 1.2-18) activities of an Israelite monarch. In the end, he disappears into heaven, literally leaving his mantle with Elisha, whom the narratives characterize in much the same way. Elisha is an agent of Yahweh, though none of the stories casts him in a major conflict with the cult(s) of Baal. He deals with monarchs (2 Kgs 3.9-20; 6.24–7.20; 9.1-3), and even more than Elijah, he responds to the specific needs of individuals not connected with the royal court. And, of course, wonders—raising the dead, purifying poisonous food and water, curing leprosy, commanding beasts (2.23-25)—continue.

What, exactly, is the religious situation which these narratives assume? The Deuteronomistic account tells us that King Ahab married a Sidonian princess, Jezebel, and thereafter built a temple for Baal in his capital city,

Samaria (1 Kgs 16.31-33). The narratives picture Jezebel as an active supporter of this Baal cult who takes drastic measures against Yahwistic resistance to it (1 Kgs 18.4, 19; 19.1-2) and Elijah as a champion of Yahweh who forces an either–or decision between these competing deities (1 Kgs 18.21, 39-40). Is this the heart of the matter, Yahweh religion against the religion of Baal? Since the royal house fostered it, should we say that the worship of Baal was a part of Israel's 'official' religion? The Omrid kings apparently did not abandon Yahwism altogether, since the Deuteronomists accused them of continuing the northern Yahwistic tradition established by Jeroboam I (1 Kgs 16.26, 31; 22.52; 2 Kgs 3.3) and the narratives speak of Jehoram consulting a 'prophet of Yahweh', Elisha (2 Kgs 3.9-12; cf. 5.8, which implies that the Israelite king sent Naaman to Elisha). Was there, then, a syncretistic 'official' religion, against which stood a 'popular', a more pure, form of the Yahweh religion found among (at least some of) the people at large?

Given the nature of our main source of information—a loose collection of narratives about two, by biblical standards quite unusual, 'men of God'—it is difficult to answer such questions with any certainty, but there would clearly be problems with formulating the matter in terms of a simple dichotomy between 'official' and 'popular' religion. Other points of view are also in evidence. For one, the narratives' portrayal of the Yahwism of Elijah and Elisha sometimes reflects assumptions compatible with the Deuteronomistic ideology which dominates the books of Kings: Yahweh has control over nature and history (he sends rain, 1 Kgs 18.1, and famine, 2 Kgs 8.1; he selects kings, 2 Kgs 9.3); when disaster strikes, it is interpreted as a punishment for human misbehavior (drought, 1 Kgs 18.17-18; illness, 2 Kgs 1.3-4); and the prophets are Yahweh's spokesmen, confronting kings and announcing his intentions (1 Kgs 18.1; 19.15-18; 2 Kgs 1.16; 3.16-19; 7.1). For another, the narratives contain references to religious beliefs and practices which appear to be at odds with the Deuteronomistic view of Yahweh religion as the theological basis for the nation's existence. They tell how these men of God cure the sick and resuscitate corpses, how they are called upon to render assistence in the daily affairs of ordinary people, and how their (sometimes capricious; cf. 2 Kgs 2.23-25) displays of power were both a source of comfort and of anxiety. Where in any of the other points of view on Yahweh religion—'official', 'popular', Deuteronomistic—is there a place for persons who act in this fashion?[1]

1.   My aim in what follows is to suggest a general social and intellectual context

The religion of Yahweh we encounter in the Elijah and Elisha narratives is a multifaceted phenomenon. How can we unravel and identify the threads that make up this tapestry? A brief review will show that we cannot rely on the more or less standard views of Israelite religion for a solution to this problem.

Israelite Religion in the Period of the Monarchy

According to Helmer Ringgren, in the period of the monarchy 'there existed side by side...the so-to-speak official religion of the Temple and monarchy (in the Southern Kingdom), a popular syncretistic religion, the religion of the great literary prophets, and the religion of the Deuteronomistic circle'.[2] The first of these was apparently the result of syncretistic tendencies that took place on several levels. G.W. Ahlström spoke of the 'symbiosis' of Yahweh and El traditions that gained impetus following the capture of Jerusalem and resulted by the time of Solomon's death in 'an official religion in Jerusalem'.[3] Besides these 'syncretistic reformulations of Yahweh religion in the royal state cult', Ranier Albertz points to 'the establishment of cults for the gods of the neighbouring states with which the royal house maintained political relations', a phenomenon he calls 'diplomatic syncretism'.[4] Solomon and Ahab are notorious for alliances of this type.

---

for interpreting the stories about Elijah and Elisha. I make no presumptions about what elements in them may reflect actual historical occurrences. Terence Collins stresses the fact that in their present form the stories have been incorporated into, and serve the purposes of, the Deuteronomistic History. In that history, Elijah and Elisha 'are archetypes of all the biblical prophets as rival figures to the kings, offering a different model of leadership with which the people can identify'. They are 'more akin to stage characters than to real people'; they are more 'typical' than historical, and 'the writers of the sixth century were not averse to using stories that were fanciful, exaggerated and even manifestly fictional'; T. Collins, *The Mantle of Elijah: The Redaction Criticism of the Prophetical Books* (The Biblical Seminar, 20; Sheffield: JSOT Press, 1993), p. 130; cf. pp. 125-39. I agree in principle with this understanding, and in this essay pursue a possible answer to the further question: what were the cultural materials out of which such 'stage characters' were created?

2.   H. Ringgren, *Israelite Religion* (Philadelphia: Fortress Press, 1966), p. 58.

3.   G.W. Ahlström, *Aspects of Syncretism in Israelite Religion* (Lund: Gleerup, 1963), p. 9; cf. pp. 13, 33-34.

4.   R. Albertz, *A History of Israelite Religion in the Old Testament Period*. I. *From the Beginnings to the End of the Monarchy* (Louisville, KY: Westminster/ John Knox Press, 1994), p. 148.

For Ringgren the second thread, popular syncretistic religion, was the result of the tendency of the Israelites who migrated into Canaan to borrow Canaanite gods.[5] Insofar as any aspect of Yahweh religion can be traced to a pre-agricultural society, it seems reasonable to assume that it would inevitably have changed to accommodate the different circumstances of a farming culture. Georg Fohrer postulates that in the period before the monarchy there was an 'organic development' of Mosaic Yahwism in which it assimilated and integrated 'Canaanite concepts and practices...in a transformation that enabled the nomadic Yahwism of the Mosaic period to survive in a settled civilization'.[6] In this agrarian setting, says Vriezen, Baalism was 'an almost invincible competitor', which might be obstructed or forced into retreat but 'could not really be overthrown'. Yahwism coped in part by adopting elements of Baalism, identifying Yahweh, for example, as the god of fertility (cf. Hos. 2.7-8, 13-14, 17-20; 14.6-9; Deut. 26.1-11). 'In that way the struggle with Baalism actually contributed to enrich men's picture of Yahweh, by making him Lord over the powers of living nature.'[7] This type of syncretism must have occurred largely as a natural consequence of living in a new cultural environment with little 'prior reflection by the people on whether they could thus give appropriate expression to the special historical experiences of liberation that they had had with Yahweh'.[8]

The long-standing debate over the nature and extent of this syncretism has been fueled in recent times by the discoveries at Kuntillet 'Ajrud— an isolated hilltop site far to the south of Jerusalem, apparently a way-station for travellers—of inscriptions referring to 'Yahweh of Samaria [another says, 'of Teman'] and his Asherah'. Some have argued that in this context 'Asherah' does not refer to the Canaanite goddess[9] or that it is 'a case...of the personification of a cult object as a goddess'.[10]

---

5. Ringgren, *Israelite Religion*, p. 96.

6. G. Fohrer, *History of Israelite Religion* (Nashville: Abingdon Press, 1972), pp. 121-22.

7. T.C. Vriezen, *The Religion of Ancient Israel* (Philadelphia: Westminster Press, 1967), pp. 169-70.

8. Albertz, *A History of Israelite Religion*, p. 85.

9. J.H. Tigay, 'Israelite Religion: The Onomastic and Epigraphic Evidence', in P.D. Miller, *et al.* (eds.), *Ancient Israelite Religion* (Minneapolis: Fortress Press, 1987), pp. 157-94; A. Lemaire, 'Who or What Was Yahweh's Asherah?', *BARev* 10.6 (Nov./Dec. 1984), pp. 42-51.

10. P.K. McCarter, Jr, 'Aspects of the Religion of the Israelite Monarchy: Biblical and Epigraphic Data', in Miller, *et al.* (eds.), *Ancient Israelite Religion*, p. 147.

William Dever and others make a strong case that the Asherah mentioned here is the Canaanite goddess, who, 'as the "Mother Goddess"...was easily identifiable in popular religion with Yahweh, the successor of El, and at least in some circles such as those at Ajrud she was evidently venerated as his consort'.[11] Along these lines, Albertz suggests that at the level of 'the local cults which were concerned above all to secure the fertility of the cultivated land, the cattle and the body, there was a need to supplement Yahweh with a female element'.[12] The inscriptions' identification of Yahweh with specific places (Samaria, Teman) also suggests that though Yahweh may be one, his cult could take a variety of forms.[13]

These local manifestations of Yahweh tended 'to become semi-independent, almost as if they were distinct deities', and yet nowhere in the Deuteronomists' accounts of the reforms of Hezekiah and Josiah is there any indication that these 'local shrines...[were considered] a threat to the concept of the unity of Yahweh'.[14]

The inscriptions from Kuntillet 'Ajrud introduce a note of ambiguity into Ringgren's parsing of Israelite religion. To which thread of the tapestry does this Yahweh belong? He is called 'Yahweh of Samaria', suggesting a connection with the 'official' cult of the Israelite monarchy. Yet his association with Asherah, who is arguably his consort, suggests the kind of borrowing of Canaanite deities which Ringgren says is characteristic of 'popular syncretistic religion'. We are two steps into Ringgren's four-part scheme, and already the distinctions are blurring.

The third thread is constituted by the religion of the writing prophets, whose point of view was 'quite different from that of the "official" religion of their period...The prophets viewed themselves as the champions of the original religion of Yahweh in its pure form, censuring the popular religion of the day as being syncretistic and corrupt'.[15] The question of the nature of this more 'pure' form of the Yahweh religion is frequently answered by reference to a certain group of Israelites who experienced liberation from Egypt and an encounter with Yahweh prior

---

11. W. Dever, 'Recent Archaeological Confirmation of the Cult of Asherah in Ancient Israel', *Hebrew Studies* 23 (1982), pp. 37-43.

12. Albertz, *A History of Israelite Religion*, p. 85.

13. J.A. Emerton, 'New Light on Israelite Religion: The Implications of the Inscriptions from Kuntillet 'Ajrud', *ZAW* 94 (1982), pp. 2-20.

14. McCarter, 'Aspects of the Religion of the Israelite Monarchy', pp. 142-43; cf. 2 Sam. 15.7 and by analogy the Ishtars of Nineveh and Arbela.

15. Ringgren, *Israelite Religion*, p. 248.

to settling in Canaan. As T.C. Vriezen puts it, the 'refugees from Egypt' developed 'a bond of fellowship and communion' with Yahweh, whom they experienced as a deity 'who governs both nature and history'. When this group settled in Canaan among their 'brother tribes' who were already there, the 'cohesion' they had developed in the desert allowed them to 'evade what was a well nigh predestined pattern of historical development' according to which newcomers who were 'socially and culturally inferior' were routinely 'assimilated to the old, culturally superior community already living in the country'.[16]

Similarly, Albertz argues that 'the origin of Yahweh religion is indissolubly connected with the process of the political liberation of the exodus group', who were not nomads but possibly *habiru*.[17] The bond between Yahweh and this group strengthened the group's social cohesiveness and was presumably 'the factor which first turned the heterogeneous bunch of fugitives into a firmly organized tribe'.[18] The exclusiveness of the Yahweh religion, manifested in continuing attempts by at least some Israelites to resist forces of syncretism, is explained by 'the extraordinary combination of social and religious factors out of which it emerged: under the extreme conditions of political liberation and a lengthy existence in the wilderness a close personal relationship developed between the Exodus group and Yahweh'.[19] Along with the prophets, the Nazirites and Rechabites were among the groups which remained 'attached to the ancient form of their faith'.[20]

Of course, speculations about the nature of the earliest forms of Yahweh religion are highly conjectural, though the construction just offered has the advantage of correlating with recent theories of how 'Israel' came to be established as an identifiable entity in the land of Canaan. But with respect to the matter of 'purity', it is difficult to conceive of even very early Yahwism as non-syncretistic. If we imagine that the liberated 'exodus group' entered Palestine at a time when that region was experiencing 'a far-reaching process of political, social and cultural change',[21] then we would expect the religion of this group to have been a participant in the dynamic process of change in which society was

16. Vriezen, *The Religion of Ancient Israel*, pp. 147, 152-53, 155; cf. 134-53.
17. Albertz, *A History of Israelite Religion*, p. 47.
18. Albertz, *A History of Israelite Religion*, p. 60.
19. Albertz, *A History of Israelite Religion*, p. 62.
20. Fohrer, *History of Israelite Religion*, p. 153.
21. Albertz, *A History of Israelite Religion*, p. 69.

being re-visioned. One may argue about the extent to which Yahweh religion was the driving force in, or was pulled along behind, the changes of this period, but everything we know about the development of cultures suggests that had it not changed it would not have survived to be an important part of Israelite life during the centuries which followed. In any event, Yahwism has a history, though its beginnings are veiled by the haze of a distant past.[22] Almost certainly this history included an early integration of El and Yahweh[23] and the development of various local cults where concerns for fertility would have been accommodated. Whatever passed (and passes) for 'purity' must have been (and still must be) in the eye of the beholder.[24]

Ringgren identifies a fourth thread, 'the religion of the Deuteronomistic circle'. The theological interpretation of national history stemming from this 'circle' now dominates much of the historical and prophetic literature in the Hebrew Bible. It is sometimes difficult to distinguish between prophetic and Deuteronomistic constructions of Yahwism, which introduces another element of ambiguity into our attempt to separate the various strands of Israelite religion. What is clear is that a situation of 'internal religious pluralism' prevailed in Israel both before and during the period of the monarchy.[25]

And where do Elijah and Elisha fit into this scheme? The tendency is to view them, and Elijah in particular, as champions of an earlier and more popular form of Yahwism against the religion of Baal and other abuses of the royal court. For Vriezen, Elijah inaugurates 'a revival of militant Yahwism...[which] sets the divinity of Yahweh so sharply over against Baal's that it does present monotheism as being, for Israel, the

22. Are the clouds perhaps those of a mountain storm? So Albertz: Yahweh 'was a southern Palestinian mountain god before he became the god of liberation for the Moses group'; *A History of Israelite Religion*, p. 52.

23. F.M. Cross, *Canaanite Myth and Hebrew Epic* (Cambridge, MA: Harvard University Press, 1973), chs. 1–3; Ahlström, *Aspects of Syncretism*; Albertz, *A History of Israelite Religion*, pp. 69-78.

24. 'Interpreting religion is a relative matter, not because there is nothing out there corresponding to it, but because there is so much out there that our concepts of it are necessarily limited to highly situated choices'; W.E. Paden, *Interpreting the Sacred: Ways of Viewing Religion* (Boston: Beacon Press, 1992), p. 123.

25. Albertz, who borrows this term from G. Lanczkowski, presents one way of envisioning the elements in this pluralism and their development and interrelationships over time in a diagram: see *A History of Israelite Religion*, pp. 19, 106.

only right and proper thing'.[26] Elijah and Elisha were part of a protest against Omrid absolutism (cf. the Naboth incident) and religious policy.

> What was new about the ninth-century prophetic movement was that it represented the combination of a defence of the traditional farmers' rights against the onslaught of the crown with a battle for traditional Yahweh religion against the syncretism ordered by the state.[27]

Fohrer says that Elijah asserted 'Yahweh's claim to sole sovereignty in Israel', but adds that he also

> introduced new elements into the faith of Yahwism to preserve its viability within the context of an advanced civilization and political order and keep it from declining into syncretism. Thus he declared that it was Yahweh, not Baal, who bestowed or withheld rain and thereby the fertility of the land...[28]

Again there is ambiguity, since we can imagine the 'men of God' so described in affiliation with any or all of the last three of Ringgren's threads.

The Idea of 'Popular Religion'

The difficulty one encounters in any attempt to trace a pattern of threads in the tapestry of Israelite religion is especially obvious when we consider the notion of 'popular religion'. It is already evident from the discussion above, and not at all surprising, that there is a wide spectrum of opinion about the characteristics of 'popular religion' in Israel. Ringgren speaks of it as 'syncretistic', and Ahlström, whom he quotes in this context, agrees.[29] Similarly, Bernhard Lang argues that during the period of the Israelite monarchy, 'the dominant religion [was] polytheistic and undifferentiated from that of its neighbours'.[30] At the other end of the spectrum, Jeffrey Tigay thinks that 'the popular/private religion was almost exclusively Yahwistic and that other deities were worshiped only in the state religion when royal policy dictated it'.[31] The

26. Vriezen, *The Religion of Ancient Israel*, p. 191.

27. Albertz, *A History of Israelite Religion*, p. 191.

28. Fohrer, *History of Israelite Religion*, pp. 230-31.

29. Ahlström, *Aspects of Syncretism*, p. 11; Vriezen, *The Religion of Ancient Israel*, pp. 160-61, 168-70; Dever, 'Recent Archeological Confirmation'.

30. B. Lang, *Monotheism and the Prophetic Minority* (Sheffield: Almond Press, 1983), p. 20.

31. Tigay, 'Israelite Religion', p. 171.

Israelites were, then, essentially monotheistic, a position argued at some length by Yehezkel Kaufmann.[32] P. Kyle McCarter stakes out a mediating position. Having established the existence of local cults of Yahweh, some of which he associated with a cult object that was personified as the goddess Asherah, he goes on to suggest that this type of cult was not, strictly speaking, syncretistic.[33]

Israelite 'popular religion' has been characterized in other ways. In one place Fohrer imagines it a phenomenon of the 'countryside' as opposed to the cities and to the capital with its 'official cultic center'.[34] He also associates it with certain 'magical notions and practices'. The instances of divination and miracle-working in the Elijah and Elisha narratives indicate 'that at least for popular tradition there was a certain connection between prophecy and magic'.[35]

At the heart of the problem, as J. Berlinerblau notes, is the fact that in biblical scholarship the term 'popular religion' has neither been precisely defined nor subjected to 'theoretical analysis'.[36] Furthermore, the term is problematic because 'it fosters the impression of one religious movement...which stands as a unified antithesis of an "official religion"'.[37] Similarly, social-scientific and historical research on non-biblical 'popular religion' has arrived at no consensus as to what the term means. However, these studies have recognized and stressed a fact which is frequently not prominent in the constructions of biblical scholars, namely that popular religious groups always exist in a reciprocal relationship with other groups. Thus,

> a nexus must exist among various religious groups in a society. No matter how dissimilar, how antagonistic 'popular' and 'official' religion actually are, it is conceded that they must exist in some sort of a relation... we must always recognize that religious groups sharing a common social space mutually affect one another.[38]

32. Y. Kaufmann, *The Religion of Israel* (New York: Schocken Books, 1972).

33. McCarter, 'Aspects of the Religion of the Israelite Monarchy', p. 149.

34. Fohrer, *History of Israelite Religion*, pp. 130-31.

35. Fohrer, *History of Israelite Religion*, pp. 159, 232; cf. Kaufmann, who however argues that biblical magic (for instance, in the prophetic legends) transmutes pagan magic; *The Religion of Israel*, pp. 78-84.

36. J. Berlinerblau, 'The "Popular Religion" Paradigm in Old Testament Research: A Sociological Critique', *JSOT* 60 (1993), p. 5.

37. Berlinerblau, 'The "Popular Religion" Paradigm', p. 7.

38. Berlinerblau, 'The "Popular Religion" Paradigm', p. 9.

Later in his study, Berlinerblau suggests that 'it would be best to structure future investigations [of Israelite popular religion] around "adjectived" Israelites—bearers of precise economic, social, sexual and geographic attributes...to delineate religiosity among *particular Israelite groups*'. Since our best sources for studying popular religious groups are texts produced by the 'biblical literati', we may define a popular religious group as *'any association of individuals living within the borders of ancient Israel who by dint of their religious beliefs, political beliefs, rituals, symbols and so on, are denigrated by the authors of the Old Testament'*. In addition, there are 'requisite groups' (such as 'women and the non-privileged classes') which we know existed but about which information is scarce.[39]

M.D. Carroll R. makes a similar point in and for another context. In a section entitled 'Understanding Latin America' from his book on Amos, Carroll argues against the 'liberationist point of view' which equates 'popular culture' with 'the "social block" of the oppressed' and distinguishes it 'from transnational or imperial culture, from national culture, from the culture of the dominant classes and even from "mass" culture'. Such a view overlooks the fact that Latin America is a rich blend of Native American and European civilizations in which distinct national cultures exist within 'a larger cultural setting in which much is shared'.[40] As a consequence, the investigation of popular religion in Latin America must be shifted from a 'terrain' or 'partisan' understanding of the phenomenon (the religion of subordinate in contrast to elite classes) to an 'object', interclass, or 'nationalistic' understanding.[41] If we make use of this kind of definition of 'popular religion', we can begin to suggest an answer to our problem.

Elijah, Elisha, and Israelite 'Popular Religion'

We can now return to the Elijah and Elisha narratives and pick up our discussion in light of these reflections. My opening description of the content of these stories referred to some of their more unusual elements—resuscitations, healing, power to command wild beasts, and the like. These do not correspond very well to any of the threads of Israelite

39. Berlinerblau, 'The "Popular Religion" Paradigm', pp. 17-18.

40. M.D. Carroll R., *Contexts for Amos: Prophetic Poetics in Latin American Perspective* (JSOTSup, 132; Sheffield: JSOT Press, 1992), pp. 96-97.

41. Carroll, *Contexts for Amos*, p. 107.

religion discussed above, and it would be convenient to ignore them. We cannot, of course, and must try instead to comprehend their place within the larger fabric of Israelite religion. To that end I will briefly recap one portion of the interpretation of these stories I have worked out in more detail elsewhere and suggest an approach to viewing them as part of the tapestry.[42]

The narratives describe how both Elijah and Elisha brought a dead boy back to life (1 Kgs 17.17-24; 2 Kgs 4.8-37). These stories characterize the two 'men of God' as powerful healers who had close contact with ordinary citizens, who could appeal to them in a crisis precipitated by someone's illness (2 Kgs 4.18-31, and by implication 1 Kgs 17.18, where the appeal takes the form of a challenge). Apart from our own possible feelings of incredulity, these stories present a problem because there is no context within the Hebrew Bible in which they can be understood.[43] However, an appropriate context for understanding such goings-on can be found in the conceptual world of shamanism, widely attested in cultures distributed around the world.

The various cultures in which shamans are found share a belief that there is a supernatural realm inhabited by powerful beings who are capable of asserting their presence in the world in ways both helpful and destructive. Shamans are inspired intermediaries whose role includes communicating with and enlisting the help of these beings. From one point of view they are essentially similar to the biblical prophets,[44] but there are important differences as well. One of these is the elaborate trances during which the shaman's behavior may be interpreted as a magical journey to the other world or an incarnation of one of the spirits.[45] Another is the central role of curing in the shamanic vocation.

---

42. T.W. Overholt, *Cultural Anthropology and the Old Testament* (Guides to Biblical Scholarship; Minneapolis: Fortress Press, 1996). Gene Tucker has for years been the editor of that series, and it was he who encouraged me to undertake writing this volume and provided me with helpful comments and skilled and timely editing along the way to its completion. I am pleased to offer this brief essay as a token both of personal gratitude and of appreciation for the many contributions he has made over the years—and will, I hope, continue to make in retirement—to our discipline.

43. The Old Testament has no other accounts of resuscitation, and in general has very little to say about healing.

44. This point is argued at length in T.W. Overholt, *Channels of Prophecy: The Social Dynamics of Prophetic Activity* (Minneapolis: Fortress Press, 1989).

45. There are indications of ecstatic behavior in the Elijah and Elisha narratives (see for instance 1 Kgs 18.46; 2 Kgs 3.15-16).

The latter observation returns us to the Elijah and Elisha stories; resuscitation is, after all, the ultimate cure. In each case the prophet performs a healing ritual (1 Kgs 17.19b-21; 2 Kgs 4.29-35), and though there are differences in details the procedures themselves are identical in structure: the patient was laid out on a bed in the prophet's chamber (1 Kgs 7.19; 2 Kgs 4.21), and when he was alone with the corpse, the prophet cried out (prayed) to Yahweh (1 Kgs 7.20; 2 Kgs 4.33), then mounted the bed and laid himself upon the body (Elijah did this three times, Elisha twice; 1 Kgs 17.21; 2 Kgs 4.34-35).

There are striking parallels to this pattern of ritual activity in ethnographic reports of shamanic curing among tribal peoples. In one account, a Northern Ojibwa shaman was summoned to cure a sick girl, but she died soon after his arrival. At once the shaman 'tied a piece of red yarn around the girl's wrist', laid her body out, and lay down beside her. He lay very still, then after a while 'began to move ever so little. The girl began to move a little also...[he] moved a little more. So did the girl. Finally...[he] raised himself into a sitting posture and at the same time the girl [did likewise]'.[46]

Unlike the Elijah and Elisha narratives which offer no explanation of the reported cure, in this case a native interpretation of the dynamics of resuscitation is available. From the Ojibwa point of view, the shaman had followed the girl's soul to the land of the dead, captured it, and brought it back before its residence there became permanent. The red yarn tied around the patient's wrist was to make his task of identifying the proper soul easier. A.I. Hallowell assures us that according to the Northern Ojibwa 'theory of the nature of things' such feats were possible, though only the most powerful shamans could perform them.

Ivan Lopatin observed a similar curing ritual in south-eastern Siberia. In this case a young boy, sick but not yet dead, was lying in his bed. The shaman sang, called upon his spirit protector, danced around the fire, and went into a trance during which the incarnated spirit spoke through him ('I am here; I have come to help these poor people. I will look at the child'). Still 'in a state of ecstasy', he approached the boy's bed and 'crouched over him' until their faces almost touched, then ran around the room beating his drum and crying out, 'I am flying...I will catch you'. From time to time he spoke in different voices, apparently representing a dialogue between spirits, and finally he cried, 'I have it; I have

46. A.I. Hallowell, *Culture and Experience* (New York: Schocken Books, 1967), p. 154.

it!', cupping his hands 'as though he held something in them'. At this point the parents rushed to the bed and pulled the blanket off the boy. The shaman jumped in beside him, and the parents covered them both with the blanket.

Again, we have an indigenous interpretation of what the participants believed had taken place. Speaking later with Lopatin, the shaman 'explained that the boy was sick because his soul had been stolen by a spirit'. The running and leaping around the room represented his flight 'into the spirit realm', where he found the offending spirit and recaptured the boy's soul and brought it back 'in the shape of a sparrow'. Lopatin confessed that he had not seen this sparrow, but both his interpreter and the boy's parents 'assured' him that they had seen it 'quite plainly'. The shaman also said 'that while lying beside the boy he had restored the soul to the body'.[47] These are not isolated examples, either in the idea that the dead can be revived, or in the particular form that the therapeutic act takes, or in the idea that the cause of the illness was the soul's leaving the body.

Although the Elisha account does not clearly explain the boy's coming back to life, saying only that his body warmed and then he winked (or sneezed) and opened his eyes (2 Kgs 4.34-5), the Elijah story links the resuscitation to the return of the *nephesh* ('soul', or 'breath'): the prophet called upon Yahweh to let the boy's *nephesh* return to his 'inward parts'; Yahweh listened, the *nephesh* returned, and the boy lived (1 Kgs 17.21-22). The similarity in physical activities, together with the native explanations of resuscitation and healing just described, suggests the possibility that the Elijah (and by inference the Elisha) narrative assumes a soul-loss theory of illness and death.

This idea seems to go against a consensus among biblical scholars that the *nephesh* and the body are not separate and detachable entities. But matters do not appear to be that simple. The word *nephesh* has a great many connotations, ranging from physical (throat, neck, breath, body, blood) and emotional (hunger, thirst, grieving, desire, agreement) associations to 'life' in the abstract and even 'corpse'.[48] It is especially

47. I.A. Lopatin, 'A Shamanistic Performance for a Sick Boy', *Anthropos* 4 (1946–49), pp. 153-74.

48. See Num. 19.11-13; cf. E.R. Brotzman, 'Man and the Meaning of *nepes*', *BSac* 145 (1988), pp. 400-409; and see A.R. Johnson, *The Vitality of the Individual in the Thought of Ancient Israel* (Cardiff: University of Wales Press, 2nd edn, 1964), pp. 3-22.

important to note that *nephesh* can be distinguished from 'flesh' (*basar*; Deut. 12.23; Isa. 10.18) and that it departs from the dying person (Gen. 35.18; the same idea, but using the term *ruach*, 'spirit', appears in Pss. 104.29; 146.4; Job 34.14-5; Eccl. 12.7). The *nephesh* is said to be poured out when one is sick (Job 30.16) or starving (Lam. 2.12). Recovery from illness can be described as Yahweh bringing up the *nephesh* from Sheol (the underworld; Ps. 30.2-3). The term *ruach* (spirit, wind) has a similar range of connotations.[49]

Furthermore, the Hebrew Bible contains clear evidence that at least some Israelites believed that a part of an individual could survive the death of the physical body. One finds, for example, references to grave offerings (Deut. 26.14; Sir. 30.18), and to diviners who employed 'ghosts' and 'familiar spirits' (Lev. 19.31; 20.6, 27; Deut. 18.11; Isa. 8.19; 19.3). Saul's consultation at Endor with 'a woman who is *master* of a ghost' (*'eshet ba'elat'ob*; 1 Sam. 28.7) is particularly striking, since she divined by the 'ghost' of a known historical figure, Samuel. Some thought that disembodied spirits (*repa'im*, 'shades') resided in Sheol (Job 26.5; Isa. 14.9-10; cf. Ezek. 32.21).[50] While scholars have been attentive to the apparent contrast between Hebrew and Hellenistic conceptions of soul and body, they have generally failed to be sufficiently sensitive to the folk background of ancient Israelite culture. For what the evidence just cited suggests is that at least some persons in the society in which the Elijah and Elisha narratives were produced would have been prepared to believe that sickness and death were the result of the loss of the soul and that curing these conditions involved recovering the errant soul and reintroducing it into the body. For persons who share the conceptual world of shamanism, the actions of Elijah and Elisha would have been perfectly intelligible and not at all out of the ordinary. Healing is one of the things shamans routinely do.

There is another famous tale of healing in this collection. The story of the Aramean commander, Naaman, in 2 Kings 5 presents an interesting mix of viewpoints. A pro-Yahwist ideology is obvious from the very beginning: the narrator tells us that Naaman was a great commander because Yahweh had given him victory (2 Kgs 5.1; cf. Isa. 10.5-6; 45.1-7), and a premise of the account is that the cure resulted in the spread of

49. Johnson, *The Vitality of the Individual*, pp. 23-37.

50. See E.M. Bloch-Smith, 'The Cult of the Dead in Judah: Interpreting the Material Remains', *JBL* 11 (1992), pp. 213-24; T.J. Lewis, *Cults of the Dead in Ancient Israel and Ugarit* (Atlanta: Scholars Press, 1989).

Yahweh's fame among foreigners (vv. 15-19). Still, this ideology does not dominate the action. One can see in the suggestion of the captive Israelite servant girl (v. 3) an indication that she was from a segment of the population with ties to Elisha, and therefore knew that holy men were healers (v. 8). The narrator does not explicitly say that the king knew of Elisha's role as a healer, but the story clearly implies that he sent Naaman along to him (v. 7). If he appears a bit apprehensive and hesitant to do so, that seems reasonable under the circumstances. Opinions about the ability of persons like Elisha to effect such dramatic cures would vary, and politically a lot was at stake. The departure from Yahweh ideology is also evident in the fact that, although Elisha uttered an oath in Yahweh's name (v. 16) and Naaman attributed his cure to Yahweh (v. 15), Elisha offered to perform the cure in order to enhance his own reputation (v. 8b). This is in marked contrast to the wonders associated with the exodus from Egypt, where it is Yahweh's reputation that is at stake, but in harmony with the activities of shamans seeking to enhance and maintain their position within their communities. Elisha refused Naaman's offer of payment, but his servant, Gehazi, acted secretly and in his own self-interest to collect the fee which is the curer's due (vv. 15-16, 19b-24). Elisha, however, knew what he had done, and as punishment afflicted him with Naaman's leprosy, thereby demonstrating his ability to harm as well as to help (vv. 25-27; recall the widow's accusation against Elijah, 1 Kgs 17.18). All of these elements—the appeal to a religious functionary to perform a healing ceremony, the cure itself and its implications for the healer's reputation, the offer to pay a fee, and the inflicting of harm—reflect the conceptual world of shamanism.

Besides these stories of resuscitation and curing, there are other features of the narratives which contribute to the conviction that, whatever other aspects there may have been to their roles in ninth-century Israelite religion, Elijah and Elisha functioned in a way closely analogous to the way shamans function in their societies. I can name, but not pursue, these here.[51] For one, there are the numerous accounts of 'miraculous' deeds (calling down fire from heaven, making axeheads float, and the like). Like the resuscitations (which might also be considered in this category), such acts of power are virtually unique to the

---

51. For a more extensive discussion see T. Overholt, *Anthropological Approaches to the Old Testament* (Guides to Biblical Scholarship; Minneapolis: Fortress Press, forthcoming).

Elijah and Elisha stories, but are relatively common in ethnographic reports of shamanic activity, where their function is to establish the authority of the shaman. The responses attributed to those who witnessed the men of God's acts indicate a similar function (see for example 1 Kgs 17.24; 2 Kgs 2.15; 4.37). Again, shamans sometimes demonstrate what seems to be an uncanny knowledge of things taking place at a distance. The stories about Elisha contain two such episodes, including the case of the unfortunate Gehazi mentioned above (2 Kgs 5.26; 6.8-12). Finally, references to the 'servants' of these two men of God and to Elisha's use of a staff in curing (2 Kgs 4.29-31) both have analogies in shamanic activities.

This line of interpretation raises a historical problem, however. Not only do the Elijah and Elisha narratives as we have them simultaneously reflect two somewhat different ideologies, but from a global perspective the shamanic worldview is also older than the Yahwistic by millennia and is typical of pre-urban societies. How can we account for its presence in monarchic Israel?

Since the development of societies is not characterized by any neat evolution from earlier (and more 'primitive') to later forms, it is reasonable (and not at all difficult) to imagine that both views were operative in Ahab's Israel. We might, therefore, think of these shamanistic elements as 'survivals', though we must be careful to avoid an outmoded understanding of that term tied to evolutionistic assumptions about progress and stages of development through which all societies are believed to pass. Judging from these stories, we are not talking about crude, fossilized, functionless remains of beliefs which earlier characterized the whole society, but beliefs and practices still living and vital in some segment(s) of the population.[52] I.M. Lewis employs a notion of survivals more adequate to our purpose. Lewis notes the presence in North African Islam of phenomena—like the veneration of saints, possession cults, and brotherhoods—which from one point of view appear to have their roots in pre-Islamic beliefs and practices. Viewed in context, however, they have become important parts of the practice of Islam in this region.[53] Another example of this kind of integration of ancient with more recent beliefs can be found in the case of a sixteenth-century

52. For a discussion of survivals, cf. J.W. Rogerson, *Anthropology and the Old Testament* (Atlanta: John Knox, 1978), pp. 23-24, 32-35.

53. I.M. Lewis, *Religion in Context: Cults and Charisma* (Cambridge: Cambridge University Press, 1986), pp. 94-107.

Italian miller named Menocchio, who was tried and eventually executed as a heretic. Carlo Ginzburg, who reconstructs this story, sees in Menocchio's bizarre 'cheese and worms' cosmogony a blending of 'popular [by which he means 'peasant'] beliefs' derived from a 'seemingly ancient oral tradition' with the teaching of the Catholic Church and ideas unleashed by the Reformation and spread by the newly developed technology of printing.[54] This is the way we should view the shamanistic pattern discernible in the Elijah and Elisha narratives. It is not a remnant of some 'pure' and exotic pre-Israelite shamanism, on its last legs in Israel and about to disappear in the evolutionary triumph of a higher religious form, monotheism. In these stories it is rather an older pattern of beliefs heavily influenced by Yahwism and a living part of it.

Berlinerblau suggests that the study of Israelite 'popular religion' should focus on 'particular Israelite groups' whose 'distinct religious orientations' are 'denigrated by the [elitist] authors of the Old Testament'.[55] That seems to me a useful principle, but it is not easy to follow in the context of the argument I have been making. Can we consider the people whom these narratives portray as sharing beliefs and practices at home in the conceptual world of shamanism to be one such popular religious 'group'? In the stories those who interact with Elijah and Elisha in a positive or sympathetic way are a heterogeneous bunch—among them a poor widow from a foreign land (1 Kgs 17), a high official in King Ahab's palace (18.1-16), a 'captain of fifty' in Ahaziah's army (2 Kgs 1.13-15), the 'people' of a city (2.19), kings in need of an oracle (3.9-20), a band of individuals of unknown composition and social status referred to collectively as 'the sons of the prophets' (2.3, 5, 7, 15, and elsewhere), the widow of one member of this band (4.1-7), the powerful wife of a landowner (4.8-37), and a captured Israelite girl working as a servant in Naaman's household (5.2-3). What sort of a 'group' is that? And where in the stories is the elitist denigration of their beliefs? On the other hand, another of Berlinerblau's propositions, that religious beliefs (he says 'groups') sharing 'a common social space mutually affect one another',[56] is clearly borne out by these stories.

The point Daniel Carroll makes about modern Latin America seems

54. C. Ginzburg, *The Cheese and the Worms: The Cosmos of a Sixteenth-Century Miller* (Baltimore: Johns Hopkins University Press, 1980), pp. xix-xxvi.
55. Berlinblau, 'The "Popular Religion" Paradigm', pp. 15, 18.
56. Berlinerblau, 'The "Popular Religion" Paradigm', p. 9.

relevant to ancient Israel as well: popular religion, at least in this instance, is apparently an 'interclass' phenomenon. The list of those sympathetic to the two men of God includes both the poorest of the poor and kings. The widow of one of the sons of the prophets stands at the periphery of the social order, the kings who seek an oracle or pass along an important foreign visitor for a cure at the center. The Shunemite woman, a wealthy landowner who needs no good word on her behalf to the authorities (2 Kgs 4.11-13), is somewhere in the middle. What unites them is belief in the power of a 'man of God' not only to champion the cause of the national deity, but also to act decisively in matters of more personal importance. Some people were more committed to these beliefs, others less; even the opinion of a single individual might change with the circumstances, as the resuscitation stories show. Hence the ambiguity about 'men of God' reflected in the stories. Such persons were thought capable of acts which benefited their recipients, and their favor was cultivated (2 Kgs 4.8-10). They were also capable of destructive, apparently capricious acts (2 Kgs 2.23-25; 5.25-27), and contact with them was potentially dangerous (1 Kgs 17.18).

From one point of view, this collection of stories presents Elijah and Elisha as 'shamans', that is, as religious intermediaries many of whose activities can best be interpreted in terms of the conceptual world of shamanism. This particular thread in the tapestry of Israelite religion comes into view most prominently in these narratives. The cast of characters just enumerated indicates that it was not the property of a special group or groups, but pervaded the whole of society. Still it was not entirely independent of the other threads of belief and practice with which it was woven. It was, rather, an integral part of a multifaceted Israelite religion during the period of the monarchy.

The Social Location of the Prophet Amos in Light of the Group/Grid Cultural Anthropological Model*

Guillermo Ramírez

The social location of the prophet Amos has been the object of extensive analysis throughout the history of critical investigation. This issue has led to a great deal of discussion and debate, especially among form critics. This paper explores the extent to which the group/grid model, a particular cultural anthropological paradigm, could shed light on the reconstruction of certain aspects of the social location of the prophet Amos. The group/grid cultural anthropological model at hand is used to explain Amos's social location from a different level of abstraction. While form criticism examines specific literary forms, actions, places and institutions, this model focuses on more inclusive and comprehensive categories for articulating the biblical social system. Hence, the group/grid model serves as a heuristic device to highlight some social features in the Hebrew text which could otherwise be overlooked.

Methodological Problems of the Sitz im Leben

It is impossible to talk about the history of form criticism, and particularly the notion of *Sitz im Leben*, without referring to the investigations conducted by Hermann Gunkel.[1] One of Gunkel's major concerns

---

*   This paper is offered with thanks to my teacher and friend, Gene M. Tucker, from whom I learned to appreciate the importance of the critical investigation of the social location of the prophetic literature.
    1.   Some of Hermann Gunkel's works are: *Die Sagen der Genesis*, 1901, reprinted as *The Legends of Genesis: The Biblical Saga and History* (trans. W.H. Carruth; New York: Schocken Books, 1964); *Israel und Babylonien* (Göttingen: Vandenhoeck & Ruprecht, 1903), translated as *Israel and Babylon* by E.S.B. (Philadelphia: J.J. McVey, 1904); 'Die israelitische Literatur', in P. Hinnberg (ed.), *Die Kultur der Gegenwart* (Berlin: B.G. Teubner, 1906); *Reden und Aufsätze* (Göttingen: Vandenhoeck & Ruprecht, 1913); *Die Propheten* (Göttingen: Vandenhoeck & Ruprecht, 1917); *Schöpfung und Chaos in Urzeit und Endzeit: Eine*

hinged upon the oral milieu giving way to the literary genre. His ultimate goal—overly comprehensive—was to interpret the pre-literary state of the biblical text within the broad spectrum of Israel's social reality. One of his most quoted statements, one which I believe expresses his understanding of the connection existing between genre and *Sitz im Leben*, declares: 'Every old literary genre has its original setting at a particular point in the folk-life of Israel'.[2] I must emphasize that Gunkel refers not to the historical period when the literary genre was originated, but to the pre-literary social milieu which witnessed the creation of the various genres.[3]

Despite Old Testament scholarship's acknowledgment of Gunkel's contribution, it is agreed that the main epistemological problem regarding the complex issues surrounding the reconstruction of the *Sitz im Leben* of biblical texts rests on its theoretical premises, that is, the correlation between the literary genre and the pre-literary milieu. This relationship cannot be reliably tested when confronted with the many variables affecting their interconnection. Investigations undertaken on this topic have examined a series of issues, such as: (1) the adequacy of the terminology employed, that is, what term best translates in the English language the German notion of *Sitz im Leben*; (2) the multiplicity and interrelationship of settings; (3) the autonomy of a genre vis-à-vis a setting; (4) the contribution and challenge of linguistics and communication of meanings; and (5) the extent to which Gunkel's specific way of attempting the reconstruction of the setting of a biblical text is comprehensive enough to acknowledge its limitations and yet be considered a useful means to help describe the complex social phenomena which lie behind the text.[4]

---

religionsgeschichtliche Untersuchung über Gen 1 und Ap. Joh 12 (Göttingen: Vandenhoeck & Ruprecht, 1921); *Die Religion in Geschichte und Gegenwart*, 1930 (trans. from Vol. I of the second edition by T.M. Homer as *The Psalms: A Form-Critical Introduction* [Philadelphia: Fortress Press, 1967]); *Einleitung in die Psalmen: Die Gattungen der religiösen Lyrik Israels* (Göttingen: Vandenhoeck & Ruprecht, 1933) (this work was completed by Joachim Begrich).

    2.   Gunkel, *Reden und Aufsätze*, p. 33. The term used here is *Sitz im Volksleben*, that is, setting in life of the people, and not *Sitz im Leben*, setting in life. The term *Sitz im Volksleben* was employed for the first time in 1906 and the term *Sitz im Leben* was employed later in 1917.

    3.   G.M. Tucker, *Form-Criticism of the Old Testament* (Philadelphia: Fortress Press, 1971), p. 15.

    4.   D. Knight, 'The Understanding of "*Sitz im Leben*" in Form Criticism', in G. MacRae (ed.), *SBLSP* 1 (Cambridge, MA: Society of Biblical Literature, 1974), p. 107.

The investigation of the idea of *Sitz im Leben* has expanded consider-ably as a result of the contributions and challenges that other disciplines have offered, especially those disciplines deriving from the social sciences. Given the difficulties encountered in trying to establish a relationship between genre and setting, other equally important dimensions of this issue need to be explored which will no doubt shed light on the overall understanding of the setting. Turning to an interdisciplinary approach to biblical studies has definitely enriched this field; yet this route has posed a number of problems which will surely be examined in forthcoming studies.

The Group/Grid Cultural Anthropological Model

In describing the model, Mary Douglas[5] introduces it as 'a tool created in order to study the complex problems anthropologists confront when analyzing culture as a subject of study and when they try to do cultural comparison'.[6] This anthropological concern shows great similarities with the interest of Old Testament scholars who seek to reconstruct and explore the possible forms of the social location of the prophets on the basis of cultural comparison. When scholars recognize their need to deepen their understanding of social backgrounds in order to enrich further the meaning of the biblical text, they too are considering culture as a subject of study and, consequently, embarking on the task of cultural comparison.[7]

The model consists of two variables: the 'group' variable, which is concerned with the outside boundary and with the external pressure society exercises over the individual members of the social group;[8] and the 'grid' variable, which has to do with the internal organization of the

---

5. Mary Douglas first introduced the group/grid model in her work *Natural Symbols: Explorations in Cosmology* (New York: Pantheon Books, 1970). Later in her work *Cultural Bias* (Occasional Paper No. 35 of the Royal Anthropological Institute of Great Britain and Ireland; London: Royal Anthropological Institute, 1978), she refined and systematized the concepts she had developed on this subject. Recently in her study *In the Wilderness: The Doctrine of Defilement in the Book of Numbers* (JSOTSup, 158; Sheffield: JSOT Press, 1993), she introduces less technical categories in order to explain the four extreme quadrants of the model (strong group/ high grid; strong group/low grid; weak group/high grid; weak group/low grid).

6. Douglas, *Cultural Bias*, pp. 1-5.

7. Douglas, *Natural Symbols* and *Cultural Bias*.

8. Douglas, *Cultural Bias*, pp. 7, 8, 16.

social structure. These two variables are combined to represent four extreme types of social environments, systems and cultural biases which altogether represent a spectrum of cultural patterns. However, they do not claim to exhaust the possibilities in which social groups can find themselves. The four different types of social environments are succinctly described as follows. 1. *The hierarchical cultural type.*[9] Members of this group express an explicit group-oriented tendency and inasmuch as they perceive themselves in the light of a collective identity, they make specific claims on their personal members. 2. *The enclavist cultural type.* Despite members' fostering of group-oriented values, they represent the periphery of the hierarchical cultural type. They may be described as the 'counter-culture'. This cultural type is profoundly sensitive to the breach between the values and structure institutionalized by the hierarchist and the social reality in which members live. 3. *The individualist cultural type.* Contrary to the first two groups, members are characterized by a clear preference for pragmatic decisions and enhancing individual accomplishments. Group membership is secondary. 4. *The isolated cultural type.* Unlike the rest of the groups, members do not foster the creation of any type of social group because of their indifference towards the formation of social boundaries. They tend to ignore the most basic rules and rites created to establish some kind of social order.

The Social Location of Amos: Three Major Hypotheses

There are three major hypotheses upon which Old Testament scholarship has focused its attention when dealing with the reconstruction of the social location of Amos. The first hypothesis relates Amos's prophecies to guilds of cultic prophets.[10] For instance, Ernst Würthwein[11] proposes

9. See Douglas, *In the Wilderness*, pp. 42-62.

10. R. Bach, 'Gottesrecht und weltliches Recht in der Verkündigung des Propheten Amos', in W. Schneemelcher (ed.), *Festschrift fur Günther Dehn* (Neukirchen–Vluyn: Neukirchener Verlag, 1957), pp. 23-34; A. Bentzen, 'The Ritual Background of Amos 1.2–2.16', *OTS* 8 (1950), pp. 85-99; W. Brueggemann, 'Amos 4.4-13 and Israel's Covenant Worship', *VT* 15 (1965), pp. 1-15; A. Gunneweg, 'Erwägungen zu Amos 7.14', *ZTK* 57 (1960), pp. 1-6; H.G. Reventlow, *Das Amt des Propheten bei Amos* (Göttingen: Vandenhoeck & Ruprecht, 1962); J.D. Watts, *Vision and Prophecy in Amos* (Leiden: Brill, 1958); E. Würthwein, 'Amos-Studien', *ZAW* 62 (1950), pp. 10-51.

11. 'Amos-Studien', pp. 16-52, esp. 27-28. In order to understand Würthwein we must see him within his scholarly framework. Würthwein is among a number of

that Amos initiated his prophetic office as a *nabi*, a prophet of weal, and as such he was expected to perform a series of stereotyped functions and to play a particular role in support and legitimation of the nation through acts of intercession (cf. Amos 7.2, 5). Contrary to these expectations, later in his career Amos emerged as a prophet of doom who continuously questioned the nation's loyalty to Yahweh (cf. Amos 1–2; 7–9).

In Würthwein's opinion, in the first two visions (7.1-3 and 7.4-6) the prophet is projected as holding the office of *nabi*, interceding in favor of his people. However, in the two following visions (7.7-9 and 8.1-2), the prophet is projected as undergoing a transformation from a prophet of weal to a prophet of doom.[12] Würthwein further contends that Amos's criticism of the cult throughout this process was not really a rejection of that prophetic sphere of life, but a critical position against some of its expressions.

The second hypothesis associates Amos with wisdom circles and village clan groups.[13] H.W. Wolff's methodology, for instance, is aimed at undermining any features which may in any way be used to associate

---

Old Testament scholars who stood out for their great appreciation of the positive role of cult in religion. See also S. Mowinckel, *The Psalms in Israel's Worship* (Nashville: Abingdon Press, 1979); A.R. Johnson, *The Cultic Prophet in Ancient Israel* (Cardiff: University of Wales Press, 1962); and Watts, *Vision and Prophecy in Amos*, pp. 19-20.

12. Würthwein, 'Amos-Studien', p. 22.

13. J.L. Crenshaw, 'The Influence of the Wise on Amos', *ZAW* 79 (1967), pp. 42-51; *idem*, 'The Wisdom Literature', in D. Knight and G.M. Tucker (eds.), *The Hebrew Bible and its Modern Interpreters* (Chico, CA: Scholars Press, 1985), pp. 369-407; *idem*, 'Prolegomena', in *idem* (ed.), *Studies in Ancient Israelite Wisdom* (New York: Ktav, 1976), p. 4; E. Gerstenberger, 'The Woe-Oracles of the Prophets', *JBL* 81 (1962), p. 261; R. Gordis, 'The Social Background of Wisdom Literature', *HUCA* 18 (1944), pp. 77-118; W.R. Harper, *A Critical and Exegetical Commentary on Amos and Hosea* (ICC; Edinburgh: T. & T. Clark, 1919); W. Irwin, 'Where Shall Wisdom be Found', *JBL* 80 (1961), pp. 133-42; J. Lindblom, 'Wisdom in the Old Testament Prophets', in M. Noth and D. Winton Thomas (eds.), *Wisdom in Israel and the Ancient Near East* (VTSup, 3; Leiden: Brill, 1955), pp. 192-204; J. McKenzie, 'Reflections on Wisdom', *JBL* 86 (1967), pp. 1-9; L. Perdue, *Wisdom and Cult* (SBLDS, 30; Missoula: Scholars Press, 1977); *idem*, 'Liminality as a Social Setting for Wisdom's Instructions', *ZAW* 39 (1981), pp. 114-27; S. Terrien, 'Amos and Wisdom', in B.W. Anderson and W. Harrelson (eds.), *Israel's Prophetic Heritage: Essays in Honor of James Muilenberg* (New York: Harper & Row, 1962), pp. 108-95; H.W. Wolff, *Amos the Prophet* (Philadelphia: Fortress Press, 1973); *idem*, *Joel and Amos* (Philadelphia: Fortress Press, 1977).

the prophet with cultic prophecy, and thus to establish a connection, be it through the literary genres, the terminology or topics employed by the prophet, between Amos and clan-based wisdom traditions.[14]

Before I hastily relate the influence of wisdom traditions upon Amos, we must first determine how we define wisdom tradition in itself and consider the need to develop certain criteria which might enable us to identify the influence of wisdom upon other texts. Certain approaches have definitely been extremist in visualizing an influence of wisdom in all of the Hebrew canon, which might easily lead to the adoption of a 'pan-wisdom' position.[15] While the ancient world was well compartmentalized and structured, it is also true that matters concerning justice to the poor, the orphan and the widow were evident in societal groups, regardless of their origin. In addition, experience was a common element to both the wisdom traditions and the cultic traditions. Neither possesses a monopoly on experience.[16]

In dealing with the problem of Amos's cultural background, we must move the scholarly discussion beyond the juxtaposition of cultic prophets and wisdom circles. We should not limit our discussion to either cult or wisdom nor ultimately regard them as mutually exclusive, that is, as belonging to two opposite poles of a single cultural world,[17] insofar as the social reality which affected the prophet Amos was much more complex than is suggested merely by identifying these two social spheres.

The first two hypotheses share a common presupposition: they identify particular groups as the supporters, preservers and modifiers of Amos's speeches and are based primarily upon the literary forms employed in the book of Amos.[18]

The third hypothesis hinges upon the study of what have been called 'central and peripheral intermediaries'. It is based on sociological and anthropological insights which view social phenomena as a result of the interaction between different societal groups. This hypothesis is a concept

14. Wolff, *Joel and Amos* and *Amos the Prophet*.

15. T. Giles, 'Amos and the Law' (PhD dissertation; Michigan State University, 1989), pp. 43ff.

16. Crenshaw, 'The Influence of the Wise upon Amos', pp. 42-51.

17. J.L. Crenshaw (*Prophetic Conflict* [BZAW, 124; Berlin: de Gruyter, 1971], p. 109) addresses this problem, though referring to a later period, when he explores the relationship between wisdom and apocalyptic literature on the issue of divine justice.

18. Wolff, *Amos the Prophet*, pp. 3-4.

originally employed in biblical studies by Robert Wilson.[19] In specifically referring to Amos, Wilson stresses that any effort to study Amos's social location is limited by the fact that most of the background information on Amos is concentrated in two small units, namely, Amos 1.1 and Amos 7.10-17; and that the complex process of redaction which the book appears to have undergone makes the reconstruction of the social location of Amos more difficult. Wilson admits that, based on the book's superscription in Amos 1.2 and, moreover, based on the analysis of the term נקד,[20] one could think that Amos belonged to a guild of cultic prophets in Jerusalem. But he also acknowledges that outside of the title נקד, the weight of evidence in support of Amos's cultic background is not conclusive. He states that it is more appropriate to conclude that the prophet was either a governmental employee in charge of a considerable herd of sheep or an independent sheep owner with a large herd.[21] In either case, Wilson views the prophet Amos as a member of the Judean upper class, if not an actual part of the political or religious establishments in Jerusalem.[22] Wilson emphasizes that Amos's Judean background is found in Amos 7.10-15, the encounter of the prophet with the priest Amaziah, a leader of the royal sanctuary of Bethel. Based on his analysis of the term חזה, 'visionary', Wilson suggests that this term was a Judahite title which was applied only to central intermediaries.[23]

From a methodological point of view, Wilson's categories may assist us in perhaps overcoming the tight polarization many studies have made between cultic tradition and wisdom tradition. I would like to emphasize,

---

19. R.R. Wilson, *Prophecy and Society in Ancient Israel* (Philadelphia: Fortress Press, 1980). See also D.L. Petersen, *The Roles of Israel's Prophets* (JSOTSup, 17; Sheffield: JSOT Press, 1981), pp. 44 and 108, n. 19. Wilson borrowed these categories from I.M. Lewis, *Ecstatic Religion* (Baltimore: Penguin, 1971). Petersen states that 'Wilson's use of these categories focuses almost exclusively on the issue of whether or not the prophet is related to the central political and religious establishment...Wilson, therefore, appropriates Lewis' categories without utilizing the full range of criteria...' I underline this limitation not in the light of Lewis's work, but on the basis of the group/grid model.

20. *Prophecy and Society*, p. 269.

21. *Prophecy and Society*, p. 269.

22. Recently, S.N. Rosenbaum proposed an opposite theory pertaining to Amos's origins, in which the prophet is said to belong to the north and not to the south. See S. Rosenbaum, *Amos of Israel: A New Interpretation* (Macon, GA: Mercer University Press, 1990).

23. *Prophecy and Society*, p. 269.

however, that these two categories must be understood from a more critical standpoint. It is important to realize that 'centrality' and 'peripherality' may be easily misunderstood if they are not placed within a broader frame of reference. One limitation in Wilson's proposal is the extent to which his definitions of 'central prophets' and 'peripheral prophets' are precise enough to explain in depth the social location of Amos. Wilson does not offer ample criteria that would assist us in perceiving cross-cultural distinctions such as those encompassed in the group/grid model.

For instance, to speak of a prophet who lives in a community culturally oriented to the individual is not the same as to speak of someone who lives in a collective-oriented society. In modern times, a person understands himself or herself as the master of his or her own thoughts and deeds. A person is encouraged to search for practical decision-making, to look for independent and mainly rationalistic bases in his or her decision-making process. The individual is seen as a free agent and independent from the deity. Reason should be the utmost light that guides each person's path. Dependence on God is, in a sense, seen as a sign of weakness. In the political sphere, the notion of *laissez-faire* prevails and the deity is not supposed to play a major role in the decision-making process. Thus, it becomes necessary to distinguish the implications of the *laissez-faire* concept as perceived and used by different cultural cosmologies throughout history.

Amos 7.10-17

There is consensus among scholars on the importance of unit 7.10-17 in reconstructing the social setting of the prophet Amos. To begin with, a framework of controversy would appear to be the most logical original setting for this type of story.[24] Amaziah's questioning of Amos's authority to address their social problems triggered the conflict between them. This is crucial in understanding the prophetic role of Amos. A similar controvertive background must have affected other levels of setting in this unit. For example, the circle of Amos's followers, those who collected, preserved and translated this story in its literary form, were likewise immersed in a controversy over defending the rights of

24. G.M. Tucker, 'Prophetic Authenticity: A Form Critical Study of Amos 7.10-17', *Int* 27 (1973), pp. 423-34.

the prophet to deliver such speeches.[25] It is important to emphasize at this point Gene M. Tucker's comments on how this text can shed light in determining the institutional background of Amos. He stresses that this speech contributes to viewing Amos's prophetic role within a more comprehensive framework. In Amos's case, this issue

> cannot be reduced to the image of the individual against the corrupt institutions of the 'state' (the king) and the 'church' (the priest). Amos does not appear out of the thin air, but he takes his stand on the basis of a traditional role and self-understanding which has institutional dimensions.[26]

Undoubtedly, the prophet must have been influenced by these institutional traditions. Nevertheless, we lack sufficient evidence to associate him with any particular tradition.

Verses 14 and 15, describing Amos's reply to Amaziah, offer a number of elements which serve as an important basis for the reconstruction of the possible social location of the prophet Amos when seen in the light of the group/grid anthropological model. Verse 14 is among the texts to have generated one of the largest number of investigations and provoked extensive debates throughout the history of interpretation of the book of Amos. It is precisely Amos's affirmation concerning his profession which deserves our attention.

The first part of Amos's reply (v. 14) consists of a nominal sentence. The problem we encounter here basically lies in deciding what criteria we should use to translate the text. A considerable number of investigators concur that it is not possible to solve the tense problem which this situation poses solely on the basis of grammatical analysis. Some of the alternatives proposed in the translation of this text are[27] (1) translate the

25. See J.L. Mays, *Amos: A Commentary* (Philadelphia: Westminster Press, 1969), p. 134; Tucker, 'Prophetic Authenticity', p. 431; Wolff, *Joel and Amos*, p. 308.

26. Tucker, 'Prophetic Authenticity', p. 434.

27. A selected group of works on the subject are: P. Ackroyd, 'A Judgment Narrative Between Kings and Chronicles? An Approach to Amos 7.9-17', in G.W. Coats and B.O. Long (eds.), *Canon and Authority: Essays in Old Testament Religion and Theology* (Philadelphia: Fortress Press, 1977), pp. 71-87; S. Cohen, 'Amos Was a *Navi*', *HUCA* 32 (1961), pp. 175-78; J.H. Hayes, *Amos: The Eighth-Century Prophet, his Times and his Preaching* (Nashville: Abingdon Press, 1988), pp. 229-40; J.L. Mays, *Amos*, pp. 133-40; H.W. Richardson, 'A Critical Note on Amos 7.14', *JBL* 85 (1966), p. 89; H.H. Rowley, 'Was Amos a *Nabi*?', in J. Fück (ed.), *Festschrift für Otto Eissfeldt zum 60. Geburtstag* (Halle an der Saale: Max Niemeyer, 1947), pp. 191-98; Tucker, 'Prophetic Authenticity', pp. 423-34; Wolff, *Joel and Amos*, pp. 311-14; T.J. Wright, 'Amos and the Sycamore Fig', *VT* 26

nominal clause as Hebrew imperfect; (2) translate it as Hebrew perfect; (3) translate the negative particle לֹא as an interrogative particle; or (4) translate לֹא not as a negative particle, but as an emphatic particle.

John Hayes's remarks on the translation and interpretation of this text are pertinent as he states that the terms 'prophet' and 'son of a prophet' must not be understood as meaning a member of the prophetic guild. Rather, the expression 'son of a prophet' is simply a way of saying 'one who belongs to the class of the prophets' and the text does not reveal any negative or derogatory views of the office and vocation of the prophet.[28] Hayes adds: 'In 2.11-12 and 3.7, Amos shows respect for the office of prophet and nowhere casts aspersion on the office. In 3.8, Amos indicates that under certain conditions anyone could and should perform the activity of prophesying.'[29] Verse 15, as part of the context, must also be taken into account when translating v. 14. Amos speaks of his new identity as a prophet. Again, Amos stresses how he perceived himself, affirming that Yahweh gave him his new identity. This is consistent with what the group/grid model associates with hierarchist cultural typology.[30] In this verse, as well as in the rhetorical questions found in Amos 3.3-8,[31] Amos accepts his original status to be different from that of the community of prophets. Thus, the prophet affirms that he was a herdsman and a tender of sycamores. It is precisely due to his respect towards a highly structured society (what cultural anthropologists would nowadays define as a stratified society) that he holds the roles played by each member of his society in such high esteem. Amos is compelled to identify his traditional role in society. However, he makes clear that his new identity as a prophet was not a decision of his own nor was it attributable to other human influences or factors, but his commitment to prophesy was instead due to Yahweh's commission (v. 15). Yahweh took him away from the flock and commanded him to prophesy. Amos is prophesying upon the authority conferred upon him by Yahweh.[32]

(1976), pp. 362-68; Z. Zevit, 'A Misunderstanding at Bethel: Amos VII: 12-17', *VT* 25 (1975), pp. 783-90.

28. Hayes, *Amos*, pp. 235-36. See also Ackroyd, 'A Judgment Narrative Between Kings and Chronicles?', pp. 71-87; Rowley, 'Was Amos a *Nabi*?', pp. 191-98; Wolff, *Amos the Prophet*, pp. 311-14.

29. Hayes, *Amos*, p. 236.

30. Douglas, *In the Wilderness*, pp. 40-62.

31. G. Ramírez, 'The Social Location of the Prophet Amos in Light of a Cultural Anthropological Model' (PhD dissertation; Emory University, 1993), pp. 150-54.

32. Tucker, 'Prophetic Authenticity', p. 432.

Amos's confrontation and impediment to prophesy in Bethel compels him to explain his original status as 'a herdsman and a tender of sycamores' (v. 14b), but immediately thereafter he also explains and clarifies his new role (v. 15). There is no explanation on the part of the prophet, however, as to how Yahweh revealed himself to him nor what rite of passage, if any, he had to undergo in order to be granted his new status.

As we analyze the interest of the prophet Amos in clearly establishing whether or not he is a prophet, and in affirming his association with the herdsmen and the tenders of sycamores in the light of the group/grid model, his assertions need not be regarded as enigmatic statements toward prophetism. Rather, Amos's concern for keeping boundaries clear (purity rules) is a positive expression which is reflective of the strong dyadic or group-oriented personality prevailing in his type of society.[33] Far from presenting a problem of prophetic identity, this expression is a result of a strictly internal organization which is common to hierarchist cultural typology's awareness that everything has its place and there is a place for everything. The creation of these types of boundaries reaffirms and provides members of Amos's group with order, security and clear personal identity. It draws a line between those who belong and those who do not belong to the group.

Bruce Malina's statements are helpful in better understanding Amos's speeches, especially that contained in v. 14 and 15. He states that 'in strong group/high grid societies (Hierarchist Cultural Typology), it is quite normal to wear one's symbolic status all the time. Titles for all ranks are permanent and enduring, and everybody who is anybody has an appropriate title.'[34] Thus we can better understand Amos's concern in explaining his personal identity if we place ourselves within the cosmological framework of a hierarchical cultural typology. To regard someone as out of place in this type of culture does not merely mean that this person is in another geographical place, but that he or she may be showing signs of disrespect for and deviance from his or her acceptable social values (purity rules), which is considered a very serious social violation.

Some scholars establish comparisons between prophetic guilds,

---

33. Douglas, *In the Wilderness*, pp. 44-49.

34. B. Malina, *Christian Origins and Cultural Anthropology* (Atlanta: John Knox Press, 1986), p. 31. The term 'hierarchical cultural type' has been taken from Douglas's latest work, *In the Wilderness*.

prophets' disciples, and Amos's prophetic call by Yahweh, disregarding the cosmological and cultural differences of hierarchical social structures. For example, H.W. Wolff's[35] distinction between what he calls an 'independent prophet sanctioned by Yahweh alone' and 'a salaried cult official' reflects Wolff's own individual-oriented cultural cosmology which has mostly prevailed in nineteenth- and twentieth-century occidental societies rather than Amos's group-oriented cultural context in the eighth century BCE.[36] We must remember that Amos belonged to a socio-cultural environment in which individuals saw themselves inserted into various groups by birth and family ties, among other factors. People were known not individually, but in terms of their family kinship, their place and group of origin, inherited craft-trades or occupations. What we see here is a fair portrayal of a quite predictable behavior on Amos's part concerning his social environment.

Conclusions

In sum, I believe that the social location of the prophet Amos entailed a cosmological understanding that privileged a set of communal values which expressed a major concern for preserving clear internal and external social boundaries. These boundaries provided members of the group with a close sense of belonging and a perception that these communal values were of such crucial importance as to require members to submit themselves to them as a means of maintaining a communal life. This is what the model defines as strong group or group-oriented cultural typology—'But Amos answered and said to Amaziah, "I was no prophet, nor was I a prophet's son, but I am a herdsman and a tender of sycamores"'. In my judgment, the conflicts between the prophet Amos and some of the upper classes of the Northern Kingdom to whom Amos addressed himself are complex enough to encompass different cultural idiosyncrasies of Amos's social world. In some instances, these idiosyncracies can be described as hierarchical cultural type and in other instances they can be described as enclavist cultural type. In our pursuit of an

35. Wolff, *Joel and Amos*, p. 313.

36. See F.E. von Deist, 'The Prophets: Are We Heading for a Paradigm Switch?', in V. Fritz *et al.* (eds.), *Prophet und Prophetenbuch: Festschrift für Otto Kaiser zum 65. Geburtstag* (Berlin and New York: de Gruyter, 1989), pp. 1-18; Hayes, *Amos*, p. 32; J.H. Hayes and F. Prussner, *Old Testament Theology: Its History and Development* (Atlanta: John Knox Press, 1985).

answer to the possible setting of the prophet Amos, we have come to the conclusion that we cannot respond to this question by limiting the social location of the prophet Amos to one single context of his complex social reality. A description of this sort would distort the very essence of what a social location is.

With respect to the enclavist cultural type I have placed Amos in, we should note that a gap evidently exists, at least in Amos's view, between the way Amos interprets and lives his social reality and the way the leaders of Israel do. We have no question that Amos was part of the social periphery when seen in the light of the Northern Kingdom context. But we must qualify this statement. To belong to the periphery of a hierarchical culture is not the same as to belong to the periphery of an individualist culture. Accordingly, we must stress that Amos reflects an enclavist culture in those instances where his speeches are addressed in relation to the upper classes of Israel.

Even though this enclavist view is not consistently applicable to Amos when other factors contained in the model are likewise analyzed, we can conclude that the model has proven of assistance in assessing with more precision the concept of peripheral prophet employed by Wilson. If we are to use the term 'periphery' to describe Amos's social location, we must clarify the differences that exist between what this concept meant in Amos's times and its connotation in modern thought. From our point of view, the prophet could hardly be driven by the social cosmology of the modern-day peripheral person. We cannot point to any single instance where the prophet intends to carry out his own will independently from Yahweh's guidance. Amos does not show any signs that he is impelled by individualistic purposes and criteria, as might be the case in modern times.

Through this model we not only perceive institutional settings (such as cultic functionaries or wisdom circles), but can recognize a wide array of cultural patterns which are part of the social system surrounding the prophet's audience as well.

STUDYING PROPHETIC TEXTS AGAINST THEIR ORIGINAL BACKGROUNDS: PRE-ORDAINED SCRIPTS AND ALTERNATIVE HORIZONS OF RESEARCH*

Ehud Ben Zvi

Within the realm of modern historical-critical studies of the prophetic books, this paper explores some questions about starting points and basic assumptions, along with the pre-ordained scripts that are likely to follow them. In plain terms, it deals with the fact that if one knows the premises of a certain scholar, one may have an idea of what his or her conclusions will look like. This being so, it is evident that those conclusions would not be compelling at all, *unless* her or his premises are the most plausible from a critical point of view.

This paper consists of two sections. The first one deals with the direct and indirect influence of a very specific understanding of the superscriptions of prophetic books. My central claim in this part of the paper is that the implicit or explicit acceptance of these superscriptions as historically valid evidence for actual authorship—unless it is clearly proven otherwise—has pre-ordained and continues to pre-ordain much of the script of the ensuing discussion, and many of its results, both directly and indirectly. Since this understanding of the superscriptions is not supported by a critical examination of the available data, neither are the conclusions that follow its acceptance, at least from a historical-critical perspective.

The second part of this paper deals with alternative horizons of research that emerge once the starting points and the sets of questions suggested by the above-mentioned approach to the superscription, and its related assumptions about the nature of prophetic texts, are set aside.

* An oral, condensed version of this paper was presented at the Hebrew Scriptures session of the 1994 Annual Meeting of the Pacific Northwest AAR/SBL that took place in Portland, OR.

I

To demonstrate that an implicit or explicit understanding of the super-scription pre-ordains much of the script of historical-critical discussions I will use a representative example, namely that of historical-critical studies of the book of Zephaniah. Zephaniah is not mentioned in the book of Zephaniah, except in the superscription. Thus it is obvious that scholars who claim something like, 'anything written in the book of Zephaniah stems from the prophet Zephaniah, son of Cushi, who lived during the reign of King Josiah, *unless it is proven otherwise*'[1] base their claim on a certain understanding of the superscription.

It seems natural that if a scholar maintains that one cannot deny Zephaniah's authorship without a convincing reason, then he or she would try to assess whether there is such a convincing reason. Thus, such a scholar would likely ponder whether contradictions, tensions and different languages found in the book *necessarily* point to more than one hand at work, that of Zephaniah and that of a redactor or redactors. If these are the starting questions, the answers, today, would tend to state that an analysis of the text shows that there is no *compelling* reason to *rule out* that Zephaniah said or wrote these words.[2] Thus, most of the

---

1.   See the characteristic expression: 'Man hat keinen Anlass Zephanja diese Worte (Zeph. 2.8-9) abzusprechen' (G. Gerleman, *Zephanja: Textkritisch und literarisch Untersucht* [Lund: Gleerup, 1942], p. 40). Gerleman did not ask whether there are reasons for attributing these verses to the prophet Zephaniah, who lived in the days of Josiah, except for a possible understanding of the superscription. Cf. 'so there is no *overwhelming* reason to assume that most of this material has been added at a later date [the emphasis is mine]' (L. Boadt, *Jeremiah 26–62, Habakkuk, Zephaniah, Nahum* [Wilmington, DE: Michael Glazier, 1982], p. 222). Cf. 'nothing in these suspect lines (Zeph 2.7) actually requires a postexilic date…one may well attribute these lines…to the prophet Zephaniah' (J.J.M. Roberts, *Nahum, Habakkuk and Zephaniah* [OTL; Louisville, KY: Westminster/John Knox Press, 1991], p. 199, see also p. 163); 'there are no compelling reasons for not accepting this period (Josiah's reign) as the time of Zephaniah…' (I.J. Ball, *Zephaniah: A Rhetorical Study* (Berkeley: Bibal, 1988), p. 285).

2.   For instance, according to Roberts, 'there is an explanatory gloss in 1.3, there appears to have been a secondary transposition of verses at 2.4-5, and there are two late universalizing glosses at 2.11 and 3.10. Apart from these few examples, the rest of the material appears to be original [*sic*]' (Roberts, *Nahum, Habakkuk and Zephaniah*, p. 163). Cf. P.R. House, *Zephaniah, A Prophetic Drama* (Sheffield: Almond Press, 1989), pp. 126-34. As it is the rule with any scholarly tendency,

book is declared, by default, Zephanic,[3] and therefore it is studied as document coming from the Josianic period. Difficult passages and expressions in Zephaniah are then explained only, or mostly, in ways that are consistent with historical reconstructions of Josianic Judah, in both political and socio-religious terms.[4] Moreover, it is often the case that such historical reconstructions are not independent of the assumed Josianic character of the book of Zephaniah. For example, Josiah's expansionist thrust towards Judah's western and eastern neighbors rests mainly on reading Zephaniah as a text that faithfully reflected either Josiah's policies or his political dreams. But this thrust is often used to

exceptions do exist. See, for instance, K. Seybold, *Satirische Prophetie: Studien zum Buch Zefanja* (SBS, 120; Sttutgart: Verlag Katholisches Bibelwerk, 1985), and B. Peckham, *History and Prophecy: The Development of Late Judean Literary Traditions* (ABRL; Garden City, NY: Doubleday, 1993), pp. 420-33.

3. Or 'authentic', a term which also implies a value judgment.

4. Among the likely results of this line of research one may mention an emphasis on the tension between the words of the prophet and the assumed synchronistic cultic behavior of the Jerusalemite elite. See, for instance, 'the point would seem to be that pagan religious mores, no matter how silly or unimportant they may appear, reflect and bring with them a far deeper and more pervasive corruption of Yahweh's religious and ethical demands than surface appearances may indicate' (Roberts, *Nahum, Habakkuk and Zephaniah*, p. 179). As a rule, scholars following this approach would tend to understand unclear expressions such as כָּל־הַדּוֹלֵג עַל־הַמִּפְתָּן in Zeph. 1.9 in terms of cultic/religious wrongdoing.

It is worth noting that there are instances in which this assumed Josianic horizon completely tips the balance in favor of quite unlikely readings. The best example is, of course, the reference to the Cushites in Zeph. 2.12. Taking into account (a) that the overwhelming majority of the references in the Hebrew Bible to Cush point to Nubia, and (b) that the other reference to Cush in the same book of Zephaniah clearly means Nubia, one may expect that such a reading would be preferred. But this reading is often rejected by scholars who accept the Zephanic assumption. Instead they propose that the term 'Cushites' refers to (a) members of a 'Bedouin' tribe somewhere in Southern Judah, on the basis of only two occurrences (see 2 Chron. 21.6; cf. Hab. 3.7) none of which is in Zephaniah (for example, R.D. Haak, '"Cush" in Zephaniah', in S.W. Holloway and L.K. Handy (eds.), *The Pitcher is Broken: Memorial Essays for Gösta W. Ahlström* [JSOTSup, 190; Sheffield: Sheffield Academic Press, 1995], pp. 238-51) or (b) to the Egyptians, (for example, B. Renaud, 'Le livre de Sophonie: Le jour de YHWH thème structurant de la synthèse rédactionnelle', *RevScRel* 60 [1986], p. 14).

I stated my position about these two issues elsewhere; see E. Ben Zvi, *A Historical-Critical Study of the Book of Zephaniah* (BZAW, 198; Berlin: de Gruyter, 1991), pp. 95-102, 76-77, 304-306.

construe the historical context necessary for the understanding of the book against its historical circumstances.

Even if one avoids such a degree of circular thinking, the fact remains that not only the questions guiding the research, but also the validity of conclusions concerning (a) the Zephanic character of the material, (b) its Josianic background, and (c) the proposed readings of difficult passages and expressions that result from conclusions (a) and (b), depend on one single premise, namely that everything in the book of Zephaniah is Zephanic unless proven otherwise. If such a premise does not hold, neither do the questions nor the conclusions reached on the basis of such a premise, either directly or indirectly. I must emphasize that the present status of Zephanic studies is certainly representative of the general situation in the study of prophetic texts, as even a cursory reading of most of the recent work in this field clearly shows.[5]

Thus, the crux of the matter is the soundness of the governing premise that the superscriptions, or titles, of these books point to a historically reliable tradition of actual authorship. It seems obvious that in the Hebrew Bible the claim of a book title, by itself, cannot be considered a decisive argument for such a kind of authorship, as the titles of the books of Isaiah and Deuteronomy clearly show, not to mention the attribution of many of the Psalms to David and other biblical figures, or later on, of the Prayer of Manasseh to Manasseh. Moreover, it is questionable, and perhaps very unlikely, that the superscription was usually meant to convey a claim of authorship, in a modern sense, to the original community.[6]

5.   See, for instance, C.R. Seitz, *Zion's Final Destiny: The Development of the Book of Isaiah, A Reassessment of Isaiah 36–39* (Minneapolis, MN: Fortress Press, 1991), p. 1; R.D. Haak, *Habakkuk* (VTSup, 44; Leiden: Brill, 1992); M.A. Sweeney, 'Concerning the Structure and Generic Character of the Book of Nahum', *ZAW* 104 (1992), pp. 364-77. (My reviews on Seitz, *Zion's Final Destiny* and Haak, *Habakkuk*, in *Shofar* 12 [1994], pp. 138-42 and 135-38, respectively.)

6.   If it were the case, the many instances of communally accepted redaction, editing, and even re-composition of biblical books (such as Jeremiah), the existence of many variants of them, and the phenomenon of pseudepigrapha would be inexplicable. For an interesting phenomenological approach to the latter, see N.G. Cohen, 'From *Nabi* to *Mal'ak* to "Ancient Figure"', *JSS* 36 (1985), pp. 12-24.

In general terms, the methodological issue at stake is one of *ad verecundiam*, that is, it concerns the critical use, or abuse, of an appeal to authority, in this case, an appeal to the authority of the writers of the superscription. As in any case of an appeal to authority, the weight of the appeal depends on both a correct interpretation

This being the case, one must critically evaluate both the original meaning conveyed by the superscription and, should the attribution be considered as a claim for authorship, the reliability of this claim from a historical point of view. Each superscription should be evaluated by itself, and always in light of the contents of the text it precedes. Thus, the text itself must not be read according to a governing assumption that attribution in the heading refers to historical authorship, either in partial or full terms. If one were do that, one would fall into circular reasoning, already assuming what one is set to investigate.

The aforementioned conclusion of this discussion is that the premise 'superscription points to historical authorship' cannot serve as a good starting point for historical-critical studies of prophetic literature. An alternative and more solid starting point is needed. Of course, a different point of departure is likely to bring along a distinct set of questions and heuristic methods.

A more solid starting point must address the issue of the message of the superscription. By attributing a text to a certain biblical character, and in many cases to a specific setting, superscriptions provide the historical community of readers with a built-in interpretive key for the text that modern historical-critical research cannot ignore. For instance, in the case of Zephaniah, the opening verse asks the historical community of readers of this book to read it as the דבר יי that came to Zephaniah at a specific point in a communally accepted 'history' of Judah.

It is worth stressing that the community of readers was not asked to listen to an oral prophetic speech or any prophetic performance, neither at the Temple nor at the gate, nor anywhere, nor to confront any flesh and blood prophet. The community was asked to read a written text about a prophet, or more precisely, about a specific 'word of God' that was given in the past to a certain character in the book. The extent to

of the statement of the authority (that is, the writers of the superscription) and the competence of the authority on the subject under discussion (that is, actual authorship, in modern terms). Since neither (a) the interpretation of attribution as actual authorship nor (b) the historical reliability of the writers of the superscription can be taken for granted, an appeal to the authority of these writers in support of a claim about historically reliable authorship rests on shaky grounds, unless one is able to support by independent evidence both (a) and (b). (From a different perspective, Lambert discussed the meaning and historical reliability of attributions of Mesopotamian texts; see W.G. Lambert, 'A Catalogue of Texts and Authors', *JCS* 16 [1962], pp. 59-77. Significantly, Lambert points there to several cases in which an attribution cannot be taken as a historically reliable claim for authorship.)

which this character may resemble an actual, historical person should be studied, not assumed.

II

Now, a text is a text, that is, 'a production, a product, made in order to be copied, to be circulated',[7] to be read by a certain public. A prophetic text, in addition, is one that is made to be read again and again, to be studied and reflected upon by a community or communities of readers (cf. Hos. 14.10). If this is our alternative starting point for historical-critical studies, a distinct set of issues and questions emerge.

First, since prophetic texts were written to be read, and since it is *only* through reading that the communicative message of the text may emerge, much emphasis should be given to the process of reading itself. Following Malina—and the research in cognitive anthropology and psychology on which he rests his position—it seems reasonable to adopt as a heuristic method what he calls the scenario model of reading comprehension. This model is reminiscent of some aspects of form criticism. In Malina's words,

> This model considers the text as setting forth a succession of explicit and implicit mental representations of scenes or schemes. These in turn, evoke corresponding scenes or schemes in the mind of the reader...The reader must perform two tasks: (1) call to mind some appropriate scene, scheme, or model as suggested by the text; and (2) then use the identified scene, scheme or model as the larger frame within which to situate the meanings proposed by the text as far as this is possible.[8]

It is expected that after reading the opening sentence or paragraph of a book, ancient readers would attempt to develop a working model of what the book was about.[9] One may assume that, in one way or another,

---

7. The quotation is from D.J.A. Clines, 'Why is there a Song of Songs and what does it do to you if you read it?', *Jian Dao* 1 (1994), p. 6.

8. See B.J. Malina, 'Reading Theory Perspective: Reading Luke–Acts', in J.H. Neyrey (ed.), *The Social World of Luke–Acts* (Peabody, MA: Hendrickson, 1991), pp. 3-23; the quotation from pp. 14-15. His position is based on studies such as R.W. Casson, 'Schemata in Cognitive Anthropology', *Annual Review of Anthropology* 12 (1983), pp. 429-62, and R.C. Anderson and P.D. Pearson, 'A Schema-Theoretic View of Basic Processes in Reading Comprehension', in P.D. Pearson (ed.), *Handbook of Reading Research* (New York: Longman, 1984), pp. 255-91.

9. A working hypothesis about the genre of the text is a necessary element of

writers at that time were aware that such was the case. This assumption is widely confirmed by reading the first words of works coming from different historical settings and showing different genre conventions, from historiographical works such as those of Herodotus, Thucydides and Xenophon, to Homer's *Iliad*, to Mesopotamian texts such as *Atrahasis* and the Erra Epic, to Egyptian instructions, and to most biblical books, including Genesis. It seems reasonable, therefore, to shift the focus of the historical-critical study of prophetic superscriptions from the slippery ground of discussions about actual authorship to that of questions about which scheme they evoked, and to the implications that a given scheme may have had for the historical, communal reading for which the prophetic books were first written.[10]

A short example may be helpful: the superscription of the book of Obadiah claims that (a) the following text should be understood as חֲזוֹן, and accordingly, that the authority and legitimacy of its message are claimed to be grounded in God, and (b) this חֲזוֹן, 'prophecy', is attributed to a 'person' named Obadiah. Such a 'person' is, of course, a character within the book, and a 'historical figure' within a communally accepted recollection of Israel's past. Thus, the very opening of the book calls forth both the narrow frame of prophetic superscriptions and the broad frame of a prophetic book. As the former is evoked in the mind of the readers, they become aware that Obadiah, the person to whom this חֲזוֹן is attributed, is introduced without any mention of the name of his father, his profession, location, or even of the time in which he lived. Since these 'information slots' are recalled by both the frame of presenting a new character in biblical literature in general and in the prophetic books in particular, and by that of a book superscription, one may reasonably assume that the text as it stands was likely to draw the attention of the original community to the haze surrounding Obadiah.[11] Thus, several key interpretive questions, such as who is Obadiah, when did he 'have' this חֲזוֹן, and against which image of the past is the reader

---

this model, but the model itself includes more data. See below.

10. Cf. J.M. Sasson, *Jonah* (AB, 24B; Garden City, NY: Doubleday, 1990), pp. 66-68.

11. It is worth noting that the presentation of Obadiah by his name alone may have conveyed a sense of informality and familiarity (cf. J. Naveh, 'Nameless People', *IEJ* 40 [1990], pp. 108-23), in a way similar to modern presentation of characters by nicknames or first names. Should this be the case, the conveyed 'familiarity' would contrast with and further underscore the haze surrounding the character.

supposed to understand this יהוה, are all brought to the forefront by the superscription. These questions are left open, as if they were waiting to be solved by the forthcoming information conveyed to the community through the reading of the book.

Significantly, immediately after introducing the two-word title of the book, the opening verse draws the attention of the readers to the LORD, to Edom, and to the relation between the two. This portion of the verse reads, 'thus says the Lord concerning Edom', or '...to Edom', or both. This type of (prophetic) messenger formula is likely to evoke in the readers the frame of prophecies against 'the nations'. The text, however, mentions only one nation, Edom. Since by the time of the composition of the book of Obadiah, 'Edom' could mean not only Edom, but also 'the nations' (see Obad. 15), at least the connoted referent remains unclear. It is worth noting that one of the main characteristics of the book of Obadiah as a whole is its clear oscillation between representative and generic terms, for instance, between 'those who have dispossessed them' and 'Edom', between 'all the nations' (16) and 'Edom' (for instance, 1-14, 18 and esp. 21).

It seems reasonable that the readers of the book of Obadiah would have recognized its genre, that is, a prophetic book. It would be extremely atypical for a book of this genre, however, to include only prophecies against 'the nations'. Genre recognition in this case evokes a scheme which leads the reading community to expect the presence of prophetic announcements concerning Judah/Israel. As we all know, they occur in the book, and they are directly related to the announcements concerning Edom or 'the nations', or both.

The issue of the heading of a prophetic book may also be approached from a slightly different angle. Neither prophetic books nor other 'biblical' books were written to be read only once. These texts were read, re-read, learned, meditated upon, and edited, or further redacted, within the community. Therefore, there is a distinct possibility that these headings served not only to evoke a more or less typical starting scheme, but also as signposts for repeated readings.[12] As such they may evoke a starting scheme that includes some knowledge of the contents of the book. (It is my contention that this is the case in Obadiah.) This

---

12. It is worth noting that the incipit of a work often serves as the work's title in colophons and lists of titles and authors in Mesopotamian literature. See, for instance, Lambert, 'A Catalogue'; W.G. Lambert and A.R. Millard, *Atra-hasis* (Oxford: Clarendon Press, 1969), pp. 32, 42.

approach leads to a clear heuristic set of questions.

Because of the above-mentioned interpretation of the superscription as pointing to actual authorship, and often also because of theological considerations, many scholars have worked under the governing assumption that prophetic texts, for the most part, go back, or must go back, to the words, the oral proclamation, of a historical prophet. Hence, prophetic texts are supposed to reflect ancient public speech intended to convince, and therefore influence the behavior of, a historical audience actually listening to a flesh and blood speaker of certain (revealed) truth. If these genre and social considerations are accepted, because of the rhetorical constraints of this kind of public address one is to conclude that prophetic speeches must have been quite straightforward if they were to achieve their goal. This model leads by necessity to historical-critical scripts in which (a) expressions that seem to be ambiguous or rich in connotations are often allowed to convey to their historical audience only one of their possible meanings, and (b) expressions that are more or less cryptic tend to be seen as textual corruption in need of emendation.

If the starting point of the scholar is that prophetic books were texts written to be read again and again, then textual ambiguities and multi-layered meanings cannot be considered an 'unexpected' presence in the text, but almost a foreseeable necessity, for their openness and incertitude significantly contribute to the feasibility of continuous re-reading. It is worth mentioning in this respect that there is empirical data showing that narratorial ambiguity has a strong impact on readers' appreciation of a text upon second reading, especially for *trained* readers.[13] One may reasonably assume that upon the tenth reading, for instance, the case would be even stronger.

The matter of trained readers has a bearing on another issue, that of the social location of those for whom these books were written. Written texts were produced and copied for people who could read for themselves, and to others. The more sophisticated the text is, the more narrow the social location of a/the public that the writers had in mind when they wrote these books.[14] It seems obvious that prophetic books

---

13. See P. Dixon, M. Bortolussi, L.C. Twilley and A. Leung, 'Literary Processing and Interpretation: Towards Empirical Foundations', *Poetics* 22 (1993), pp. 5-33.

14. Of course, they could have had more than one public in mind. See C.S. Parpola, 'The Assyrian Tree of Life: Tracing the Origins of Jewish Monotheism and Greek Philosophy', *JNES* 52 (1993), pp. 161-208; E. Ben Zvi, 'The Dialogue between Abraham and YHWH in Gen. 18.23-32: A Historical-Critical

directly address, and are the product of, a highly educated group. Much can be said about how a sharpened awareness of this sociological feature may influence historical-critical analysis, but as this topic demands—at the very least—a separate paper, I will focus here only on two narrow issues.

First, it is extremely unlikely that biblical prophetic texts were composed or redacted within and for social groups that knew of only one piece of religious literature: the one they were writing, rewriting or learning from. If many texts were known and read within each community, it is reasonable to map networks of similar ideas conveyed by similar languages across biblical texts. Assuming that it is more likely that the historical and social background of a text would be closer to those of texts showing similar languages and idioms, and expressing similar concepts and social horizons, than to those showing none of the above, this mapping may help to discern different groups of texts, writers and original communities of readers.

Thus, on the one hand, within a given prophetic book, networks of similar expressions pointing to related ideas characterize it as an integrated and distinctive work, despite clear evidence of editorial or redactional activity (see, for instance, expressions such as בֶּן־אָדָם in Ezekiel, קְדוֹשׁ יִשְׂרָאֵל in Isaiah, and the network of references to Zion in the latter).[15] These networks contribute to the shaping of a communal interpretive key for the reading of these texts, namely that each text should be read as a separate whole. On the other hand, this can hardly be the communicative message of similar networks that cut across limits of biblical books, genre and assumed superscriptional time. These networks most likely reflect a shared language and theology/ideology. Hence, these networks may serve to reconstruct historical social groups or communities, along with their literature, and their theological/ideological outlook.[16]

The second issue is that if the community of readers is mainly one of re-readers, one must assume that they were well aware of the main outline of these books. Readers did not wonder, for instance, whether Abraham convinced God to spare Sodom and Gomorrah in Genesis 18,

Analysis', *JSOT* 53 (1992), pp. 27-46, esp. pp. 44-45.

15. The presence of distinctive language may also serve the purpose of characterizing and 'individualizing' the persona of the prophet to whom the book is attributed. Tompkins has recently called attention to a similar tendency in Thucydides's speeches. See D.P. Tompkins, 'Thucydides Constructs his Speakers: The Case of Diodotus', *Electronic Antiquity* 1.1 (1993), pp. 1-8.

16. I applied these research guidelines elsewhere; see Ben Zvi, *Zephaniah*.

nor whether Jonah would die after he was thrown to the sea. If so, their reading was not guided by a desire to know 'the end of the story',[17] or the lesson one may learn only from the 'the end of the story'.

To sum up, whereas it is certainly true that the communities for which these texts were written re-read them for a number of reasons, some of them of a sociological nature,[18] such a continuous re-reading was directly related to the ability of these communities to draw meanings from a communal and interpersonal reading of the text. Significantly, this reading was informed by a conceptual framework that included much knowledge about any section of the book being read at any given time. This necessitates a certain level of freedom and ambiguity in the text, as I mentioned before. It also creates a certain mode of close reading of the prophetic text that is very different from the one proposed by (a) those working within a model of an aural audience listening to the proclamation of the prophet,[19] (b) those who treat the text as a piece of literature that is being read for the first time, or written without having in mind a community of continuous re-readers, and (c) those who assume a very limited contextual knowledge on the part of the readers.[20]

17. Cf. K.M. Craig, Jr, *A Poetics of Jonah: Art in the Service of Ideology* (Columbia, SC: University of South Carolina Press, 1993), pp. 75-79.

18. For instance, defining the community as the one that shares some religious texts and teachings, the latter being directly related to a communal understanding of the former.

19. Of course, there is no denying that there were prophets in Israel. The point advanced here is that the audience of prophetic books confronts a written work about a prophet, not a living prophet.

20. See, for instance, 'Jonah and the Lord both come on stage with a complete absence of preliminaries, much like God in the very first chapter of Genesis. Who is the Lord and who is Jonah, the son of Amittai? Without any overt exposition, *the reader can only piece it together based on the action and conversation itself*... Likewise, the Lord does eventually emerge as the creator God who apparently controls the natural order...[emphasis mine]' (Craig, *Poetics of Jonah*, p. 63). I addressed this issue in a review of this book soon to be published in the *Canadian Journal of Comparative Literature*.

I am glad to dedicate this paper on prophetic literature and methodology to my teacher and good friend, Prof. Gene M. Tucker. I know that both issues are close to his heart. May this paper be worthy of the person it honors.

I would also like to thank many of the participants in session and post-session discussions of the Prophets and History Section of the Society of Biblical Literature during recent years for their helpful comments and vigorous debate about many of the issues discussed in this paper.

IDEOLOGY AND IDEOLOGIES IN ISRAELITE PROPHECY

Norman K. Gottwald

As recently as a decade or so ago it was uncommon to encounter the term 'ideology' in biblical studies. Nowadays, it appears frequently, either offhandedly or as a technical term in so-called ideological criticism. In popular speech 'ideology'/'ideological' are usually disparaging labels bearing the sense of 'prejudicial' or 'falsifying', in contrast to 'non-ideological' as 'objective' or 'truthful'. This use of 'ideology' as a dismissive gesture requires biblical interpreters to specify their understanding whenever they use the word, and especially when they build arguments that depend substantially on its use.

In fact, 'ideology' has carried multivalent meanings since its coinage at the end of the eighteenth century.[1] There appear to be four primary

---

1. M. Fander, 'Historical-Critical Methods', in E. Schüssler Fiorenza (ed.), *Searching the Scriptures*. I. *A Feminist Introduction* (New York: Crossroad, 1993), pp. 205-24; N.K. Gottwald. 'Social Class and Ideology in Isaiah 40–55', *Semeia* 59 (1992), pp. 43-57; D. Jobling. '"Forced Labor": 1 Kings 3–10 and the Question of Literary Representations', *Semeia* 54 (1992), pp. 57-76; I.J. Mosala, *Biblical Hermeneutics and Black Theology in South Africa* (Grand Rapids: Eerdmans, 1989); H. Mottu, 'Jeremiah vs. Hananiah: Ideology and Truth in Old Testament Prophecy', in N.K. Gottwald and R.A. Horsley (eds.), *The Bible and Liberation: Political and Social Hermeneutics* (Maryknoll, NY: Orbis Books, rev. edn, 1993), pp. 313-28; D. Penchansky, 'Up For Grabs: A Tentative Proposal for Doing Ideological Criticism', *Semeia* 59 (1992), pp. 35-41. For elucidation of ideological criticism as it is emerging in biblical studies, I recommend 'Ideological Criticism', in *The Post Modern Bible* by the Bible and Culture Collective (New Haven: Yale University Press, 1995), pp. 272-308. For helpful historical and conceptual clarification and criticism of the concept of ideology, I have drawn on C. Geertz, 'Ideology as a Cultural System', in D.E. Apter (ed.), *Ideology and Discontent* (New York: Free Press, 1964), pp. 49-76; J. Larrain, 'Ideology', in T. Bottomore (ed.), *A Distionary of Marxist Thought* (Cambridge, MA: Harvard University Press, 1983), pp. 219-23; W.J.T. Mitchell, *Iconology: Image, Text, Ideology* (Chicago: University of Chicago Press, 1986); E. Shils, 'Ideology. I. The Concept and Function of Ideology', in *The International Encyclopedia of the Social Sciences*, VII (New York: Free Press,

senses in which 'ideology' is currently employed in the humanities, including biblical studies.

1. An ideology is a fairly coherent system or pattern of ideas or beliefs, at times virtually equivalent to 'philosophy' or 'worldview', and in biblical studies the term is sometimes used as a more neutral or secular substitute for 'theology'. In this usage, ideology belongs to the history of ideas. To the extent that most people entertain notions about the meaning of life, they may be said to have at least an implicit or rudimentary ideology. Attention is focused, however, on an explicit body of ideas systematically developed by leading thinkers. In any case, whether rudimentary or elaborated, ideology is treated in total or relative independence of the social position of the ideologists. The truthfulness of ideas is taken to be established by codes of religious revelation, logical reasoning and/or appeal to common human experience.

2. Ideology is a system or pattern of ideas or beliefs that corresponds to the life conditions and self-interests of particular groups of people. In this usage, ideology belongs to social history and cultural criticism. Whereas in the first sense of ideology the emphasis is on sets of ideas in themselves, in this second sense the emphasis falls on the connection of sets of ideas to social conditions and self-interests. It is recognized that many, probably most, ideologists are unaware of the connections between their ideas and their social contexts. The ideas advanced are likely to be taken as self-evident, resting on presuppositions that may be accepted by one social group but questioned or rejected by other social groups. The truthfulness of ideas is to be established on one level as the truth of a particular sector of society, but the assumption of a universal truth is thrown into radical question since it is not evident which social group has the higher truth claim when ideas clash, as they customarily do. It is characteristic to acknowledge that the truthfulness of ideas is settled only proximately in the realm of politics and popular culture; in short, by some combination of social force and persuasion.

3. Ideology is a form of consciousness that takes the surface appearances of social relations to be reality in ignorance of the actual social dynamics in which the ideologists are, as it were, immersed or entrapped. This is the concept of ideology as 'false consciousness' which views the

1968); J.B. Thompson, *Studies in the Theory of Ideology* (Berkeley: University of California Press, 1984); R. Williams, 'Ideology', in R. Williams (ed.), *Keywords: A Vocabulary of Culture and Society* (New York: Oxford University Press, rev. edn, 1983), pp. 153-57.

world 'upside down'.[2] As with the preceding notion, this view of ideology belongs to social and cultural criticism, but differs in that criticism in this case goes beyond merely establishing links between ideas and group interests. Ideological criticism becomes an attempt to uncover the actual social relations masked by the limiting and self-serving group interests expressed in the ideas. The posited false consciousness is usually not thought to be a strategy of cultivated duplicity, a matter of bad faith, but is rather recognized as a worldview imbibed as 'natural' from the social context. By means of the understanding of ideology as false consciousness, an effort is made to get beyond the arbitrariness of group ideologies. The truth value of particular ideologies must be tested by their effectiveness in showing how society actually works beneath the surface of tradition, habit, common sense, and political and social propaganda. Ideology in this sense necessarily pushes toward some implicit notion of the common good, even if a universal truth cannot be established in the abstract.

4. Ideology is seen as a set of strongly held but impractical ideas about social relations, which if put into practice would be damaging to society or, even if one is sympathetic to them, simply impossible of attainment. To be ideological in this sense is to be 'subversive', 'fanatical', 'dogmatic', or 'delusional'. Ideology is extremism, rigidity and unreasonableness in group thinking.

Where does Israelite prophecy fit in this map of ideology? Can biblical prophecy be regarded as ideological in any of the senses I have delineated? Moreover, does prophecy show any signs of awareness of these ideological categories long before the term 'ideology' was coined?

Prophetic Ideology as a System or Pattern of Ideas

In this weakest sense of ideology, Israel's prophets certainly do display structures of thought that offer a more or less coherent view of the world. These structures of thought are not laid out deductively and they are far from exhaustive in the topics covered. Likewise, the prophetic books do not display a single harmonious view. Nonetheless, we can

---

2.   Mitchell, *Iconology: Image, Text, Ideology*, pp. 160-208. The well-known Marxist optical metaphor for ideology as false consciousness is the camera obscura (or dark room). Mitchell provides an illuminating analysis of what Marx had in mind in employing this metaphor. He draws on related pre-Marxist metaphors and argues for a close link between the camera obscura and commodity fetishism, another of Marx's central metaphors.

identify certain thought patterns that characterize most, if not all, prophetic books. These 'master ideas' may be glossed by a paraphrase of
the typically theocentric discourse of prophecy:

- Israel's deity is sovereign over history and society.
- Israel as a people, a social entity and body politic, is obligated
  to obey the revealed will of its deity.
- Israel repeatedly breaches its sociocultural, political and cultic
  obligations to deity in ways that permeate and undermine the
  whole social body.
- Israel's breach of its obligations threatens, or has actually
  already incurred, the withdrawal of divine protection and guidance and the dissolution of the people as a whole.
- It is possible—and in the case of some prophets certain—that
  Israel, after painful corporate loss and suffering, may/will recognize its condition as deserved punishment and discipline, and
  may/will take up its obligations once again, assisted in this
  conversion by mercy of the deity.

In characterizing this general ideology of prophecy we are attending
to prophetic books as finished wholes. When redaction history is taken
seriously, it is acknowledged that 'prophetic' ideology in this fashion is a
literary construction derived from the canonical corpus of prophetic
writings. This means that the weight given to one or another of the
above general features varied, not only from book to book, but within
books. The intra-literary variations are attributable to stages in the
growth of the prophetic traditions.

It is plausible, for example, to reconstruct three or more stages in the
evolution of a prophetic book, as the 'original' prophets—Amos (Coote),
Micah (Mosala), Isaiah (Barth, Clements, Sheppard) and Jeremiah
(Mowinckel, Hobbs) in particular—became fountainheads for subsequent
elaborations and additions to their thought. Thus, some prophetic voices,
especially prior to the exile, lack a clear articulation even of the
possibility—much less the certitude—of Israel's eventual salvation. The
first stages of Amos and Micah, and possibly also of Isaiah and Jeremiah,
appear to end on the 'tragic' note of Israel's demise, whereas the final
form of their books—indeed, of all prophetic books—strike the 'comic'
note of ultimate redemption.[3]

3. N.K. Gottwald, 'Tragedy and Comedy in the Latter Prophets', *Semeia* 32
(1984), pp. 83-96.

Awareness of the involved historical development of prophecy, with its multiplicity of voices intertwined in a series of books spread over at least six centuries, leads us on to ideology in the second sense.

Prophetic Ideology as Ideas Linked to Social Conditions and Interests

The rich variety and nuances of prophetic ideology appear to be grounded securely in the social and historical circumstances of their particular settings and the group interests with which they identify and for which they speak as well as the group interests they oppose.

It is commonplace for most readers of the Bible, particularly those who hold a high view of it as Scripture, to read prophetic thought as universal truth unconnected with social conditioning. To do so, however, requires that we ignore one of the most distinctive features of prophetic thought. Prevailingly, the earliest stages of prophecy identify with and speak for those who have been socially and politically marginalized, viewed as victims of powerful political and economic institutions and their leaders. The mechanisms of victimization through onerous taxation, exorbitant interest, debt foreclosure, corruption of the judiciary, and conspicuous consumption by elites[4] are typical of bureaucratic kingdoms within the tributary mode of production throughout the ancient Near Eastern world and beyond.[5] Given the continuum of socioeconomic conditions in the ancient Near East, it is nonetheless striking that in its ideological tendencies the prophetic corpus of Israel stands in sharp contrast to the literature that has survived from those kingdoms. Elsewhere,

---

4. M.L. Chaney, 'Bitter Bounty: The Dynamics of Political Economy Critiqued by the Eighth-Century Prophets', in R.L. Stivers (ed.), *Reformed Faith and Economics* (Lanham, MD: University Press of America, 1989), pp. 15-30; N.K. Gottwald, 'From Tribal Existence to Empire: The Socio-Historical Context for the Rise of the Hebrew Prophets', in J.M. Thomas and V. Visick (eds.), *God and Capitalism: A Prophetic Critique of Market Economy* (Madison, WI: A-R Editions), pp. 11-29 (Reprinted with the title 'The Biblical Prophetic Critique of Political Economy: Its Ground and Import', in N.K. Gottwald, *The Hebrew Bible in its Social World and in Ours* [Semeia Studies; Atlanta: Scholars Press, 1993], pp. 349-64).

5. T.F. Carney, *The Shape of the Past: Models and Antiquity* (Lawrence, KS: Coronado Press, 1975); J.H. Kautsky, *The Politics of Aristocratic Empires* (Chapel Hill: University of North Carolina Press, 1982); G.E. Lenski, *Power and Privilege: A Theory of Social Stratification* (Chapel Hill: University of North Carolina Press, 1984).

the criticism of dominant elites is absent or muted; in Israelite prophecy the criticism of abusive leaders is loud and clear.

This outright identification of prophets with the victims of systemic injustice signifies that the prophetic voices speak from direct experience of the plight of the hard-pressed peasant populace. They empathically judge the vital interests of these victims to be determinative for the ongoing health of Israel as a social whole. The extent to which particular prophets were personally victimized—or themselves actually came from sectors of the populace typically wronged—is difficult to determine because of the dearth of autobiographical or biographical information concerning them. Attempts to minimize the prophetic social criticisms on the assumption that the prophets were largely upper class in origin are no more than a red herring. Even if it could be shown that prophets were of privileged background, social history discloses many cases in which persons of high-class background have become spokespersons for the underprivileged. These considerable 'exceptions' warn us against a rigid mechanical correlation between ideas and group interests. Whatever their social origins—and they were likely to have been various—the prophets speak concretely and vividly of unjust institutions and practices they have witnessed and they do so with a keen sympathy for the inherent dignity and worth of the common people who suffer the wrongs they portray in excruciating detail.

Furthermore, in their identification with Israelite underclasses, the prophets understand the abusive behavior of the upper classes not simply as the deeds of single individuals. They identify the abuses as group behavior backed by a group ethos that functions to protect group interests. These unjust leaders benefit from the wealth and power they derive unfairly from others, and at the same time they vehemently justify their advantages over others as legitimate or at least permissible. Prophets tirelessly flay the hegemonic practices of Israelite leaders fueled and justified by an ideology that brazenly grounds their privilege not only pragmatically but also in the ultimate sanctions of religion.

This predilection to identify with and give voice to the suffering subjects of the Israelite kingdoms continues as a major strand throughout all the later layers of prophecy, even when it is muted or mixed with other emphases. Some of the ideological themes that nuance and qualify this 'option for the underdogs' deserve comment.

Occasionally prophets will acknowledge that the oppression and corruption practiced by leaders has infected the whole populace through demoralization and outright imitation of their leaders' vices (Isa. 3.12b; 9.16-17a; Jer. 5.1-5). This phenomenon of the brutalized poor who internalize the oppressors' logic and behave unjustly toward one another is a familiar one in many societies.

Certain prophets appeal to one sector of the leadership to correct the abuses of other sectors, notably when Israelite kings are held up as exemplars of justice and virtue, even when particular kings are condemned for their failure of office (Isa. 9.2-7; 11.1-10). This phenomenon corresponds to royal initiatives to reform the administration of justice and to cancel debts which were occasionally launched at the beginning of a king's reign.[6] The political wisdom in such reform measures was to allay social unrest in the populace and to rein in the aggrandizing power of bureaucrats and big landholders who threatened at times to become too independent of the crown or actually to overthrow the incumbent monarch.

As prophecy unfolds during and after the exile, a major emphasis on community rebuilding parallels the remarkable survival of a Judahite community and its needs for supportive institutional and social symbolic structures. Within this restoration milieu, the balance in prophetic commentary and advocacy shifts from social criticism toward social construction based on a reformed cult. This shift takes place not necessarily because there are no grounds for further social criticism, as Isaiah 56–66 and Malachi make abundantly clear. It is rather that two new complementary concerns emerge: to motivate deported Jews to return to Judah,[7] and to solidify the cultic domain as the framework for Jewish identity and just social relations since there was no longer an independent Jewish state.

Nonetheless, there does appear to be a subtle shift in prophecy from an initial emphasis on social justice as the precondition for cultic correctness toward an emphasis on cultic correctness as the way to secure social justice. Our analysis of the role of cult in prophetic thought will be affected by the growing recognition that a rather unified normative cult of Yahweh was much slower to develop than was once thought.[8] As a result, we now see that the pre-exilic prophets were reacting to a variety

6.   Chaney, 'Bitter Bounty'.
7.   Gottwald, 'Social Class and Ideology in Isaiah 40–55', pp. 43-57.
8.   P.R. Davies, *In Search of 'Ancient Israel'* (JSOTSup, 148; Sheffield: JSOT Press, 1992); M.S. Smith, *The Early History of God: Yahweh and the Other Deities in Ancient Israel* (San Francisco: Harper & Row, 1990).

of alternative and competing cults,[9] whereas post-exilic prophets faced a more unified cult that had sloughed off or marginalized features that were operative in pre-exilic times.[10] This may mean that post-exilic prophets were moved to focus heavily on rallying support for the reconstituted cult as 'the last best hope' for Israel, even as they criticized the corruption and social blindness of many cultic officials.

The several qualifications I have identified in grounding the ideology of prophecy in social conditions and self-interests leads us on to a view of ideology as erroneous thinking.

Prophetic Ideology as False Consciousness

There are two points to consider. First, do the prophets describe the ideas of their opponents as the equivalent of false consciousness? Secondly, do the prophets themselves display ideas that can be regarded as false consciousness?

If we take false consciousness to mean a spurious reliance on the surface appearance of social relations, with a corresponding failure to look deeply into all the effects of social behavior, especially one's own, then it is clear that the prophets charge the leaders they criticize with precisely that failure of insight, what Hosea calls 'lack of the knowledge of God' (4.1, 6). This knowledge is not at all a restricted theological notion about God, but an awareness of the societal obligations stemming from deity which constitute the very foundation of Israel's corporate life.

The abusive leaders are complacent in their privilege, exercising their authority self-confidently and reveling in their wealth unashamedly precisely because they think they are the bulwarks of society and that what is good for them is automatically good for all their subjects. They do not look sufficiently beyond their power and abundance to take into account what they are doing to ordinary people. The welfare of those over whom they have power does not figure in their social calculus. 'They do not grieve over the ruin of Joseph [i.e., Israel as a socio-religious whole]!' (Amos 6.6). When they hear complaints, they dismiss them as idle grumbling, and when they face direct condemnation by

9. S. Ackerman, *Under Every Green Tree: Popular Religion in Sixth Century Judah* (HSM, 46; Atlanta: Scholars Press, 1992); S.M. Olyan, *Asherah and the Cult of Yahweh in Israel* (SBLMS, 34; Atlanta: Scholars Press, 1988).

10. B. Schramm, *The Opponents of Third Isaiah: Reconstructing the Cultic History of the Restoration* (JSOTSup, 193; Sheffield: JSOT Press, 1995).

prophets, they claim divine endorsement for their practice. They scoff at the warning that any serious reversal of fortune, much less divine punishment, will befall them. 'Is not Yahweh in the midst of us? No evil shall come upon us' (Mic. 3.11). To this frequently expressed sentiment, the prophets replied sharply, 'Do not trust in these deceptive words: the temple of Yahweh, the temple of Yahweh, the temple of Yahweh, saying, We are delivered!' (Jer. 7.4, 8).

Frequently prophetic discourse flays the superficial and mechanistic manner in which not only political and social leaders, but more sadly religious leaders as well reassure one another that all is well in the body politic.[11] Concerning the prophets who trade on these reassurances, Jeremiah reports Yahweh as saying, 'They fill you with vain hopes' (23.16) and 'They steal my words from one another' (23.31).

So deeply entrenched are these leaders in the web of their self-serving practice and its ideological justification that they have lost the capacity to discern right from wrong. 'Woe to those who call evil good and good evil!' (Isa. 5.20). While in some cases prophets attempt to reason with the leaders, in many instances they cease argument or admonition and only announce a coming judgment. This determination of leaders to ignore social and political realities is portrayed in a richly figurative vocabulary, such as 'making a covenant with death' (Isa. 28.14), or as 'eating the fruit of lies' (Hos. 10.13), as being 'joined to idols' (Hos. 4.17), or as 'a spirit of harlotry within them' (Hos. 5.4). Idolatry and harlotry in prophetic usage often extend beyond their primary religious and sexual meanings to serve as metaphors embracing the whole range of socioeconomic, political and religious sins they condemn. Idolatry as metaphor alludes to the pursuit of wealth, power and prestige as selfishly grasped ends. Harlotry as metaphor alludes to the breach of social obligations accepted by Israel in its covenant with Yahweh, as also to the alacrity and abandon with which leaders seek the gratification of their most immediate and pressing desires without regard to consequences.

In their passionate condemnation of false consciousness in others, do the prophets themselves betray false consciousness? A number of allegations have been made about the gross onesidedness of the prophetic condemnations of Israelite leaders and institutions. It is sometimes claimed that they vastly overstated the political and social abuses in Israel, tarring whole groups of leaders with the infractions of a few. It has also been asserted that the plight of the peasants in Israel was not

11. See Mottu, 'Jeremiah vs. Hananiah', pp. 239-46.

nearly so desperate as the prophets assert. The argument has even been mounted that the monarchy was in the process of extending economic prosperity to most Israelites but that the harping of the prophets, together with the Deuteronomic Reformers, undermined and destroyed the monarchy's progressive economic measures in mid course.[12]

Such claims, while not easily assessed, are certainly appropriate as challenges to a sacralizing of prophetic thought. They direct our attention to the objections that those criticized by the prophets hurled back at them. It has to be remembered that only in retrospect, after the destruction of both Israelite kingdoms, were the views of critical prophecy accepted as the ideology of reconstituted Judah. During the lifetimes of most of the prophets, their analyses and prescriptions were hotly disputed and more often than not rejected by those in a position to change social and political conditions.

This much can be said about presumed false consciousness in the prophets. Since we do know a fair amount about how bureaucratic monarchies and tributary modes of production functioned in the ancient Near East, we are in a position to make a proximate judgment about how well the prophets understood the workings of power and wealth in their society and the resulting impact on all sectors of the populace. On such a comparative reading, it seems fair to say that the prophets exposed the oppressive features of their society with remarkable acumen. In making this assessment of prophetic realism about their society, we should doubtless allow for prophecy's polemical rhetoric, loaded with hyperbole, irony and satire, which may well have downplayed credit to a minority of leaders who sympathized with the prophetic critique and tried to change oppressive conditions. There remains of course the issue of possible prophetic naïvety in thinking that they could persuade leaders boxed in by social structural constraints to change their ways on the basis of moral and religious appeals. In this regard, the prophets may have underestimated the ideological entrenchment of their opponents.

One other factor speaks against a facile false consciousness in prophecy. Although prophetic books are very sparse in autobiographical information or self-reflection, in Jeremiah we do encounter agonized misgivings about whether his analysis of institutions and leaders was correct (15.15-21; 20.7-18). Was he self-deluded, possibly even deluded by God? Even the savage judgments of Amos are interrupted by his

---

12. M. Silver, *Prophets and Markets: The Political Economy of Ancient Israel* (Boston: Kluwer-Nijhoff, 1983).

plaintive plea for God to spare Israel, 'O Adonai Yahweh, cease I beseech you! How can Jacob stand? He is so small!' (Amos 7.5). These hints at self-reflection suggest that prophets may not have come lightly to their unhappy conclusions and that they did in some measure resist the dire conclusions to which their penetrating look beneath the surface of social life ultimately led them.

Something needs to be said here about prophetic attitudes toward sex and gender. There are points at which prophets attack upper-class women as exemplars of rampant greed and ostentatious consumption (Amos 4.1-3; Isa. 3.16-17). On the other hand, they speak for the rights of widows and come to their aid (1 Kgs 17.8-16; 2 Kgs 4.1-8). Moreover, Hosea delivers a stinging rebuke to men who scapegoat women with sexual looseness while they themselves set the worst possible examples in their sexual behavior (Hos. 4.11-14).[13] However, in the process of targeting male Israelites as acting like loose women, the prophet falls back upon and reinforces a condescending view of women as prone to evil. This tendency is amplified by Jeremiah (2.23-25, 33) and Ezekiel (chs. 16; 23) to the point of obscenity and misogyny.[14] Feminist criticism not only rightly warns us about the misogynist effect of these texts on those who take the prophetic voice as Scripture,[15] but it also serves to warn us against lifting up—or worse still, of unconsciously absorbing— any element of prophetic ideology literally and naïvely without evaluating it in its original context and with reference to criteria that we have thought through for our own time and place.[16]

There is yet another sense in which prophets have been charged with false consciousness, and that is in their theological interpretation of social historical developments. Prophetic rhetoric reads God as the ultimate, and often proximate, controller of human affairs, as do all the voices within the Hebrew Bible. This may be regarded as the ultimate in false consciousness, and has been so regarded by Feuerbach, Marx and Nietzsche among others, since in what sense can God be said to act in

---

13. P. Bird. '"To Play the Harlot": An Inquiry into an Old Testament Metaphor', in P.L. Day (ed.), *Gender and Difference in Ancient Israel* (Minneapolis: Fortress Press, 1989).

14. M.E. Shields, 'Circumcision of the Prostitute: Gender, Sexuality, and the Call to Repentance in Jeremiah 3.1–4.4', *BI* 3.1 (1995), pp. 61-74.

15. J.C. Exum, 'The Ethics of Biblical Violence against Women', in J. Rogerson and M. Davies (eds.), *The Bible in Ethics: The Second Sheffield Colloquium* (JSOTSup, 207; Sheffield: Sheffield Academic Press, 1995), pp. 248-71.

16. Mosala, *Biblical Hermeneutics and Black Theology in South Africa*.

history? Furthermore, even if God has such a role in history, is it not audacious for a prophet to speak for God with such apparent certitude?

To explore this set of issues would require us to examine the role of religion in ancient Israelite society. It can at least be said that prophets were not alone in speaking for God. The notion that God spoke through representative Israelite leaders was a given in the culture; the prophets did not invent the notion but carried it forward by risking contentious minority counter-versions of the voice of God. Religious language and symbols were the dress in which all the parties debated the ground and conditions for sustaining community for the benefit of its members.[17] Prophetic ideology pushed the boundaries of community membership to include a more serious regard for all those affected by the attitudes and behavior of leaders. One can choose to believe that a high deity was or was not backing the ground and conditions under debate, but the prophets are not to be faulted for believing in the ultimate importance of the issues they advanced.

Prophetic Ideology as Impractical Utopianism

Since the prophets were generally facing institutions and functionaries who already held power within prevailing political and social systems, they had the disadvantage of opposing a hegemonic ideology that was solidly established as the official version of the truth about Israelite society. From the standpoint of the leaders they indicted, the prophets were labeled 'troublemakers' (1 Kgs 17.17), 'conspirators' (Amos 7.10), and 'madmen' (Jer. 29.26). Because of the intense social conflicts in which they participated, the prophets were seen less as idle dreamers than as dangerous subversives. In mounting their counter-ideological attack on an abusive and corrupt leadership, it was the prophetic aim 'to turn the tables' on hegemonic ideology by contending that it was those in power who were the actual subversives engaged in systematically undermining the ground and conditions of communal peace and justice. Elijah's retort to Ahab's jibe, 'Is it you, you troubler of Israel?', catches the ideological contest succinctly: 'I have not troubled Israel; but you have, and your father's house' (1 Kgs 17.17-18).

17. B.O. Long, 'Social Dimensions of Prophetic Conflict', *Semeia* 21 (1981), pp. 31-53; N.K. Gottwald, 'Problems and Promises in the Comparative Analysis of Religious Phenomena', *Semeia* 21 (1981), pp. 103-12; Mottu, 'Jeremiah vs. Hananiah'.

In the polarized conflicts involving prophets and their opponents, each side was struggling for ideological supremacy by demonstrating their views as 'inside' and their enemies' views as 'outside'.[18] Only a later community consensus elevated the prophetic judgments to 'gospel truth'—judgments which during the lifetimes of the prophets had usually been a decidedly minority position. Of course majority and minority are deceptive categories when applied to an ancient Near Eastern kingdom. There were no democratic votes on prophetic ideas. It is possible that they had a large sympathetic following among common people whose voices we do not directly hear in the biblical text. We also garner from the book of Jeremiah that prophetic sympathizers were found among some persons in government.[19] However, to be in the majority in the sense of speaking for public policies that were enacted was seldom the prophetic position. Haggai and Zechariah, in their promotion of a rebuilt temple after the exile, appear to have been exceptional in this regard.

In the last analysis, the only way to form a judgment about how 'extreme' or 'fanatical' or 'impractical' the prophets were is to try to grasp the contours of the social and political alternatives they favored. That is no easy task. Prophetic speech is a dense intermixture of 'occasional' speech addressed to specific situations and audiences and more generalized theological and ethical assertions. Prophets do not give us developed and nuanced encompassing accounts of how they think society and government should be arranged, much less detailed blueprints. Perhaps the one exception is the sketch of restored Jerusalem in Ezekiel 40–48, but its program is more visionary than pragmatic.

The upshot is that in making our own judgments about the validity of prophetic ideologies for their time, as well as their instructiveness for us, it is inescapable that our own ideologies will enter into the picture in weighing evidence that is both spotty and laden with emotion. To the degree that the prophets form part of our ecclesial and cultural Scripture and to the degree that rather similar structural issues about society, politics and religion are vigorously controverted in contemporary society, it is certain that they will continue to fascinate and challenge us. In our attempt to understand prophets on their own turf and to evaluate what they signify for us, ideological criticism will prove to be an invaluable

18. R.R. Wilson, *Prophecy and Society in Ancient Israel* (Philadelphia: Fortress Press, 1980).

19. Long, 'Social Dimensions of Prophetic Conflict'; Gottwald, 'Problems and Promises'.

aid—if only because it will constantly remind us that in grappling with prophetic ideologies we are also grappling with our own sense of what is true and right for us individually and communally.[20]

20. Y. Leibowitz, *Judaism, Human Values and the Jewish State* (Cambridge, MA and London: Harvard University Press, 1992), pp. 88-105; Penchansky, 'Up For Grabs: A Tentative Proposal for Doing Ideological Criticism', pp. 35-41.

Part II

PARADIGMS

W.F. ALBRIGHT AS PROPHET-REFORMER:
A THEOLOGICAL PARADIGM INSCRIBED IN SCHOLARLY PRACTICE

Burke O. Long

When embarking on his graduate training in 1913, William Foxwell Albright saw himself as taking up a crusade to ward off both scientific anti-clericalists who rejected the Bible's claims and anti-intellectual clerics who wholeheartedly accepted them. This purpose took shape not superficially, or in popularizing spin-offs of technical study, but in the very sinews of his critical practice carried out over a very long career. The crusade was given energy by a notion of biblical prophets which Albright seemed to incorporate into his self-image as a quiet reformer.

Since Gene M. Tucker maintained a career-long interest in the Hebrew prophets, frequently writing and lecturing on the subject, it seems appropriate on the occasion of his retirement from active teaching to honor him with a song on the prophetic theme. I also sing the song in a different key, for I wish to explore not Albright's study *of* biblical prophets, but how his particular notion *about* biblical prophets was inscribed in the very stuff of his scholarly practice.

Albright believed unreservedly in the methodologies of modernist science. He knew the limits of science, but also was convinced of its possibilities for achieving objective knowledge about ancient history and civilizations, especially the 'lands of the Bible'. Within this framework he contributed as few others did to creating a twentieth-century American biblical archaeology that could stand before the bar of critical and scientific scholarship. Yet linked to his discovery and synthesizing of new information from artifact and inscription were constellations of ideological commitments which surfaced in struggles to maintain or oppose formations of knowledge-based social power. From this perspective, Albright is like all scholars. And yet, because he holds such an unrivaled place in American scholarship, his encoding of a prophetic image into critical work offers a paradigmatic opportunity to view a chapter in the history of biblical scholarship in a new way. I wish to offer a narrative, not of disembodied ideas, but of contested claims to knowledge expressed through ideologically charged social and political processes.

The Flaming Chariots of his Angels

The day after Christmas, 1913, only weeks after beginning his graduate studies at Johns Hopkins University, William Foxwell Albright urgently told his mother of a new discovery. Though blind to it earlier, he now saw an intimate connection between biblical criticism (the 'higher criticism' of historical and source analysis) and the preachings of social gospel, or the 'new Social Movement'. The biblical prophets, or as might be said nowadays, a certain hermeneutical construal of these Old Testament figures, were key to Albright's realization.

On one side Albright pictured Christian orthodox 'conservatists', who saw the prophets as 'religious preachers alone', leaving no room for social reform. In fact, wrote the young and confident Albright, the prophets were 'largely social reformers' whose inspired and 'burning words' had been covered by centuries of accretion, 'comfortable blankets of eschatology, fatuous optimism, and what-not'. He continued:

> I regard it as a striking instance of Divine guidance that our young ministers of tomorrow will leave the seminaries with no such false mirages of 'Bible Religion' as in recent past, and usually at present. The prophets handled social injustice with ungloved hands, and preached the most remorseless·logic, but the glossators have robbed fully half of the force of their bolts.[1]

By 'cursing the higher critics', Albright continued, warming to his subject, the orthodox—Albright meant the anti-scientific literalists—hold back the progress of Christ's kingdom and allow the pristine truth about the prophets to languish in obscurity. However, the higher critics 'will finally lay bare to the world the flaming chariots of his [Christ's] angels, which drive thru the Bible just as Jehu-like today as ever, tho muffled and smoked by accumulated misunderstandings'.

The higher critic—Albright now seemed to be placing himself onto

1. Letter, W.F. Albright to 'Mother' (Zephine Viola Foxwell Albright), December 26, 1913; *Albright Papers*, Library of the American Philosophical Society, Philadelphia. I am grateful to the Society, which awarded me a Mellon Fellowship during 1991–92 to consult Albright's papers, and to the Library's staff, who extended friendly and professional assistance.

the canvas of naysayers and prophets—must be a reformer inflamed with a prophet's passion and armed with a scientist's cold scrutiny. Suggesting a reluctance to serve, like the biblical prophets of old, Albright saw himself as henceforth becoming a prophet-crusader, seeking not social reform, but historical truth:

> I am afraid that hereafter, instead of considering Biblical Criticism as an unfortunate necessity, tho not without great eventual good, involved by our search for truth, I shall see it as a crusade, which must be forced upon the attention of the world (with caution, and not with too unrestrained zeal).

Although he is not entirely clear, Albright seems to have thought of himself as a biblical critic who would seek to reclaim truth that had been lost, or simply obscured by verdant growth of later tradition. Perhaps a popular Protestant notion of prophet as one who calls for religious renewal through repristinized practice had insinuated itself into the rush of words Albright wrote to his mother. Indeed, in a published essay, he implied that Elijah was such a figure, one of those prophetic 'adherents of the pure faith inculcated by Moses' who reacted with 'sorrow' to the apostasies during the Omride dynasty.[2] Much later, when all of Europe was engulfed in World War II, Albright expressed his conviction much more clearly. The eighth-century Israelite prophets were not primarily social revolutionaries, he wrote, but 'first, and last, *religious* reformers' (emphasis mine). Alluding to anxious public discussion at the time about totalitarianism and militant communism—the debate continued the anti-socialist, anti-foreigner hysteria of the 1920s and foreshadowed ideologies of the Cold War—Albright dismissed suggestions that the biblical prophets had been precursors to socialism or communism. They were in no sense innovators. 'Their task', he wrote, 'was not to preach a new monotheistic or henotheistic theology, but rather to demand a return to the purer faith of their forefathers, which was in acute danger of becoming canaanitized'.[3]

This sense of prophetic mission, to reclaim the generative truth of beginnings, seems closest to what the young Albright expressed in 1913 as a crusade of the historical critic. Actually, some two years earlier, while an undergraduate at Upper Iowa University, Albright pre(con)figured

2. W.F. Albright, 'Archaeological Discovery in the Holy Land', *BSac* 79 (1922), p. 409.

3. W.F. Albright, 'The Archaeological Background of the Hebrew Prophets of the Eighth Century', *JBR* 8 (1940), p. 135.

this reformist biblical critic as a scientifically minded Christian who would harness the power of science to draw religion back to its essential core. In an effusive essay entitled 'Modernism', Albright eulogized science as a calling devoted to illuminating 'vast stretches of the unknown darkness around us' and fostering global unity, the 'kindly glow of human brotherhood', through material advance.[4] Glancing briefly at 'phases of progress', Albright asked rhetorically, 'Has our religion alone been unaffected by this great period of transformation and revaluation?' Some resist these inevitable changes, he wrote, but not he. Taking on the roles of both scientist and Christian apologist, Albright then exhorted his readers:

> Let the chaff go, men may quarrel over the chaff-like grain, but the essentials are with us...The human God—this is the Desire of Nations—deity incarnate, suffering with us, [came] to save us from our lower selves. What concept nobler, what better able to inspire men with enduring moral zeal. Here lies the heart of our faith—a heart thru which modernism may attune itself with the pulse-beat of suffering humanity. Let the battle rage around this stronghold![5]

Some years after writing these words, Albright finished his graduate training at Johns Hopkins. Widely read in mathematics, physics and biology—Albright had actually taught science for a year to high school students—and now given the tools of historical philology by a teacher who exemplified the Germanic ideals of a *wissenschaftlich* university, Albright at last seemed ready to embark on his reformist crusade, and mount the chariots of Christ's flaming angels.[6] He explained to Sam Geiser, a close friend from Upper Iowa days, that he was laying the foundations for a 'Christ-myth rationalism', a scientifically explained Protestant Christianity Triumphant. At the time, Albright was preparing a series of new publications in which

> ...the prehistory of our Christology will be worked out as thoroly [sic] as possible, for the first time. Needless to say, polemics will be avoided, nor will a direct reference to the New Testament be made until all the train has

4.   'Modernism—The Genius of Our Day', *Upper Iowa Academician* (c. 1911). Offprint copy among the *Albright Papers*.

5.   'Modernism', p. 2.

6.   On Albright's relation to the culture of science, see B.O. Long, 'Mythic Trope in the Autobiography of William Foxwell Albright', *BA* 56.1 (1993), pp. 42-44. Also see L. Running and D.N. Freedman, *William Foxwell Albright: A Twentieth Century Genius* (New York: Morgan, 1975), p. 287.

been laid...For years I have tried to find common ground, where
scientific rationalism and evangelical faith can meet. Now I seem to find
it. During the coming years I shall, if God wills that my eyesight be
spared, devote myself quietly to my technical researches, incidentally
building a structure too strong for the batteries of mistaken apologetics.
When it is all over, orthodoxy will rub its eyes and say, wonderingly,
'What was I afraid of? It all seems so reasonable now!' Such are the laws
of progress in our society.[7]

I believe it would be a mistake to dismiss these statements as simply
overwrought infatuations of youth. In the first place, Albright began his
career when many American Protestants were creating forms of theology variously adapted to new forms of social and secular philosophy.
Christian biblical critics found themselves at the center of religious con-
troversies, and the decade of the 1920s brought forth strident internal
struggles between the 'modernists' and the 'fundamentalists'. Under the
circumstances, it was not at all unusual for biblical scholars to shape their
work in some measure to meet the needs of Christian apologia, either to
resist many of the social and intellectual changes sweeping through
America from the 1880s to World War I, or to create bodies of biblical
knowledge that would aid the causes of progressive theology.[8]

The second reason why Albright's sense of mission is not to be dismissed too lightly is that after twenty-two years of extraordinarily productive and focused scholarly work, he actually realized these youthful
ambitions. He did it soberly, grandly, and with an unrivaled assemblage
of 'all the train'. During World War II, Albright published two substantial books: *From the Stone Age to Christianity* and *Archaeology and the
Religion of Israel*.[9] In both, Albright organized massive additions to
knowledge about the ancient Near East, many of which were his own
discoveries, in the service of that 'prehistory' to Christology which he

7.   Albright to S. Geiser, October 8, 1918.
8.   For the wider picture, see W. Hudson, *Religion in America* (New York:
Charles Scribner's Sons, 3rd edn, 1981), pp. 265-92; S. Ahlstrom, *A Religious
History of the American People* (New Haven: Yale University Press, 1972), pp. 763-
804; S. Persons, 'Religion and Modernity', in J. Smith *et al.*, *The Shaping of
American Religion* (Princeton: Princeton University Press, 1961), pp. 369-401;
M. Marty, *Pilgrims in their Own Land: 500 Years of Religion in America* (Boston
and Toronto: Little, Brown, 1984), pp. 297-317.
9.   *From the Stone Age to Christianity: Monotheism and the Historical Process*
(Baltimore: Johns Hopkins University Press, 1940); *Archaeology and the Religion
of Israel* (Baltimore: Johns Hopkins University Press, 1942).

had envisioned at the age of 27. The books seemed also to have been conceived as successors and correctives to the non-theistic works of James Henry Breasted, especially *The Dawn of Conscience*.[10] Albright opposed what he would later call Breasted's 'non-religious teleology', while embracing a Breasted-like ambition to create a unified history of Western religion from its prehistoric beginnings down to early Christian times.[11]

The purpose of *From the Stone Age*, Albright wrote, was to trace 'our Christian civilization of the West to its earliest sources'. In the 1948 translation into German, Albright added that he hoped thereby to 'deliver a small contribution to Christian theology of the future'.[12] Two years later Albright wrote that his purpose in publishing *Religion of Israel* was 'nothing less than the ultimate reconstruction, as far as possible, of the route which our cultural ancestors traversed in order to reach Judeo-Christian heights of spiritual insight and ethical monotheism'. He was mainly concerned, he said, 'with the religion of the Old Testament, of which the religion of the New was only the extension and fulfillment'.[13]

One may read both of these works as, in part, reformist projects which encoded Albright's passion as prophet-historical critic. By transposing traditional theological claims for the uniqueness and truth of biblical revelation into the idiom of objectivist historical narrative, Albright tried to reinstate a condition of belief that had been weakened by a broad range of twentieth-century events. For example, in both narratives, Albright projected ancient Israel, conceived unproblematically as an ethnic unity, in opposition to the Canaanites who were pictured, just as simplistically, as culturally and religiously deficient, if not depraved.

10. New York and London: Charles Scribner's Sons, 1933.

11. Albright greatly admired Breasted, but was troubled by his 'meliorism', his strong humanistic faith in a natural order which through human effort becomes better and better. See Albright's memorial tribute, 'James Henry Breasted, Humanist', in *American Scholar* 5 (1936), pp. 287-99. I have been unable to locate among Albright's papers a document in which, as D.N. Freedman reported to me, Albright had compared his own accomplishments with those of Breasted.

12. *From the Stone Age*, p. 32. See *Von der Steinzeit zum Christentum* (Bern: Francke, 1949), p. 7. Pagination in *From the Stone Age* refers to the Anchor Books edition (Garden City, NY: Doubleday, 1967) in which the original text was updated mainly with a new introduction and a few additional endnotes.

13. *Religion of Israel*, p. 4. Pagination refers to the Anchor Books edition (Garden City, NY: Doubleday, 1969), the text of which is virtually unchanged from the 1942 edition.

The Canaanites were a people given to 'orgiastic nature-worship', and 'gross mythology', a people whose

> cult of fertility in the form of serpent symbols and sensuous nudity… were replaced by Israel, with its pastoral simplicity and purity of life, its lofty monotheism and its severe code of ethics.[14]

Similar contrasting constructions ruled Albright's aesthetic judgments. Assyrian-Babylonian poetry had a 'curiously monotonous effect', but Israelite poets took inherited literary conventions, used them 'even more effectively' than their neighbors had, and preserved 'most of the beauties and few of the crudities of older national literature'. Even though the emotional heights of biblical poetry could be found in Mesopotamia, Albright wrote, 'biblical literature maintains a much higher average level of feeling'.[15]

In short, Albright reclaimed his truths about the Bible but valorized them more *against* their environment than *in* it. Or to paraphrase St Paul, the Israelites—Albright seems to have conflated the focalizing theological perspective of the canon with historical Israel—the Israelites lived *in* their world, but not *of* it.

Moreover, an ancient structure of Christian (prophetical) historiography ruled *From the Stone Age*. Headings for individual chapters, such as 'Praeparatio', or 'When Israel was a Child…', or 'In the Fullness of Time…' all invoked Christian and specifically Patristic hermeneutics as approved frameworks for properly grasping the import of this scientifically grounded history of ancient religion. The Old Testament was preparation for the New, or in different terms, the Old Testament prophetically configured Christ, or in the idiom of historiography, the religious ideas of the ancient peoples of Near Asia evolved, haltingly, unevenly, 'organismically', from primitive beginnings to the highest truths of Christianity. In addition, various remarks suggested that the purposive directionality in history that Albright saw was heavily weighted toward Christian self-characterization. Albright detected, for example, a 'certain movement in the direction of theological universalism' in Mesopotamian and Egyptian religion, and its flowering in Mosaic

---

14. *From the Stone Age*, p. 281. On the theologically vested stereotyping of the Canaanites, see D. Hillers, 'Analyzing the Abominable: Our Understanding of Canaanite Religion', *JQR* 75 (1985), pp. 253-69.

15. *From the Stone Age*, p. 281; *Religion of Israel*, pp. 14, 21.

monotheism.[16] It is difficult to miss the specifically Christian interest in such a representation, not only in tracing the course of theological universalism through biblical Israel to the early church, but in eventually valorizing constructions of Christian truth as superseding ancient Judaism whose monotheistic vision had been clouded by lingering ethnic particularism.[17]

Albright believed that the cultural and religious ideas of West Asian peoples demonstrably evolved from primitive beginnings to the highest (and never-to-be-surpassed) truths of Christianity. Accordingly, he built a narrative of intellectual and cultural movement toward Christianity out of a theological position: a Jesus-centered, supersessionist reading of all that had gone before—Hebrew, Greek, and their ancient Near Eastern antecedents. Wearing the hats of Christian and historian, Albright finally asserted at the end of *From the Stone Age* that the 'Church Fathers saw truly when they represented these aspects of paganism [the pre-Christian elements of culture] as part of the divine preparation for Christianity'.[18] Albright had ridden the flaming chariots of Christ, and, like the prophets of old, called Christians (who were then engaged in a life-and-death struggle with totalitarianism) back to the pristine roots of their Christology: 'We need reawakening of faith in the God of the majestic theophany on Mount Sinai, in the God of Elijah's vision at Horeb, in the God of the Jewish exiles in Babylonia, in the God of the Agony at Gethsemane'.[19]

Re(un)covering Primal Poesies

In 1922, Albright—he was then the Director of the American School of Oriental Research in Jerusalem—published what would become a very influential study of early Hebrew poetry.[20] Despite criticisms which

16. *From the Stone Age*, p. 213.
17. Albright's version of this theological view came to the surface in *From the Stone Age*, pp. 391-92, where he imagined the strictly monotheistic Pharisees as praiseworthy, but nevertheless just deficient enough to allow for Christian triumph, or in the idiom of Darwinism, something of an evolutionary dead-end. The Pharisees were 'not at all suited to become the vehicle of a great evangelistic movement', Albright wrote, because they were weighed down with a 'mass of secondary regulations and restrictions'.
18. *From the Stone Age*, p. 399.
19. *From the Stone Age*, p. 403.
20. 'The Earliest Forms of Hebrew Verse', *JPOS* 2 (1922), pp. 69-86.

recent studies have made possible,[21] Albright's essay at the time offered an innovative attempt to set what he took to be the regularities of early Hebrew prosody in the context of Babylonian, Egyptian and Assyrian verse, and to arrange examples of biblical poetry chronologically according to changes in their formal characteristics. This line of inquiry, with its implications for Albright's drive to recover historically reliable information from the Bible, would culminate nearly half a century later in his extended treatment of 'Verse and Prose' in *Yahweh and the Gods of Canaan*,[22] but not before a string of studies by Albright and some of his students had refined his method and amplified his original work.[23]

Albright suggested in his 1922 article that the original version of the Song of Deborah (Judg. 5), and to a lesser extent, David's lament over Jonathan (2 Sam. 1.19-27), represented Canaanite poetry deeply imprinted with the stylistic conventions of earlier Mesopotamian and Egyptian verse. Post-Davidic poetry, he asserted, exhibited a breakdown of this classical style, and was influenced by late Assyrian and Babylonian models that streamed into Israel along a cultural highway running through Syria and Phoenicia. Since Albright presumed that older Babylonian poets strictly adhered to a regular accentual verse unit, he could posit (or rather, be 'struck' by as he wrote) the conformity of Judges 5 to this system of regular meter and 'climactic parallelism'. In

21. See, for example, J. Kugel, *The Idea of Biblical Poetry* (New Haven: Yale University Press, 1981), pp. 37-39; A.J. Hauser, 'Two Songs of Victory: A Comparison of Exodus 15 and Judges 5', in E.R. Follis (ed.), *New Directions in Biblical Hebrew Poetry* (JSOTSup, 40; Sheffield: JSOT Press, 1987), p. 282 n. 5.

22. *Yahweh and the Gods of Canaan: A Historical Analysis of Two Contrasting Faiths* (Garden City, NY: Doubleday, 1968), pp. 1-52.

23. Albright, 'The Earliest Forms of Hebrew Verse'; 'The Song of Deborah in the Light of Archaeology', *BASOR* 62 (1936), pp. 26-31; 'The Oracles of Balaam', *JBL* 63 (1944), pp. 207-33; 'The Song of Habakkuk', in H.H. Rowley (ed.), *Studies in Old Testament Prophecy* (Edinburgh: T. & T. Clark, 1950), pp. 1-18; 'A Catalogue of Early Hebrew Lyric Poems (Psalm LXVIII)', *HUCA* 23 (1951), pp. 1-39; 'Some Remarks on the Song of Moses in Deuteronomy XXXII', *VT* 9 (1959), pp. 339-46; 'Archaic Survivals in the Text of Canticles', in D.W. Thomas and W.D. McHardy (eds.), *Hebrew and Semitic Studies Presented to Godfrey Rolles Driver* (Oxford: Oxford University Press, 1962), pp. 1-7. Among the work of Albright's students, see above all F.M. Cross, Jr, and D.N. Freedman, 'The Blessing of Moses', *JBL* 67 (1948), pp. 191-210; 'The Song of Miriam', *JNES* 14 (1955), pp. 237-50; and *Studies in Yahwistic Poetry* (Missoula, MT: Scholars Press, 1975). See also D.N. Freedman, *Pottery, Poetry, and Prophecy* (Winona Lake, IN: Eisenbrauns, 1980).

effect, Albright believed that he had established an objective basis for discerning older, more original, elements of poetic style, and thus had launched what were to become increasingly refined efforts to date early Hebrew verse typologically. He relied not upon the cluttered and often puzzling biblical text for his notion of the original, but upon actual examples of Babylonian poetry that pre-dated Israel's literature.

Thus, after meticulously reconstructing David's lament, Albright wrote, 'It must be emphasized that the preceding arrangement of the poem has not been reached as a result of any *a priori* theory, but that it simply imposes itself upon the reader who knows what to expect in ancient verse-forms'.[24]

For my purposes, it is not necessary to enter into a full discussion of the details of Albright's article, many of which he later corrected anyway. Suffice it to observe that his learning and philological rigor were inextricably bound up with a network of values, assumptions and aesthetic judgments, some of which seem very problematic nowadays, at least for some scholars. One might question, for example, Albright's value-laden narrative of literary change, in which early material, presumed to set the 'classical' standard of perfection (understood as strictness of prosody and regular 'climactic parallelism'), degraded into nonstandard verse in which the classic style was said to have been corrupted or fallen into disuse.[25] Also, a certain over-confident arbitrariness crept

24. 'The Earliest Forms of Hebrew Verse', p. 83.

25. Albright argued that the Babylonians and Assyrians were 'really strict in matters of prosody'. Thus he tended to emphasize regularity of accentual scansion where he saw it, and to devalue that which was more complicated and divergent from the 'norm'. Two examples of second-millennium Babylonian verse were put forth as 'classic', Albright having explained the widespread absence of such 'exact metrical form' in later materials as the result of wooden translations from older poetry, which 'free verse' then became a 'secondary Assyrian poetic fashion' ('The Earliest Forms of Hebrew Verse', pp. 69-70). Given this implicit narrative of change and decay, it is not surprising to find that Albright posited a similar golden age in Egypt: 'Just as in Babylonia, the most [formally] perfect prosodic development is found about 2000 BC, during the great literary revival of the Twelfth Dynasty' (p. 72). So with biblical poetry: Albright saw a classical and formally perfect Hebrew style in the Song of Deborah, reconstructed 'with the excision of only a few variant lines and obvious glosses' and with alteration of accentual stress in accordance with the general rule in Babylonian verse. The later lament of David, though it still showed a 'dominant structure' (reconstructed) in accord with the classic pattern, had devolved from this classic style, and one heard only echoes of the old climactic parallelism, now falling into disuse (p. 84).

into excisions and rearrangements of textual material, and Albright's attribution of high style to verse already identified as 'classic' frequently seemed to drive the analysis toward achieving what he first assumed. [26]

More pertinent to my interest is that as Albright reconstructed those original lines of poetry, and assumed, or perhaps felt drawn to, the normative power of a supposedly early and 'classical' pattern, he seemed to encode in the very stuff of philological science that highly regarded paradigm of historical critic as prophet-crusader. He sought to recover, and was convinced that, at least provisionally, he had exposed the pristine and originary beneath a palimpsest of textual history. In subsequent years, as Albright came back again and again to this small body of verse, he would argue on grounds of antiquity and supposed regularities of oral tradition that these selfsame poetic texts preserved some historical information with which to evaluate the historical reliability of later prose traditions. In the larger context of Albright's published work in which he repeatedly sought to recover accurate history from the Bible, evidentiary quest blended with apologia. Albright could affirm not only that real, objective history had been caught by some literary details, but that these same details carried the affective weight of a trustworthy Bible. And if trustworthy for history, so too for religious and moral truths. Carrying the weapons of philological science and clothed with the armor of disinterested method, prophet-crusader Albright uncovered the purity and antiquity of Israel's poesies and set them *in*, but not *of* their environs.

'The literary poetry of Israel', he asserted in a final rhetorical flourish to his 1922 article, 'does not owe its beauty to Bedu models, but to the fact that it was able to clothe the formally elegant models of the ancient Orient with a spontaneous and freshly exuberant life'.[27] As noted above, Albright's wartime books, *From the Stone Age* and *Archaeology and the Religion of Israel*, wove similar aesthetic judgments into a fabric of intellectual history, where the ancient Hebrew poesies, uncovered, would be taken up into a larger narrative, the growth of monotheism towards its Christian *telos* in late antiquity.

---

26. See, for example, 'The Earliest Forms of Hebrew Verse', nn. 1, 4 and 7 on p. 75. Albright seemed to shape the poem to hypothesis when he wrote that Burney's restoration of meter 'suffers from the frequent occurrence of more than two unaccented syllables before the ictus; it is very improbable that a poem so perfect in structure would tolerate a metrical anomaly of this nature' (p. 74).

27. 'The Earliest Forms of Hebrew Verse', p. 86.

The Renaissance of our Day

In May 1944, Albright delivered two lectures at Gettysburg Seminary. Only skeletal notes remain—the words were penciled onto the reverse of a 3 × 5 inch, elegantly printed invitation to the event. They are enough, however, to suggest the absent body of a sweeping narrative in which Albright located himself on a map of modern, critical biblical study. The configured self as prophet-reformer shows up again, but this time with a suggestive allusion to a pattern rooted in the Protestant Reformation.

Lecture One	*Lecture Two*
The OT after a Century of Progress	What Does the OT Mean for us Today?
1. The impact of the new on established order	1. The OT in the history of the Christian Church
2. The philological phase	A. The OT as 1st century scriptures
A. The Enlightenment and its effect	B. Growth of NT
B. The Hegelian phase—Wellhausen	C. Eclipse of both: Outgrown tradition
C. Religionswissenschaft—Gunkel	D. The reformation and the Bible
D. The current situation—Pfeiffer and Irwin	E. The higher criticism of OT and NT
3. The archaeological phase	F. Eclipse of both, overgrown by tradition
A. Beginnings—to 1890	G. The renaissance of our day through archaeology and philology
B. Development—to 1930	2. The notion of two collections
C. Synthesis—to our day	A. The OT—summary
4. As I view the OT	B. The NT—summary
	C. Notion—not equal but complementary

The first lecture implied a familiar modernist narrative of scientific progress. The 'established order' of Old Testament knowledge, which was in its time challenged by philological science, had now in turn been rendered obsolete by the 'new order' of archaeological research. However, those scholars who represented a before-'archaeological phase' on the timeline of philological advancement, especially Julius Wellhausen, belonged to a bygone era. Wellhausen's heirs, (Robert) Pfeiffer and (William) Irwin, even though still working at leading research institutions in the 'current situation', were relegated to obsolescence at the margins of progress, as the 'archaeological phase' takes hold in a 'new synthesis'. Of course, the primary narrative voice was Albright's. He constructed the narrative and provided the triumphal interpretation of its central character, the Bible as scientific object—'As I view the Old Testament'.

The second lecture seemed to construe archaeology and comparative Semitic philology as decisive influences in the history of Christian appropriation of the Bible. An overgrowth of ecclesiastical tradition early on 'eclipsed' the original Scriptures of the church. However, the Protestant Reformation cut away such tradition by appealing directly to unencumbered Scripture and thus prepared the way for modern historical and literary studies of the Bible. Transmuting that religious desire for paradigmatic beginnings into historical quest for origins, higher critics such as Wellhausen excavated for earliest texts and first meanings. Tradition built up again, however, 'overgrowing' even this reformist drive, until scientific archaeology and philology should appear to shape a reforming 'renaissance of our day', poised to help regain direct access to the ancient text. Without such a modern reformation, or prophetic recovery, Albright seemed to imply, the question put as title for the lecture, 'What Does the Old Testament Mean for us Today?' could hardly be answered, at least not correctly.

Considering his prominence among biblical archaeologists at the time, Albright's implication would have been clear to his audience: Albright the archaeologist, Albright the unrivalled master of comparative philology, Albright the reformer, not only told the tale, but made the tale possible. He recovered truth that, recalling the phrase he used as a young man, had been 'muffled and smoked by accumulated misunderstandings'.

Imbedded in this reformist narrative was a map of scholarly territory in which flesh and blood Old Testament scholars represented ideological struggles. Because Wellhausen never took very much account of the stirrings of nascent archaeology, he symbolized a tradition of literary and philological scholarship that Albright characterized as inward-looking, self-referential, and finally unscientific, or rather, not scientific enough. Wellhausen also employed an evolutionary view of historical development (Albright labeled Wellhausen a 'Hegelian' and thought he had imposed a rigid dialectical scheme on cultural history) and on this basis drew conclusions that, when Albright reduced them to a few theologico-historical issues, were viscerally disturbing. The traditions about the earliest Hebrew ancestors, said Wellhausen, for the most part were creations of a much later age and thus were historically unreliable. (As seen above, Albright presumed and often sought to confirm a historically trustworthy Bible.) Moreover, because these ancestral traditions were written so late they actually obscured the primitivity of religious and intellectual development that characterized the ancestral Hebrew people. According to Wellhausen, the credit for achieving the high ethical monotheism to which Christianity was heir belonged not to Abraham and Moses, but to their later descendants, the great Old Testament prophets. (From an early age, Albright believed that authentic monotheism had begun with Moses, and that, as seen above, the biblical prophets were not innovators, but reformers who called for restoration of Mosaic ideals in an age which threatened their dissolution).[28]

Robert Pfeiffer of Harvard held a place on the map and in Albright's narrative because he represented the legacy of Wellhausen in the mid-twentieth century. To Albright, Pfeiffer embodied the end of that era, despite their very similar training in Semitics.[29] Pfeiffer had only very limited experience in field archaeology, however, and perhaps for this reason was more wary than Albright of the claims made for the direct relevance of archaeology to understanding the Bible. Consequently, when he wrote his *Introduction to the Old Testament*,[30] published just after Albright's equally commanding *From the Stone Age to Christianity*, Pfeiffer made little reference to those discoveries that most likely would

28. J. Wellhausen, *Prolegomena to the History of Ancient Israel* (Edinburgh: A. & C. Black, 1885; translated from the 1878 edition). Albright set forth his opposition to Wellhausen's constructions of the history of Israelite religion in many publications. See especially, 'Archaeology Confronts Biblical Criticism', *The American Scholar* 7 (1938), pp. 176-88; his critiques of Wellhausen are sprinkled in sections of several books, including *The Archaeology of Palestine and the Bible* (New York: Fleming Revell, 1932); *From the Stone Age*; *Yahweh and the Gods of Canaan*.

29. Born in Italy, Pfeiffer studied in Berlin and Tübingen, and took his divinity degree with the Protestant faculty in Geneva. He received a PhD from Harvard in 1922 and a Master of Theology the following year. He taught Bible and Semitic languages at Harvard and Boston University, was made Curator of the Semitic Museum in 1931, and directed the Harvard-Baghdad School excavations at Nuzi in modern-day Iraq during 1928–29. See *Directory of American Scholars* (3rd edn, 1957), p. 585.

30. Cambridge, MA: Harvard University Press, 1941.

have exemplified the 'archaeological phase' in Albright's lecture and which he so skillfully used in *From the Stone Age*. This decision—there were substantive debates going on at the time about how far the mute artifacts of archaeology could legitimately inform biblical interpretation—handed Albright the perfect symbol.

In Albright's published review of Pfeiffer's *Introduction*, the book seems to be both a text 'out there' which other people may read, and a paradigmatic cipher in the framing perspective through which Albright mapped the territory of biblical studies for his own readers.[31] Although a 'monumental' and 'important landmark', Albright wrote, the work marked 'the end of an era'. Since it belonged to the passing epoch, it did not draw upon 'the new linguistic data or new philological techniques, thanks to which our approach to problems of Hebrew linguistic and literary history has been revolutionized in the past few years'.

Indeed, Albright took the book as something to be corrected and updated, even praised faintly, while simultaneously defining it as a negativized antagonist to 'our approach'. Adopting the tone of one who was firmly positioned in the vanguard of the new era, Albright measured Pfeiffer's work unproblematically 'in the light of recent progress', implying that the *Introduction* in the main was mired in stagnation. Seeding the review with various compliments and noting certain points of agreement, Albright nevertheless reserved his passion for courteous but forthright indictment. Pfeiffer was 'surprisingly uninfluenced by the archaeological discoveries of the past two decades', and (invoking the mythic parent of such deficiency), fell again and again 'under Wellhausenist influence'. In a variety of ways Pfeiffer (and the readers of the review) were told that he was uninformed or out of date.

In a letter to Pfeiffer, however, Albright put his opinion a bit more delicately: 'The mass of material and the bibliography and indices will be invaluable. Of course, I do think it is the last of the 1880–1941 type of Introduction, since epigraphic discoveries are revolutionizing the entire field with unexampled rapidity, in spite of the war.'[32] He was more candid with W.S. Ferguson, Dean of Harvard's faculty of the humanities, in sentencing the book (and Pfeiffer) to an after-life of antiquarian curiosity. The *Introduction* would 'retain its importance for many years as a summation of the historical criticism of biblical literature up to the close of this phase of Old Testament research'. Citing examples of

31. The review appeared in *JBL* 61 (1942), pp. 111-26.
32. Albright to R. Pfeiffer, December 14, 1941.

recently published inscriptions, Albright added, 'to one familiar with the discoveries of recent decades, there is thus something strangely unreal about the entire book'. And yet—here Albright seemed to suggest in Pfeiffer a perverse resistance to instruction—the 'omission of all this material is deliberate, not in any way the result of ignorance'.[33]

Pfeiffer responded to the published review with generosity and deference. Yet he firmly attributed the absence of archaeological references in his book to a considered decision about a debatable point. He was skeptical of the claims made for the relevance of such finds to interpreting the Bible. 'I agree with Woolley,' he wrote, 'when he said that the Bible contributes more to the interpretation of archaeological finds than vice versa.' The cache of letters found at Lakish, a site not far from Jerusalem, were a case in point. 'I am familiar with your brilliant interpretation of these difficult texts and I would utilize it were I writing a Hebrew dictionary or a Biblical commentary; but I find nothing in them of basic significance for a presentation of Jeremiah's times, life, and religious thought.'[34]

There the matter stood: Pfeiffer held back and refused to embrace the substance of the 'progress' that Albright so fervently encoded in his reformist reading of the rise of modern archaeology; Albright just as tenaciously dismissed such refusal, with the added suggestion that the objectivities of 'science' demanded no other conclusion than the one he himself had drawn. One might say that the 'renaissance' with which Albright identified had swept away Pfeiffer, and in its place were prophet-reformer Albright's new truths about the Bible.

In his Gettysburg lecture, Albright also associated William A. Irwin with the passing era of Wellhausenian literary approaches. In some ways he seemed an even more potent symbol than Pfeiffer. Not only was Irwin tainted with a socio-anthropological approach to the Bible and theological liberalism, both of which Albright viewed as characteristic of the University of Chicago, but he belonged to a line of intellectual succession that was not at all rooted in the traditions of German philology as these had been imparted to Albright by his teacher Paul Haupt.

A graduate of the University of Toronto, Irwin had studied at the University of Chicago under John Merlin Powis Smith (1866–1932), a

---

33. Albright to W.S. Ferguson, November 29, 1941. Ferguson had asked Albright for an evaluation of Pfeiffer's qualifications for election to the American Philosophical Society.

34. R. Pfeiffer to Albright, July 2, 1942.

pupil and then close associate of William Rainey Harper, the Yale-trained scholar who had served as the University's first president.[35] From Smith, Irwin received thorough schooling in Wellhausenian historical criticism of the Bible. In 1930, succeeding his teacher at the Divinity School and Oriental Institute, Irwin extended Smith's deep interest in intellectual and social history, and worked within a faculty which, on the whole, was removed from, although not ignorant of, the field activities of biblical archaeologists. Since most archaeologists at the time were connected with old-line institutions in the mid-Atlantic and New England states,[36] factional rivalry, or at least the perception that the youthful Midwest was resolutely independent of the East Coast centers of biblical scholarship, seemed a part of Irwin's and Albright's uneasy relationship.[37]

35. R. Storr, *Harper's University: The Beginnings. A History of the University of Chicago* (Chicago: University of Chicago Press, 1966); J. Wind, *The Bible and the University: The Messianic Vision of William Rainey Harper* (Atlanta: Scholars Press, 1987).

36. The University of Chicago was an early corporate supporter of the American Schools of Oriental Research, and J.H. Breasted, the renowned Egyptologist from the Oriental Institute at Chicago, served as Trustee of ASOR from 1926–35. Yet for many years the management of the schools was primarily in the hands of a committee whose members rarely came from any school outside the eastern United States. Moreover, the Chairs of the committee from 1902–21 were all easterners, and with reorganization of ASOR in 1921, two men, James Montgomery (University of Pennsylvania) and Millar Burrows (Yale University) served lengthy terms as President. It was not until 1949 that a scholar from the University of Chicago, Karl Kraeling, was chosen to lead ASOR. Irwin's only official contact with the world of biblical archaeology, and then only indirectly, was in 1934 when he served as a representative of the Oriental Institute at the Megiddo excavations in Palestine. For a sketch of Irwin's career, see the *National Cyclopaedia of American Biography*, 53 (New York: White, 1971), pp. 213-14.

37. In 1891 a regional section of the national Society of Biblical Literature was established in Chicago; in late fall the following year, members decided, in the words of Harold Willoughby, a Chicagoan, to reorganize themselves 'in typically independent midwestern fashion', as the Chicago Society for Biblical Research, completely independent of the SBL. Although open to guests from other regions of the country, and indeed the world, the new Society's proceedings were controlled by scholars based in the Midwest. See H.R. Willoughby (ed.), *The Study of the Bible Today and Tomorrow* (Chicago: University of Chicago Press, 1947), p. ix. This particular publication of the Society assessed the state of biblical studies in the post-war period, and even though Albright and his pupil G.E. Wright contributed to the volume, they in no sense dominated its perspective. The presumed supremacy of an archaeological-background approach as the pre-eminent path to reliable knowledge about the Bible,

Projected onto the symbolic landscape of Albright's reformist narrative, however, Irwin represented those faults and lapses characteristic of the passing 'before archaeology' age. Albright guarded the claim that Moses came to the exalted notion of monotheism that was to characterize forever Judaism and Christianity. In so doing, he maintained covertly a form of Christian dogma: the unity of revelation through the Old and New Testaments; or, in Albright's historicized expression, Mosaic monotheism, though expressed without benefit of Greek rationalism, was nevertheless consistent with Christian trinitarian formulations.[38] Irwin, following in the steps of Wellhausen and other scholars at the time, ascribed much less exalted features to Israelite religion, and located the highest pre-Christian achievements of monotheistic thought with the prophet Isaiah.[39]

a cause for which Albright tirelessly campaigned, was relativized in many of the essays by full reference to other approaches to the Bible. Rejection of one of Irwin's papers by the editors of *JBL* (Albright's opinion was decisive in the matter) once led to an exchange in which Irwin, professing to speak for many of his Chicago colleagues, raised the specter of political exclusion. Albright, Chair of the journal's Editorial Board, and Erwin Goodenough, Chief Editor, both vigorously denied the charge. However, Albright in private tossed a vague accusation back toward Chicago, saying that he and several of his younger colleagues (he probably meant his own former students) had had 'the most incredible recent experiences and adventures with the Chicago organ, *AJSL*, episodes that make Irwin's one experience with *JBL* look pale by comparison' (Albright to E.R. Goodenough, July 3, 1939.) Irwin never published an article in *JBL*, which for years had been managed by scholars in the East. Most of his work appeared in periodicals published by or closely associated with the University of Chicago, such as *JR* (successor to *Biblical World* [1893–1918] and *American Journal of Theology* [1897–19201), *JBR* and *AJSL*, succeeded in 1942 by *JNES*. See the bibliography of Irwin's works in E.C. Hobbs (ed.), *A Stubborn Faith: Papers on Old Testament and Related Subjects Presented to Honor William Andrew Irwin* (Dallas: Southern Methodist University Press, 1956), pp. 164-70.

  38. Following publication of *From the Stone Age*, a few scholars hotly debated how best to describe Mosaic theism: was it truly monotheistic or not? Albright admitted privately to H.H. Rowley something of the theological commitments that had been masked by the scholarly language of historical dispute: 'We [I and my opponents] can never agree on a definition of monotheism [in speaking about Moses] for the very simple reason that I refuse to accept a definition which denies monotheism to orthodox trinitarian Christianity'; Albright to H.H. Rowley, May 25, 1942.

  39. See, for example, Irwin's review of Albright's *From the Stone Age* in *JR* 21 (1941), pp. 318-19 and *Christian Century* 58 (March 5, 1941), pp. 322-23.

In the name of science and its claims to objective knowledge, Albright rejected studies of the Bible that were not firmly controlled by the presuppositions and derived data of archaeological research. Albright continually drew upon such information to support his views about the antiquity and historical reliability of many biblical materials that others mistrusted, and to depict the history of biblical religion.[40] Irwin approached the Bible with similar claims to scientific objectivity, but primarily with the assumptions and interests of a literary-historical scholar. Thus, he worked extensively with reconstructed documentary sources of the Bible and editorial changes or additions to the biblical text. He also reconstructed original forms of biblical poetry, stripped of its overlay of corruptions and editorial expansions. The Bible itself, that is, text *as writing*, offered Irwin—as it did Wellhausen—his privileged object and paradigm for scientific study.[41] For prophet-crusader Albright, 'biblical science' meant accepting the principles, even the substance, of Wellhausenist source theory, but emphasizing the study of cultures to which the Bible pointed and through which it could be more accurately understood. To Albright, Wellhausen (and his heir Irwin, through his teacher J.M.P. Smith) represented biblical criticism that was outmoded, speculative and unchecked by those empirical facts that Albright was convinced archaeology offered. New, reliable, truly scientific biblical study meant the 'backgrounds approach', a study of the world *around* the Bible so as to understand better the world *in* the Bible. For this, nothing less than the passion and acumen of the prophet-reformer was demanded to usher in the 'renaissance of our day'.

40. See his 'Archaeology Confronts Biblical Criticism', pp. 176-88.

41. Irwin's lecture, 'Fifty Years of Old Testament Scholarship', *JBR* 10 (1942), pp. 131-35, 183, delivered at the 50th anniversary meeting of the Chicago Society of Biblical Research, concentrated on literary studies of the Bible during the years 1891–1941. While extolling gains in understanding that had been made possible by archaeological finds, Irwin failed to mention many particulars or the contributions of Albright. See also W.A. Irwin, 'The Significance of Julius Wellhausen', *JBR* 12 (1944), pp. 160-73, esp. p. 164. Irwin's *The Problem of Ezekiel: An Inductive Approach* (Chicago: University of Chicago Press, 1943) is illustrative of his approach. He took great care to arrive at what to him were objective literary and stylistic criteria with which to discriminate original from spurious material in the biblical book; yet in the spirit of scientific inquiry, he claimed no finality for his results, and remained open to further consideration of the argument and the internal literary evidence on which it was based (pp. vii-xi).

Conclusions

I have argued that William Foxwell Albright took a particular theological construction of the Hebrew prophets as paradigmatic for his own sense of self, and that this artifact of autobiography was encoded variously as strands of apologia within his scholarly discourse. As a prophet-crusader seeking to lay hold of repristinized truth, Albright—he was also historical critic and archaeologist—set out to restore confidence in the Bible's trustworthiness and to chart the 'prehistory' of triumphant Christology; as prophet-crusader—he was also historically oriented textual critic—Albright sought to hear the pristine voices of the Hebrew poets and so confirm their pre-eminence as speakers of religious and aesthetic value, and their reliability as archivists of at least some bits of objective history. As prophet-reformer—he was also archaeologist and philologian—Albright located himself on a map of modern biblical study and claimed to usher in, like the Protestant reformers, a 'renaissance' of progress leading to true historical and religious understanding of the Bible.

My argument should not be taken as an effort to reject the scientific aspects of biblical criticism which Albright practiced. And it would be foolish to impugn his innovative and foundational contributions to the field at the time. Rather, I suggest the importance of inquiring into constellations of ideological commitments which, like attachments to values and paradigms of modern science, become ingrained in critical work and visible in struggles to maintain or resist formations of knowledge-based social power. I have primarily woven a fabric of theological, historical and reformist purposes in this essay, but I could imagine other tapestries as well. My main purpose has been to depict the production of scholarly knowledge not as the achievement of unambiguously objective truth, but as the organization of socially constructed facts and meanings. In the case of Albright, who held a central place in American biblical studies, these contestatory dynamics emerged in his acts of historical recovery, philological analysis, ideological mappings, and assertions of Christian triumphalism, especially against the rising totalitarianism of the 1930s and 40s.

Such a perspective on the history of biblical studies is, of course, a peculiar construction of our own late-twentieth-century age, when confidence in the ideals and political innocence of objectivist notions of scholarly knowledge has weakened. Mine is not a counsel of despair, but of hope. I suggest one way to conceive and write a history of knowledge-making while owning up to various contests of vested interest that make knowledge possible, and inevitably, open to challenge.

RITUALIZING, RITE AND PENTATEUCHAL THEOLOGY*

Frank H. Gorman, Jr

Introduction

As is well known, the priestly ritual material located at the heart of the
Pentateuchal story (Exod. 24.15–Num. 10.10, excluding Exod. 32–34)
has not received serious attention in Protestant theological discussions of
that material.[1] Indeed, 'ritual'[2] has received, for the most part, a negative

*   It is with pleasure that I dedicate this article to Professor Tucker and extend
my thanks for all that he has taught me. I also want to thank the Faculty Scholars
program of the University of Kentucky for a Mellon Fellowship awarded for the
academic year of 1994–1995 which provided the occasion for the writing of this
article.
    1.   I have discussed the exclusion of 'ritual' from biblical studies in 'Ritual
Studies and Biblical Studies' (forthcoming in *Semeia*). Important discussions are
also found in R.A. Oden, Jr, *The Bible Without Theology* (San Francisco: Harper &
Row, 1987), pp. 1-39; J.D. Levenson, *The Hebrew Bible, the Old Testament, and
Historical Criticism* (Louisville, KY: Westminster/John Knox Press, 1993), pp. 1-
61, 82-126; H. Eilberg-Schwartz, *The Savage in Judaism* (Bloomington/Indianapolis:
Indiana University Press, 1990), pp. 1-28, 49-66; S. Briggs, 'The Deceit of the
Sublime: An Investigation into the Origins of Ideological Criticism of the Bible in
Early Nineteenth-Century German Biblical Studies', *Semeia* 29 (1992), pp. 1-23;
R. Rendtorff, 'The Images of Postexilic Israel in German Biblical Scholarship from
Wellhausen to von Rad', in M. Fishbane and E. Tov (eds.), *Sha'arei Talmon*
(Winona Lake: Eisenbrauns, 1992), pp. 165-73.
    2.   It is now widely recognized that 'ritual' is a scholarly construct, often used in
an uncritical fashion, that has its own history and ideological biases (see T. Asad,
Genealogies of Religion [Baltimore: Johns Hopkins University Press, 1993], pp. 55-
79; C. Bell, *Ritual Theory Ritual Practice* [New York: Oxford University Press,
1992], pp. 13-66; J.Z. Smith, *Drudgely Divine* [Chicago: University of Chicago
Press, 1990]). Because of this, the use of 'ritual' as a general category is problematic
and points to the need for terminological clarification (see R. Grimes, *Ritual
Criticism* [Columbia, SC: University of South Carolina Press, 1990], pp. 7-27).

evaluation and has been viewed as an 'outsider' to theological construction in the context of biblical studies. This study is, as the title
suggests, an attempt to explore what attentiveness to the dynamics of a
specific ritual enactment might contribute to a theological reading of the
Pentateuchal story.

There are three primary reasons for examining the conjunction of rite[3]
and 'theology'[4] in the Pentateuch. One very important and obvious
reason has to do with the central place that the ritual materials have in
the Pentateuch.[5] Without suggesting that 'ritual' should become the
unifying 'center' of Pentateuchal theology, the centrality of the ritual
materials must be taken seriously in our theological readings of the
Pentateuch.[6] 'Ritualized' activity was of crucial importance for those
persons or groups responsible for the production of the Pentateuch.
Texts that reflect and are, to some extent, shaped by ritualized activity
are not limited to the priestly traditions (for example, Gen. 15; 22; Exod.
19–24.14). Ritualization and rite, and not only confession, played an on-

3.   I use 'rite' to refer to a concrete enactment that is located in the context of
specific institutional structures, meanings, goals, and with institutional authorization
(cf. Grimes, *Ritual Criticism*, pp. 9-10). 'A ritual enactment' and 'a ritual process'
refer to specific and concrete enactments and processes. 'Ritualizing' and 'ritualization'
have to do with human enactments that range from creative and emergent actions to
more patterned activities. Both recognize that gesture is part of the human 'becoming'
and that such activity is shared to some extent with the 'animal' or 'natural' world
(see Bell, *Ritual Theory*, pp. 69-93; T.E. Driver, *The Magic of Ritual* [San Francisco:
Harper Collins, 1991], pp. 12-31).
4.   The quotation marks reflect the recognition that 'theology' like 'ritual' is a
difficult term with a lengthy, ideological history of its own. I use it to refer to various
types of 'constructive' discourse generated by persons with fairly specific institutional locations (such as members of specific faith communities or specific professional communities) which, for those undertaking 'theological readings' of biblical
texts, require not only a detailed reading of the text but also a detailed reading of the
self and the community within which the self is located.
5.   See E.G. Newing, 'A Rhetorical and Theological Analysis of the Hexateuch',
South East Asia Journal of Theology 22 (1981), pp. 1-15; F. Gorman, *The Ideology
of Ritual* (JSOTSup, 91; Sheffield: JSOT Press, 1990), pp. 39-60.
6.   In that ritualizing and rites are context specific, they will not provide a
generalized center for a unified reading. Insightful ('theological') discussions of
'commandment' and 'law' are found in J. Levenson, 'The Theologies of
Commandment in Biblical Israel', *HTR* 73 (1980), pp. 17-33, and O. Kaiser 'The
Law as Center of the Hebrew Bible', in Fishbane and Tov (eds.), *Sha'arei Talmon*,
pp. 93-103.

going role in the development and production of the Pentateuchal traditions.[7]

A second reason for including the ritual materials in our theological discourse on the Pentateuch recognizes that the history of the exclusion of (and hostility toward) 'ritual' reflects both theological and ideological biases.[8] Both in the New Testament and in the theology of the church fathers, a negative view of Judaism and its rites provided one means by which the church could mark out its identity in opposition to Judaism.[9] The polemic of the early church against Judaism was further developed and intensified in the Protestant Reformation's attack on the 'rituals' of the Catholic church. The biases against 'ritual', and clearly this meant bias against both Judaism and Catholicism, were retained and developed in the 'neutral' and 'objective'construction of Protestant biblical scholarship in the seventeenth and eighteenth centuries.[10] It must be asked in a critical and self-reflective way if the ongoing neglect of the 'ritual' materials which fails to include them in theological readings of the Pentateuch does not reflect, to some degree, older ideological and theological biases?

Finally, recent developments in 'ritual studies' provide both theoretical and methodological insights that prove useful in the study of the Pentateuch.[11] First, it is clear that 'ritualizing' activity is constitutive, to

7.   Biblical scholars have tended to place more emphasis on the 'words' of worship than on the 'actions' of worship. This has functioned to privilege word over enactment and reason over activity (see Bell, *Ritual Theory*, pp. 13-93).

8.   I have discussed some of the details of this history in 'Ritual Studies and Biblical Studies'.

9.   For discussions of 'Judaism' in the early church and the church fathers, see R.R. Ruether, *Faith and Fratricide* (New York: Seabury, 1974); E.P. Sanders, *Paul and Palestinian Judaism* (Philadelphia: Fortress Press, 1977), pp. 33-59; S. Sandmel, *Anti-Semitism in the New Testament?* (Philadelphia: Fortress Press, 1978); C. Klein, *Anti-Judaism in Christian Theology* (London: SPCK Press, 1978); A.T. Davies (ed.), *Anti-Semitism and the Foundations of Christianity* (New York: Paulist Press, 1979); G.I. Langmuir, *History, Religion, and Antisemitism* (Berkeley and Los Angeles: University of California Press, 1990), pp. 275-305.

10.   Important discussions are found in H.G. Reventlow, *The Authority of the Bible and the Rise of the Modern World* (trans. J. Bowden; Philadelphia: Fortress Press, 1984), and W. Baird, *History of New Testament Research. I. From Deism to Tübingen* (Minneapolis: Fortress Press, 1993).

11.   Important examples include J.D. Shaughnessy (ed.), *The Roots of Ritual* (Grand Rapids: Eerdmans, 1973); E.G. d'Aquili *et al.* (eds.), *The Spectrum of Ritual* (New York: Columbia University Press, 1979); F. Staal, 'The Meaninglessness of Ritual', *Numen* 26 (1979), pp. 2-22; R.L. Grimes, *Beginnings in Ritual Studies*

176   *Prophets and Paradigms*

some degree, of human life and existence. Failure to take this into account will diminish the depth of our theological discourse. Secondly, it is important to reflect on the nature of human activity and its role in the production of the self and society.[12] Human beings do not only think themselves into and through existence; they also enact their existence. Thirdly, ritual studies raise important issues regarding the relationship between the production of rites and the production of texts concerned with and/or generated by rites.

This paper will discuss the larger ritualized process that is 'set into motion' when a person discovers an irregular skin eruption on her or his body (see Lev. 13–14).[13] The person must be examined by a priest who declares the skin eruption either clean or unclean. If unclean, the person must leave the community and remain outside the camp. When there is a change in the skin condition, the priest re-examines the person and if the priestly declaration is 'but now clean', an eight-day rite of restoration[14] is enacted which moves the formerly unclean individual back into the larger social body. The purpose of the study is to ask what this particular and concrete ritualized process offers to the construction of Pentateuchal theology.

(Lanham, MD: University Press of America, 1982); T.W. Jennings, 'On Ritual Knowledge', *JR* 62 (1982), pp. 111-27; V. Turner, *From Ritual to Theatre* (New York: Performing Arts Journal Publications, 1982); J.Z. Smith, *To Take Place* (Chicago: University of Chicago Press, 1987); Grimes, *Ritual Criticism*; Driver, *The Magic of Ritual*; Bell, *Ritual Theory*; R.L. Grimes, 'Reinventing Ritual', *Soundings* 75 (1992), pp. 21-41; C. Humphrey and J. Laidlaw, *The Archetypal Actions of Ritual* (Oxford: Clarendon Press, 1994).

12. See M. Bakhtin, *Toward a Philosophy of the Act* (trans. V. Liapunov; ed. V. Liapunov and M. Holquist; Austin: University of Texas Press, 1993), and P. Bourdieu, *Outline of a Theory of Practice* (trans. R. Nice; Cambridge: Cambridge University Press, 1977).

13. For exegetical discussions, see J. Milgrom, *Leviticus 1–16* (AB; Garden City, NY: Doubleday, 1991), pp. 768-889; Gorman, *Ideology of Ritual*, pp. 151-79; B.A. Levine, *Leviticus* (Jewish Publication Society Torah Commentary; Philadelphia: Jewish Publications Society, 1989), pp. 76-92; J.E. Hartley, *Leviticus* (WBC; Dallas: Word Books, 1992), pp. 170-201.

14. On 'rites of restoration', see F. Gorman, 'Priestly Rituals of Founding: Time, Space, and Status', in M.P. Graham, W.P. Brown and J.K. Kuan (eds.), *History and Interpretation* (JSOTSup, 173; Sheffield: JSOT Press, 1993), pp. 48-50.

The Concrete and the Particular

Efforts to construct critical discourse concerning a specific rite must recognize that it is enacted by real flesh-and-blood persons in concrete, specific and particular contexts. Our discursive practices concerning rites must focus on the specific actions of real persons and the concrete moments of life in which they enact their existence. This requires, in part, that we reflect on the concrete construction of the self in the context of the concrete processes of social life.[15]

The present situation arises when a person discovers a disfigurement of the skin and comes before a priest for a purity ruling and declaration.[16] The person is physically marked and institutionally defined. The institutional declaration takes place not only as priestly utterance but also as social construct. Thus, a person experiences a 'marked' body which is then declared unclean by a priest with the 'prescribed' consequence of expulsion from the social body. It is only after the skin condition has changed, a priest declares the person clean, and an eight-day rite has been enacted that the individual is restored to her or his previous social status.

The scholarly search for general categories and classificatory systems all too often fails to give attention to the experience of the 'concrete, flesh-and-blood' person. It is certain that 'dis-location' and 're-location' of the self are not experienced as abstractions or general categories by the individual. For one whose body is evaluated in such a way that expulsion is the consequence, it is a brutal form of analysis that fails to consider and take seriously the specific and particular experience of social exile and marginalization[17] which, in all probability, was experienced, in this situation, as a form of death.[18]

15. See Bakhtin, *Philosophy of the Act*; Bourdieu, *Theory of Practice*, pp. 72-158; Bell, *Ritual Theory*, pp. 69-117; P.M. Cooey, *Religious Imagination and the Body* (New York and Oxford: Oxford University Press, 1994), pp. 63-85, 109-29.

16. For discussions of the precise nature of the skin lesions, see D.P. Wright and R.N. Jones, 'Leprosy', *ABD*, pp. 277-82, and Milgrom, *Leviticus*, pp. 771-808.

17. See Cooey (*Religious Imagination*, pp. 87-108) for a discussion of the body as site of social discourse and as arbiter between universality and particularity. Cooey's work develops themes present in E. Scarry, *The Body in Pain* (New York and Oxford: Oxford University Press, 1985). On the relation of the body and social discourse, see M. Foucault, *The History of Sexuality*, I (trans. R. Hurley; New York: Vintage Books, 1978).

18. See E. Feldman, *Biblical and Post-Biblical Defilement and Mourning* (New

I would certainly not want to argue that we can 'know' precisely what an Israelite experienced in this ritualized and institutionalized expulsion and restoration.[19] Without knowing the precise nature and content of the Israelite 'experience' of an 'unclean body', it would have included emotional, affective and cognitive responses. I suggest two resources that may contribute to our 'understanding' of this experience. First, various psalms reflect the movement of particular rites and, in that way, reflect the ritualized experience of the participants.[20] Ritualized activity is one means of constructing the self—the complex and dynamic self that includes emotions, physicality and cognition—which then acts upon the rite and 're-constructs' it. Secondly, we must listen to the voices of those in our own cultural contexts who experience bodily 'marks' and social exclusion. For example, important insights might be heard in the words of individuals with cancer and AIDS who speak of the experience of the 'diseased' body and the social exclusion that often results.[21] Although social and cultural differences exist, there are significant similarities.

In the present situation, the body as site of physical disruption becomes site for priestly evaluation which then becomes a means for social exclusion/inclusion.[22] The body is a vehicle for determining social status and location and the individual's concrete existence within the community takes place through the body as site of priestly declaration. The self is constituted, in part, in terms of the body and the body, in turn, is constituted, in part, in terms of social practice and discourse. It is important that we reflect on the ways in which the physical body is the

York: Yeshiva University/Ktav, 1977), pp. 37-41; Gorman, *Ideology of Ritual*, pp. 131-32, 161-79.

19. Nor would I argue that we can 'know' precisely the experience of a person who stands before us. Although 'knowing' may not be possible, 'understanding' in meaningful ways certainly is, for example, through empathetic and imaginative sharing of lived experiences.

20. See G.A. Anderson, 'The Praise of God as Cultic Event', in G.A. Anderson and S.M. Olyan (eds.), *Priesthood and Cult in Ancient Israel* (JSOTSup, 125; Sheffield: JSOT Press, 1991), pp. 15-33.

21. For reflections on illness, the body and society, see S. Sontag, *Illness as Metaphor* (New York: Farrar, Straus & Giroux, 1978), and *AIDS and its Metaphors* (New York: Farrar, Straus & Giroux, 1989). On the experience of AIDS, see J.E. Fortunato, *AIDS: The Spiritual Dilemma* (San Francisco: Harper & Row, 1987), and M. Callan, *Surviving AIDS* (New York: Harper Collins, 1990).

22. See n. 17.

site of political, theological, religious and social discourses that function to define and value the individual.[23]

In the present situation, the self comes into being and emerges at the intersection of concrete enactment and institutional and social structures. In this ritualized process, the body is a means of negotiating the relationship between the self and society. This process indicates one of the ways in which ritualization functions to locate the concrete individual within a specific social situation.

The Body and Ritualized Activity

Discursive analysis of ritualized processes must emphasize the centrality of the body in the production of ritualized activity.[24] It is impossible to enact a rite without a body because ritualized activity is enacted with, by and through the body. Ritualizing has to do with 'bodying forth', the gesture, 'standing forth', and the positioning of the self.[25]

The centrality of the body in ritualizing activity points to the concrete nature of ritualizing activity and rite. The body is located and positioned; it is here and not there. The positional and locative nature of enactment requires, as already discussed, that analysis take the concrete and particular seriously. In ritualized processes, the self bodies forth its existence. Although specific rites may include transcendent concerns, social constructs and more inclusive messages, ritualized activity must be understood to have primary reference to itself as bodily enactment.[26]

Attentiveness to ritualization suggests that the production of theological discourse must take the bodied existence of human selves seriously. Human beings do not exist in society apart from bodies—very concrete

23. See E. Grosz, 'Bodies and Knowledge: Feminism and the Crisis of Reason', in A. Alcoff and E. Potter (eds.), *Feminist Epistemologies* (New York and London: Routledge, 1993), pp. 187-215.

24. On religion and the body, see the essays in J.M. Law (ed.), *Religious Reflections on the Human Body* (Bloomington/Indianapolis: Indiana University Press, 1995). On the body, society and meaning, see J. Benthall and T. Polhemus (eds.), *The Body as a Medium of Expression* (New York: E.P. Dutton, 1975); T. Polhemus, *Social Aspects of the Human Body* (Harmondsworth: Penguin, 1978); M. Johnson, *The Body in the Mind* (Chicago: University of Chicago Press, 1987); J. Gallop, *Thinking Through the Body* (New York: Columbia University Press, 1988); Grosz, 'Bodies and Knowledge', pp. 187-215.

25. See Grimes, *Ritual Criticism*, pp. 7-15; Bell, *Ritual Theory*, pp. 94-117.

26. I have discussed institutional and symbolic meanings of several priestly rites in *Ideology of Ritual*.

and specific bodies that are constituted in part through biology, in part through social discourse, and in part through personal reflection and activity. In addition, the body becomes a site for the play of power.[27] The priest can exclude or include on the basis of an investigation of the appearance of the body. The body, declared unclean, becomes a possible corrupter, a 'disease', of the social body. The present situation views the body as a locus of fear—the body can corrupt, make unclean, contaminate. Such ritualized and institutional concern for the 'unclean' body continued (continues?) to survive in the West in its suspicion of the body as source of temptation and sin and as matter to be brought under rational control. Contemporary theological reflection and discourse must re-evaluate the long-standing fear and suspicion of the body—this includes, for example, dualistic notions of the self, the association of women with the 'weak' and 'tempting' body, and the belief that the body is inconsequential to the true 'inner' or 'spiritual' self—and affirm in positive ways the bodied nature of human existence.

Enactment: Situations and Strategies

Critical discourse on ritualized processes must focus on the nature of activity and enactment. What constitutes 'ritual' activity and how is it distinguished from 'non-ritual' activity? Two aspects, in particular, need attention: the 'ritual' moment and a strategy for ritual enactment.[28]

Ritualized activity is situational and locative and is called for and called forth by concrete ritualized moments. Ritualized processes emerge out of, are generated by, and function as responses to very specific social situations as they are experienced by individuals who are caught up in, and who are, in part, constructed by the concrete moments of existence within a community. Human location within specific situations and social moments gives rise to ritualized activity, that is, the moments of ritualization and the strategies for ritualization. The 'ritual' moment is constituted by all the persons, powers, structures and situations that come together and generate 'the calling forth' of and 'the call for' enactment.

---

27. See Bell, *Ritual Theory*, pp. 197-223, for a discussion of social power, ritualization and the body.

28. Bell (*Ritual Theory*, pp. 81-83) discusses four features of practice: it is situational; it is strategic; it reflects a 'misrecognition' of what it is doing; and it involves agency and the will to act.

Ritualized activity is not only situational, it is also strategic.[29] Ritualized processes and rites provide strategies for action within concrete social situations. The movement back and forth between situational moment and ritualized enactment, ritualized enactment and situational moment, is dialectical and generative.[30] The concrete individual engages a social moment, that is, actualizes a strategy of enactment, and in, by and through that engagement reconstitutes the moment. At the same time, the ritually reconstituted moment will then engage the individual in a moment of reconstitution. The strategic give and take of ritualized moment and concrete enactment, the mutual construction and reconstruction of situation and individual, more accurately characterizes ritualizing processes than do the more traditional definitions of 'ritual' as formal, prescribed, fixed, static and repetitious rules for behavior. These traditional descriptors may be reflected in some cases, but they are not essential to the production of ritualized activity.[31]

Taking the eight-day rite (Lev. 14.1-20) of restoration as an example, it is clear that the text does not give detailed information concerning the enactment of the rite. The text makes no effort to 'prescribe' every action and leaves the situation open for individual and creative enactment. There is a basic 'patterning' presented in the text, but it does not present 'a' pattern which can then be transformed into 'the' pattern.[32] The text details what is necessary for the rite to be enacted, but it leaves room for individual interpretation and creative variation in the concrete enactment of the rite. The text envisions a constructive practice that consists of a patterning, that is, an open-ended framework of possibilities, and a concrete enactment. Rather than lamenting that the text fails to provide necessary information for interpretation, we must recognize that the text says what it 'needs' and 'wants' to say. In this way, the text itself indicates that ritualizing is an open-ended set of possibilities and not a formal scheme to be repeated without variation.

Inability to observe the enactment of these 'textual rites' creates both theoretical and methodological problems. 'Observation', however,

---

29. Bell, *Ritual Theory*, pp. 88-93.
30. Bakhtin, *Philosophy of the Act*.
31. See Bell, *Ritual Theory*, pp. 88-93; Grimes, 'Reinventing Ritual', pp. 21-38.
32. G.A. Anderson ('Sacrifice and Sacrificial Offerings [OT]', *ABD*, pp. 882-86) discusses the 'scripturalization of the cult' and the canonical shaping of the sacrificial texts.

especially when related to matters of 'interpretation', has its own problems.[33] First, earlier views of observation were based on the assumed neutrality and objectivity of the scholarly observer/interpreter. Such views pitted the objective observer against the subjective participant and privileged scholarly cognition (= interpretation and explanation) over indigenous activity. This view, in its efforts to construct a 'science' of fieldwork, failed to recognize that scholarly activity, involving research, interpretation, reporting, writing and publication, is itself a cultural production undertaken by 'subjective participants'. Secondly, one must ask what it is that must be observed for accurate reflection and how many times 'it' must be observed to guarantee a correct interpretation. Thirdly, recent ritual studies suggest that participation is a better vantage point for engaging ritualized activity than the neutral, objective, transcendent observer.[34]

It is more appropriate to address critically what is available than to lament what is not available. I offer three suggestions. First, in terms of method, we must be attentive to the relationship that exists between ritualizing activity and the production of 'ritual' texts. In what ways did ritualized activity become generative of ritual texts and what were the social, cultural and historical factors that gave rise to the production of ritual texts?[35] Secondly, in terms of theology, we must draw on our imagination,[36] our ability to image our way into a text and through a rite, as a means of engaging 'ritual' texts in such a way that we discover

33. The status and nature of 'observation' is receiving critical discussion in anthropology. The following are helpful: M. Auge, *The Anthropological Circle* (Cambridge: Cambridge University Press, 1982); Bell, *Ritual Theory*, pp. 19-66; J. Fabian, *Time and the Other* (New York: Columbia University Press, 1983); G.E. Marcus and M.M.J. Fischer, *Anthropology as Cultural Critique* (Chicago: University of Chicago Press, 1986).

34. See Grimes, *Ritual Criticism*, pp. 15-27, 210-33.

35. G. von Rad ('The Problem of the Hexateuch', in *The Problem of the Hexateuch and Other Essays* [trans. E.W. Trueman Dicken; London: SCM Press, 1984], pp. 1-78) recognizes a relationship between 'legend' and 'cult' in the formation of the Sinai materials, but argues that 'the legend unquestionably preceded the cultus' (p. 22) and that the central feature of the 'rite' associated with Sinai was the declaration of the word of Yahweh to the listening people (p. 23). The confessional basis of the texts is emphasized in the traditioning process.

36. For recent discussions of imagination, biblical texts and theology, see W. Brueggemann, *Texts Under Negotiation* (Minneapolis: Fortress Press, 1994), pp. 1-25, and L.G. Perdue, *The Collapse of History* (Minneapolis: Fortress Press, 1994), pp. 263-98.

something not only about 'texts' and 'rites' but also something of our own ritualized ways of being in the world. Thirdly, we must, as biblical scholars, reflect critically on our own ritualized practices of thinking, writing, assembling and communicating.[37]

Ritualized enactment is locative, positional, strategic and provisional. It is probing, searching, experimental and tentative. It takes place in an open world of possibilities in which concrete individuals in concrete moments struggle to find a place to 'take a stand'. Such ritualizing takes place without absolute rules and without absolute guarantees of 'successful' outcomes, whatever 'success' might mean in any given ritualized moment. Certainly, ritualized processes like that presented in Leviticus 13–14, which are grounded in and supported by powerful social institutions, will provide strategies that offer successful outcomes. They work. Without question, institutional rites attempt to provide certainties.[38] One should not, however, argue that these institutional certainties are necessary for determining and defining ritualized activity. Indeed, it is appropriate, one might say necessary, to ask just how much certainty such institutional structures actually do provide. Particularly in the contemporary Western context, one might argue that institutional structures and the rites associated with them provide for many persons one of the primary causes of ambiguity, uncertainty and anguish.

Conclusions and Suggestions

It is clear that the 'ritual' materials in the Pentateuch cannot be ignored if our readings of the Pentateuch are to have integrity. Ritualization is found both in the content of the Pentateuch and in the processes that led to its formation. Further, ritualization is an important aspect of human existence. Engaging the ritual materials is not simply a matter of under-standing texts, but also a matter of understanding ourselves.

The discursive analysis of ritualized activity in relation to Leviticus 13–14 has taken place within two interactive and dynamic contexts. In one, ritualized enactment is located and discussed along a continuum that moves between generative and emergent human ritualizing and

37. Grimes, *Ritual Criticism*, pp. 210-33.
38. On cultural order and priestly rites, see Gorman, *Ideology of Ritual*, pp. 13-30. For a critical discussion of the history of 'culture' and 'order' in anthropological discourse, see C. Herbert, *Culture and Anomie* (Chicago: University of Chicago Press, 1991).

institutionally constructed and structured rites. This is not an either/or question but a matter of evaluating each enactment in terms of its tentative human gesturing and its institutional patterning. In the other, ritualized enactment is understood to be generated in the mutual interaction and constitution of the individual self and the larger social context. Ritualized activity is a moment in which the concrete individual engages the social world in such a way that each becomes generative and constructive of the other.

I offer four suggestions for ways in which attentiveness to the Pentateuchal 'ritual' materials might contribute to contemporary theological readings of the Pentateuch. Two have to do with our readings of the Pentateuchal texts and two have to do with our readings of ourselves.

First, if our understanding of the Pentateuch rests to a degree on its formation and production, then we must be attentive both to the 'groups' that stand behind the texts and to the processes that functioned to produce them. If Israelite religion was constituted, in part, by ritualizing, then the texts generated by the practice of that religion will reflect its ritualizing. We must examine the relationship between rites and the production of texts in such a way that rites are viewed both as generative background and as productive activity. What were the ritualizing activities that gave rise to the production of the Pentateuch?

Secondly, the concrete nature of enactment suggests that we should read the Pentateuchal texts with an eye to the concrete and particular enactments of the persons located in the story.[39] This means, in part, that we give less attention to the meta-narratives, be they literary or theological, that have been proposed to hold together and unify the diverse stories and characters of the Pentateuch. The world of ritualization is tentative, ambiguous and open and the 'worlds' of the individuals in the Pentateuch may be less than unified. We must be attentive not only to the differences that exist between the Pentateuchal traditions but also to the fissures found in the enacted lives and worlds of the individual Pentateuchal characters.[40] Our theological discourse must reflect the open-ended and uncertain worlds produced by concrete texts and focus less on the quest for the unified world of the Pentateuch.

39. On the importance of the specific text and the little dramas found in the biblical texts, see Brueggemann, *Texts Under Negotiation*, pp. 57-72.

40. I would argue that certain fissures and ambiguities are found in the 'rebellion' stories in Num. 16–17 and in the story of the bronze serpent in Num. 21.1-9, both of which reflect obvious ritualizing activity.

Thirdly, we must reflect critically on our own concrete location and the particular social moments in which we find ourselves. As suggested, this means, in part, recognizing and taking seriously our bodied existence— we are here and not there—and finding a positive and valuable place for the body in our theological discourse. Further, we must be attentive to the ways in which we enact our own existence and not simply to the ways in which we think about our existence. For example, we must not only think about the de-centering of our world at this particular moment in history and the ambiguities that emerge out of that de-centering, we must also find a place to stand forth and enact the self in such a de-centered and ambiguous world.[41]

Fourthly, we must reflect critically on our production of Pentateuchal readings, be they, for example, theological, historical, postmodernist or narrative, and our production of theological discourse as it relates to these readings of the Pentateuch. This entails critical reflection on the highly ritualized ways in which those within the scholarly community read, write, report, communicate and assemble. What activities are involved in the production of 'scholarship' and 'theology'? Additionally, however, our reflection on production must take seriously our own concrete location within those professional institutions associated with the academy.[42] Our scholarly activities are deeply embedded in and dependent on various types of institutional support, available economic resources, and the ongoing existence of a community or communities that affirm, tolerate and sustain our activities. We must recognize the communities

41. It is important to recognize that ritualizing takes place in many contemporary quests for liberation and is not, as is often implied, opposed to the enactment of justice. For example, the marches and demonstrations associated with the struggles to obtain civil rights for African Americans, women, and the gay and lesbian communities reflect ritualizing characteristics (see Driver, *The Magic of Ritual*, pp. 12-31). Many feminists have found ritualizing and rites to be important in the discovery and construction of self, voice and community (see, for example, B.G. Walker, *Women's Rituals: A Sourcebook* [San Francisco: Harper & Row, 1990]; M. Procter-Smith, *In Her Own Rite: Constructing Feminist Liturgical Tradition* [Nashville: Abingdon Press, 1990]).

42. E. Schüssler Fiorenza, 'The Ethics of Biblical Interpretation: Decentering Biblical Scholarship', *JBL* 107 (1988), pp. 3-17; W. Brueggemann, 'At the Mercy of Babylon: A Subversive Reading of the Empire', *JBL* 110 (1991), pp. 3-22; F.F. Segovia, '"And They Began to Speak in Other Tongues": Competing Modes of Discourse in Contemporary Biblical Criticism', in F.F. Segovia and M.A. Tolbert (eds.), *Reading from this Place* (Minneapolis: Fortress Press, 1995), pp. 1-32.

that provide us occasion and context to generate and produce 'biblical and theological scholarship'. We must see ourselves as the indigenous, subjective and concrete individuals involved in the production of cultural rites who are, at the same time, the critical observers involved in the production of interpretive and theological discourse.

A MATTER OF LIFE AND DEATH:
A COMPARISON OF PROVERBS 1–9 AND JOB

Suzanne Boorer

It has long been recognized that the book of Job polemicizes against the retributive justice framework that underlies the book of Proverbs.[1] However, the divergence between Job and Proverbs goes much further and deeper than this. They stand over against each other in terms of their intrinsic view of the world. Proverbs presents a dualistic way of thinking in which aspects of the world tend to be polarized into opposites. In contrast, the book of Job advocates a non-dualistic view of reality. The implications of this for the way life is to be lived are far reaching.

This basic difference in worldview is clearly illustrated in the contrasting place assigned to life and death in Proverbs 1–9 and the book of Job.[2] Proverbs 1–9 only will be the focus of my discussion rather than the whole book of Proverbs. These chapters are generally seen as com-

---

1. See especially the influential article by M. Tsevat, 'The Meaning of the Book of Job', *HUCA* 37 (1966), pp. 73-106; and the more general discussions in, for example, J. Crenshaw, 'The Human Dilemma and the Literature of Dissent', in D.A. Knight (ed.), *Tradition and Theology in the Old Testament* (Philadelphia: Fortress Press, 1977), pp. 235-58, especially pp. 253-54; *idem, Old Testament Wisdom: An Introduction* (Atlanta: John Knox, 1981), pp. 116-18; G. von Rad, *Wisdom in Israel* (Nashville: Abingdon Press, 1984), pp. 128-37, 220; R.E. Murphy, The *Tree of Life: An Exploration of Biblical Wisdom Literature* (Garden City, NY: Doubleday, 1990), pp. 116-17; C. Fontaine, 'Proverbs', in C. Newsom and S. Ringe (eds.), *The Women's Bible Commentary* (London: SPCK; Louisville, KY: Westminster/John Knox Press, 1992), p. 146.

2. Even though it is quite probable that the book of Job has a complex tradition history, especially given the marked differences in style and content between the prose and the poetry, for the purposes of my discussion and in line with recent trends (see for example the recent commentaries by N. Habel, *The Book of Job* [London: SCM Press, 1985] and D.J.A. Clines, *Job 1–20* [Dallas: Word Books, 1989]) the book of Job will be taken as a literary whole in its final form.

prising a distinct section within the book of Proverbs since they consist of longer poems in contrast to the material contained in chs. 10–30. However, a brief survey of the references to life and death in chs. 10–31 reveals that conclusions can be drawn that are in line with those that will be reached with regard to chs. 1–9, though at times quite different terminology is used: namely, that life and death are perceived in a dualistic framework as opposites. Death is associated with what is negative—the wicked, the fool, or negative behaviour (for example, 2.25; 10.21; 11.7, 19b; 15.10; 21.6). Life is associated with what is positive—the wise, heeding and keeping the instruction of the wise, positive behaviour, and the fear of Yahweh (for example, 10.11, 16, 17; 11.30; 15.24; 19.23; 22.4). Life and death (and their various associations) are set over against each other as mutually exclusive alternatives (for example, 11.19; 12.28; 13.14; 14.27; 15.24; 19.16). In particular, the perception of the relationship of life and death to each other, and, flowing from this, how one obtains life, is markedly different in these two texts. It is the intention of this article to tease out these differences and to explore their implications for living.[3]

---

3. A discussion of the range of meaning associated with life and death in the Old Testament or even in the wisdom literature lies outside the scope of this article. Suffice to say that it is generally recognized that life and death are used not just to connote something physical. They also have a qualitative dimension. For example, L. R. Bailey *(Biblical Perspectives on Death* [Philadelphia: Fortress Press, 1979], pp. 40-41) states that death is often used as a metaphor for those things which detract from life as Yahweh intends it, among them illness, persecution, despair…and, correspondingly, life is life to the full as Yahweh intended it. These are clearly important connotations of death and life as used in the wisdom literature and Proverbs in particular. For a detailed discussion of the shades of meaning associated with life and death in the Old Testament, see Bailey, *Biblical Perspectives on Death*; H. Gese, 'Death in the Old Testament', in *Essays on Biblical Theology* (Minneapolis: Augsburg, 1981), pp. 34-59; K. Richards, 'Death', *ABD*, pp. 108-10; R. Martin-Achard, *From Death to Life* (Edinburgh and London: Oliver & Boyd, 1960); G. von Rad, *Old Testament Theology*, I (London: SCM Press, 1975), pp. 387ff.; H.W. Wolff, *Anthropology of the Old Testament* (London: SCM Press, 1974), pp. 97-118; J.C. Burns, 'The Mythology of Death and the Old Testament', *SJT* 26 (1973), pp. 327-40; B. Vawter, 'Intimations of Immortality and the Old Testament', *JBL* 91 (1972), pp. 158-71; J.J. Collins, 'The Root of Immortality: Death in the Context of Jewish Wisdom', *HTR* 71 (1978), pp. 177-92.

Life and Death in Proverbs 1–9

Proverbs 1–9 operates with a dualistic worldview in which life and death are mutually exclusive. This is evident from the use of words for life/ living (חַי; חָיָה) and death/dying/Sheol[4] (שְׁאוֹל; מוּת; מָוֶת) their associations, and the interplay of these in the text.

Life (חַי; חָיָה) is associated with (keeping) the commandments, teaching, instruction, words or sayings of the parent (3.2; 4.4, 10, 13, 22-23; 6.23; 7.2) and with wisdom and personified wisdom or Woman Wisdom (3.18, 22; 8.35; 9.6). In some contexts life and its associations are contrasted with death, which is often associated with the Strange Woman.[5] The term 'Strange Woman' is used here and in the following discussion to designate the poetic figure of the negative woman variously described in Proverbs 1–9. Although this figure appears in various guises in the text, in places labelled for example as אִשָּׁה זָרָה מִנָּכְרִיָּה (2.16; 7.5); שִׂפְתֵי זָרָה (5.3); מֵאִשָּׁה זָרָה מִנָּכְרִיָּה (7.5, parallelling אִשָּׁה זוֹנָה), 6.26); and אֵשֶׁת כְּסִילוּת (9.13), it will be assumed here that these all refer to the same figure. Thus in 8.35 life associated with finding Woman Wisdom is set in opposition to death associated with hating Woman Wisdom (8.36). In 2.19 and 5.6 the paths of life are set in opposition to the path of the Strange Woman that is associated with death (2.18-19; 5.5-6). Indeed, keeping the commandment of the parent, associated with life, preserves the son from the Strange Woman (6.23-24; 7.2-5).

Correspondingly, then, death (שְׁאוֹל; מוּת; מָוֶת) is associated with sinners who are 'like Sheol' (1.12, see 1.10), with the wicked (5.23, see 5.22), with those who hate Woman Wisdom (8.36), and with the Strange Woman (2.18 [see 2.16]; 5.5 [see 5.3]; 7.27 [see 7.5]; 9.18 [see 9.13]). With regard to the Strange Woman, death is associated more specifically with her way, symbolized by her feet or steps (5.5) and paths (2.18), and with her

---

4.   Sheol, as the place of death, functions symbolically to connote death in these texts.

5.   G. Yee ('"I Have Perfumed my Bed with Myrrh": The Foreign Woman (*'issa zara*) in Proverbs 1–9', *JSOT* 43 [1989], pp. 53-68, especially p. 54) has argued convincingly for this position on the grounds of similarity of attributes and the macrostructure of Prov. 1–9. This view is also held by, for example, R. Murphy, 'Wisdom and Eros in Proverbs 1–9', *CBQ* 50 (1988), pp. 600-603, especially 603; C. Camp, *Wisdom and the Feminine in the Book of Proverbs* (Sheffield: Almond Press, 1985), pp. 115-17; R.C. Van Leeuwen, 'Liminality and World View in Proverbs 1–9', *Semeia* 50 (1990), pp. 111-44, p. 134 n. 12.

'house', a metaphor for womb[6] (2.18; 7.17; 9.18). Often, in the context, death and its associations are contrasted with those things associated with life. For example, the Strange Woman, associated with death, stands in contrast to wisdom, knowledge, prudence, understanding or the commandments of the parents in 2.18; 5.5; 7.27. In addition, within the broader context, death associated with the Strange Woman stands in opposition to the son's own wife (5.5 [see 5.15-19]), to Woman Wisdom who is associated with life (9.18 [see 9.16] and 7.27 [see 8]), and to the path of life (2.18).

This opposition between life and death and their associated symbols has often been noted: in particular, there has been much attention given recently to the opposition between Woman Wisdom and the Strange Woman, associated with life and death respectively. For example, N. Habel refers to the Strange Woman as the 'binary opposite' of wisdom;[7] C. Camp speaks of the Strange Woman as 'formulated "over against"... Wisdom';[8] R. Murphy sees the Strange Woman as 'the opposite to Lady

---

6.   See C. Newsom, 'Woman and the Discourse of Patriarchal Wisdom: A Study of Proverbs 1–9', in P.L. Day (ed.), *Gender and Difference in Ancient Israel* (Minneapolis: Fortress Press, 1989), pp. 142-60, 149, and R. Alter, *The Art of Biblical Poetry* (New York: Basic Books, 1985), p. 182.

7.   N. Habel, 'The Symbolism of Wisdom in Proverbs 1–9', *Int* 26 (1972), pp. 131-57, especially pp. 141, 156. Although Habel in this article sees the nuclear symbol in Prov. 1–9 as 'the way', he also gives prominence to the symbolism of the two women companions who form binary opposites.

8.   Camp, *Wisdom and the Feminine in the Book of Proverbs*, p. 117. Camp's later attempt to collapse or merge the two opposed women into a unity in her article 'Wise and Strange: An Interpretation of the Female Imagery in Proverbs in Light of Trickster Mythology', *Semeia* 42 (1988), pp. 14-36 can be criticized on the grounds of a certain confusion between experience outside the text with what the text itself states. It cannot be argued, as Camp attempts to do, that the similar characteristics of the two women, validated in experience, point to the same figure. The obvious 'surface opposition' between the two figures as portrayed in the text that Camp acknowledges (p. 23) cannot be collapsed into 'a subtle underlying unity' (p. 19) because of the ambiguity in experience leading to difficulty in recognition of the two women who present themselves in similar ways. The text is clear—Wisdom leads to life and the Strange Woman to death. The position Camp is striving to maintain here of a 'paradoxical, but experientially validated, unity' of good and evil (p. 33) lies closer to the perspective of the book of Job as will become clear in the following discussion. For a similar criticism of Camp in this respect (referring to a similar argument in C. Camp, 'Woman Wisdom as Root Metaphor', in K.G. Hogland *et al.* [eds.], *The Listening Heart: Essays in Wisdom and the Psalms in Honor of R.E.*

Wisdom', 'a foil for presenting the charms of Wisdom', and 'the epitome of all that Lady Wisdom is not';[9] and G. Yee perceives the Strange Woman as 'the ultimate antithesis of Lady Wisdom'; 'the speeches of the *'issa zara* destructively lead to death, as Wisdom's call leads to life'.[10]

Given the prominent number of references to death associated with the Strange Woman (2.18; 5.5; 7.27; 9.18) and the antithesis of Woman Wisdom to her, exploration of the symbolism of the Strange Woman will help to clarify further the dualistic perspective of Proverbs 1–9.

There is a certain amount of agreement in recent discussions of the Strange Woman that, whatever her identity, she symbolizes, or provides a metaphor of, disorder, chaos, even evil; that is, whatever represents a threat to, or disruption of, the social order or well-being of the society. She stands opposite Woman Wisdom who symbolizes order, the social and created order, that is life-giving. For example, Camp describes the Strange Woman as embodying 'the forces of "chaos"',[11] as 'a full-blown force of evil',[12] as 'a metaphorical vehicle for the disruptive and chaotic forces that threaten the shalom of individual and society',[13] as 'a symbol for every danger that threatens the well-being of the community';[14] that is, of the patriarchal society, for 'her deviant sexual behavior...is a symbol of the forces deemed destructive of patriarchal control of family, prosperity and society'.[15] Yee also sees the Strange Woman as the personification 'of all that is evil and destructive in society'[16] or a personification of forces that 'continually threaten to disrupt the social

Murphy [Sheffield: JSOT Press, 1987]), see Van Leeuwen, 'Liminality and World View in Proverbs 1–9', pp. 112, 133 n. 5.

9.   Murphy, 'Wisdom and Eros in Proverbs 1–9', p. 603.

10.   Yee, '"I Have Perfumed my Bed with Myrrh"', p. 53. For a similar view see also Newsom, 'Woman and the Discourse of Patriarchal Wisdom', p. 150, who states with reference to the Strange Woman and Wisdom, 'As death belongs to one, life belongs to the other', and Van Leeuwen, 'Liminality and World View in Proverbs 1–9', p. 134 n. 12.

11.   C. Camp, 'What's So Strange about the Strange Woman?', in D. Jobling, P.L. Day and G.T. Sheppard (eds.), *The Bible and the Politics of Exegesis: Essays in Honor of Norman K. Gottwald on his Sixty-Fifth Birthday* (Cleveland: Pilgrim, 1991), pp. 17-31, 27.

12.   Camp, 'What's So Strange', p. 26. See also Van Leeuwen, 'Liminality and World View in Proverbs 1–9', p. 116, who aligns the Strange Woman with evil.

13.   Camp, *Wisdom and the Feminine in the Book of Proverbs*, p. 120.

14.   Camp, 'What's So Strange', p. 28.

15.   Camp, 'What's So Strange', p. 27.

16.   Yee, '"I Have Perfumed my Bed with Myrrh"', p. 56.

order'.[17] However, she goes further, seeing a cosmic dimension in this: 'Her very alienage becomes a metaphor for the disruption of the social order of the created world, leading to death itself.'[18] The Strange Woman then is set over against Wisdom who personifies 'everything that is good, life-giving and of God's very self'.[19]

C. Newsom explores the symbolic dimension of the Strange Woman in terms of her otherness within the male discourse of a patriarchal society. Woman, as man's other, is on the margin of the patriarchal society, at the limit of that order. Thus the Strange Woman is identified with the ultimate boundary, death, and merges with the chaos that threatens that society at the boundary. Her opposite, Woman Wisdom, also at the boundary but on the inside, functions as an ideal that protects the symbolic order of the patriarchal society and shields it from chaos, the Strange Woman.[20] Finally, R. Van Leeuwen also focuses on the significance of boundaries, cosmic and social, in the interpretation of the symbolism of Proverbs 1–9, including that of the Strange Woman and her opposite Wisdom. Underlying the metaphors of Proverbs 1–9, he argues, is a worldview that reflects an order of creation that is reflected in, or regulates, social norms, an order that assigns everyone and everything their proper limits, time and place. Wisdom is associated with order, both cosmic and societal order, and prescribes life within boundaries. Love of Wisdom which leads to life, and is also equated with what is good, is staying within the prescribed limits. The Strange Woman is 'a liminal figure', the symbol of what lies out of bounds: to follow her means to cross a forbidden boundary, and this is evil and entails death.[21]

These explorations of the symbolism of the Strange Woman as chaos, as that which threatens order and life, both cosmic and social, as symbolized by her opposite Woman Wisdom, reaffirm and add depth to the intrinsic worldview of Proverbs 1–9 stated above.

This dualistic worldview, however, is not presented in Proverbs 1–9 simply as a treatise on the nature of reality. Rather, it is presented in a

17. G. Yee, 'The Theology of Creation in Proverbs 8:22-31', in R.J. Clifford and J.J. Collins (eds.), *Creation in the Biblical Traditions* (CBQMS, 24; Washington: CBAA, 1994), pp. 85-96, 93.

18. Yee, 'Theology of Creation', p. 87.

19. Yee, '"I Have Perfumed my Bed with Myrrh"', p. 56.

20. Newsom, 'Woman and the Discourse of Patriarchal Wisdom', pp. 142-60, especially pp. 148, 156-57.

21. Van Leeuwen, 'Liminality and World View in Proverbs 1–9', pp. 111-44.

didactic style, in such a way as to persuade the son, the next generation, not only to accept this dualistic point of view of the parent but more especially to live, given this, in such a way as to grasp life.[22]

The way to live, as exhorted by the parent in various symbolic ways, is to embrace life and to avoid its opposite, death; that is, to follow the way of order, wisdom, life and to avoid absolutely the way of chaos. Disorder, anarchy and whatever threatens life and leads to death is the way of the Strange Woman.[23] Indeed embracing wisdom/order/life will preserve one from its opposite, chaos/disorder/death.[24]

The means of persuasion are: first, by spelling out the consequences of following Wisdom (and the parent's instruction and so on) in terms of life,[25] and of gravitating towards the Strange Woman (and the wicked and so on) in terms of death;[26] and secondly, by active exhortation to follow the instruction and commandments of the parent and to embrace Wisdom (for example, 4.4-9; 7.2-4) and to avoid the Strange Woman (for example, 5.8) and others associated with death (for example sinners, 1.10).

In sum, Proverbs 1–9 presents a dualistic worldview in which life and death are mutually exclusive opposites. And the practical implication of this is that one embraces life not only by actively seeking to embrace it but in particular by avoiding death.[27]

Life and Death in the Book of Job

The symbolism in the book of Job is different from that in Proverbs 1–9: for example, although in Job the Strange Woman, symbol of chaos in

22. See, for example, Murphy, *The Tree of Life*, p. 15; Yee, '"I Have Perfumed my Bed with Myrrh"', p. 55; and especially the helpful analysis of the dynamic present here by Newsom, 'Woman and the Discourse of Patriarchal Wisdom', pp. 143-46. Van Leeuwen ('Liminality and World View in Proverbs 1–9', p. 115) sums up the function of Prov. 1–9 as follows: '[it] is first of all a protreptic one which invites the youth into a life of wisdom. The secondary, paraenetic function of Proverbs 1–9 is to remind "sages" of their basic world view and to confirm them in it.'

23. This is a difficult task in practice, given the similar characteristics of Woman Wisdom and the Strange Woman and hence the ambiguity involved, but nevertheless the goal is clear.

24. See, for example, Prov. 1.33; 6.23-24; 7.2-5; 8.36.

25. See, for example, Prov. 1.33; 3.1-2; 4.8-9; 8.35.

26. See, for example, Prov. 1.18-19; 5.22-23; 7.26-27; 9.18.

27. As Van Leeuwen ('Liminality and World View in Proverbs 1–9', p. 130) puts it: 'In this world there are two contrary lives: for Wisdom, Good and Life or for Folly, Pseudo-good, and Death'.

Proverbs, is nowhere to be found, Job has its own symbols of chaos in the sea (Yam), Behemoth and Leviathan (for example, Job 3.8; 7.12; 38.8; 40.15–41.34).[28] However, when this difference in symbolism is taken into account a significantly different perception of the relationship of life and death and how one comes to embrace life emerges from the book of Job than that presented in Proverbs 1–9. And underlying this is a very different worldview and way of thinking.

In radical contrast to Proverbs 1–9 where to embrace wisdom or to be wise is to embrace life and order and to avoid chaos and death, in the book of Job the wise one par excellence, portrayed in the figure of Job (1.1), embraces death and embodies chaos, and it is this very one who gains life. Indeed, it is from Job's embracing of death and chaos, and not from avoiding it, that life emerges.

Amidst the complexities of interpreting the book of Job,[29] our starting point will be the Yahweh speeches (38.1–40.2; 40.6–41.34)—the intrinsic worldview reflected in these, and the place of life and death and chaos portrayed in them. The Yahweh speeches form the climax of the book

---

28. There is some debate about the identity and symbolism of Behemoth and Leviathan. M. Pope (*Job* [Garden City, NY: Doubleday, 1973], pp. 268-70, 276-78), E.M. Good (*In Turns of Tempest: A Reading of Job* [Stanford, CA: Stanford University Press, 1990], p. 361), and Habel (*The Book of Job*, pp. 559, 560-61) maintain that Behemoth and Leviathan represent mythical symbols of chaos. In contrast R. Gordis ('Job and Ecology [and the Significance of Job 40.15]', *HAR* 9 [1985], pp. 189-202), J.G. Gammie ('Behemoth and Leviathan: On the Didactic and Theological Significance of Job 40.15–41.26', in J. Gammie *et al.* [eds.], *Israelite Wisdom: Theological and Literary Essays in Honour of Samuel Terrien* [Missoula, MT: Scholars Press, 1978], pp. 217-18, especially pp. 219-20), and Alter (*The Art of Biblical Poetry*, pp. 94, 106-107, 140) maintain that Behemoth and Leviathan are simply creatures (even if spoken of in heightened terms as Alter maintains). I favour the view that Behemoth and Leviathan, whilst still part of God's creation (Job 40.15), symbolize chaos.

It should also be noted here that, as we shall see, in Job chaos is associated with both death (for example, 3.8) and life (for example, 38.8) whereas, as we have seen, in Proverbs the Strange Woman, symbol of chaos, is associated with death only over against order and life.

29. The complexities of interpreting this sophisticated and multi-dimensional text are legion, and I acknowledge that many different interpretations, both with regard to details and the text overall, are possible. I seek here only to present one possible interpretation of this multivalent and ambiguous text. I am currently preparing a fuller discussion of some of the ideas put forward here in relation to the issue of hope and the book of Job.

of Job, that towards which the dynamic of the preceding speeches moves.[30] Because of this and the fact that they are presented as speeches of Yahweh and therefore seek to portray the divine perspective, it can be said with some justification that what they present carries more significance and authoritative weight than other views struggled with in the rest of the book. This applies to the place they give to life and death and chaos and to the intrinsic worldview that they present.

The cosmic design presented in these Yahweh speeches includes the realm of death (38.17). It occurs as one of the list of cosmic phenomena presented to Job—albeit in the form of rhetorical questions that show up Job's ignorance (38.1–39.30)—all of which form part of Yahweh's total creative design, the world that Yahweh created and has control over. Moreover in this cosmic design death and life are intertwined: for example, the young eaglets live and grow by gulping the blood of the slain (39.30). Furthermore, Leviathan, the sea monster, the traditional symbol of chaos and threat to life, is very much alive as part of Yahweh's universe (ch. 41).[31] Leviathan too has a place in this cosmic order as controlled and limited by Yahweh (41.1-5),[32] and so does Yam (38.8-11). Indeed in 38.8-11, Yam, or the sea, traditional symbol of chaos and threat to the created order,[33] is not only portrayed as an intrinsic part of Yahweh's creation but, when limited by Yahweh, as utterly inseparable from life. Thus, in 38.8-11 the creation of life is imaged as the birthing of an infant (38.8) that is nurtured and protected by swaddling it and placing it in a playpen (38.9, 11). But this infant is a baby sea monster, the sea, symbol of chaos and threat of destruction to life; its protective bands are cloud (38.9, ענן) which can also be symbolic, at least for Job, of destruction (3.5); and the bars or doors of its playpen (38.10), which 'hedge it in' (סוך) (38.8 paralleling 38.10-11), restraining and limiting it, can symbolize either protection and security (see סוך in 1.10) or imprisonment (see סוך in 3.23). Hence in the poetic imagery of the

30. This is commonly held: see for example C. Westermann, *The Structure of the Book of Job: A Form-Critical Analysis* (Philadelphia: Fortress Press, 1981), pp. 4-6, and most discussions of the book as a whole as well as commentaries, for example, Tsevat, 'The Meaning of the Book of Job'; Alter, *The Art of Biblical Poetry*, pp. 85-110; Habel, *The Book of Job*.

31. On the symbolism of Behemoth and Leviathan, see n. 30.

32. The verse numbers given here and in what follows will be the English rather than the Hebrew numbering.

33. See Martin-Achard, *From Death to Life*, pp. 43-44 for a discussion of the association of death/Sheol with chaos/the sea.

passage birth/nurturing/protection are inseparable from chaos/destruction/
imprisonment for the same symbols encompass both. Chaos and the
birthing of life are inseparable; life emerges and is sustained and nurtured
by the limiting of chaos.[34]

From this brief discussion of some of the imagery of the Yahweh
speeches concerned with life and death or traditional symbols of chaos
and destructive threat to life, it can be seen that these speeches reflect a
universe and view of reality that is paradoxical and non-dualistic. There
is no life and nurturing without chaos and even death (39.30), expressed
most clearly in 38.8-11 by using the same symbolism for chaos and life. In
this non-dualistic worldview, as R. Alter puts it, 'God's creation involves
a necessary holding in check of destructive forces and a sustaining of
those same forces because they are the forces of life'.[35]

But how are life and death and their associated symbols portrayed in
the speeches of Job and the friends leading up to the authoritative climax
of the Yahweh speeches in which a non-dualistic worldview is portrayed
in which life/nurturing and chaos/destruction/death are inseparably held
together?

Job has much to say about death. In the dynamic movement of the
Job speeches, Job begins with a death wish and the rejection of life.[36] In
ch. 3 this is expressed in radical form in the desire for his very origins to
be blotted out: Job curses the day/night of his birth/conception (3.1-10)
and laments that he had ever been born or at least had not died at birth
(3.11-26). As one of the curses he calls on death shadow (צלמות) to
claim the day of his birth (3.5), and in lament form asks, 'why did I not
die (מות) at birth?' (3.11). The obverse of this—the rejection of life
because of its misery—is given, again in lament form, in Job's question
as to why life (חי) is given to those in misery/the bitter in soul who are
then described as longing for death (מות, 3.20-21).

These themes of longing for death and rejection of life are taken up in

34. See the discussion of this passage by Alter, *The Art of Biblical Poetry*,
pp. 99-100. See also Habel, *The Book of Job*, pp. 538-39.

35. Alter, *The Art of Biblical Poetry*, p. 100. For further discussion of the para-
doxical nature of the universe portrayed in Job 38 see Alter, *The Art of Biblical
Poetry*, pp. 98-100, 102, 106, 110; Habel, *The Book of Job*, pp. 531-35; and
A. Brenner, 'God's Answer to Job', *VT* 31 (1981), pp. 129-37, especially p. 132.

36. For a discussion of Job's death wish, see B. Zuckerman, 'The Art of Parody:
The Death Theme', in *Job the Silent* (New York: Oxford University Press, 1991),
pp. 118-35, 260-69. See also the observations concerning Job's dissent from Proverbs
regarding death by Crenshaw, 'The Human Dilemma', pp. 235-58, 252-54.

the subsequent Job speeches of chs. 6–7 and 9–10. In 6.8-9 Job expresses the hope that God will kill him because he has no strength or resources to sustain him in life and no future to make this worthwhile. Again, in 7.2, Job expresses his death wish in terms of the common ancient Near Eastern view of humankind as a slave: Job, like a slave whose lot in life is only misery, longs for death, for the shadow, the end of his slavery and misery, the reward or wages of his labours.[37] And in 7.15 Job states that he chooses death rather than his bones. Again, alongside this, Job's rejection of his life is clearly stated. In 7.16 Job states that he rejects life,[38] and repeats this again explicitly in 9.21 ('I reject my life', אמאס חיי) and in 10.1.

The same line of thought comes to expression in these Job speeches in chs. 3, 7 and 10 in his descriptions of Sheol, the realm of death. Predictably, for Job Sheol is the place of rest, the place of escape from the misery and slavery of life (3.13-15, 17-19), the place to which, after this transitory life of misery and oppression by God (7.7-8, 14-21a; 10.20), he can escape permanently away from God's oppressive presence (7.9-10, 21b; 10.21-22).

Ironically for Job God is the source of his life (10.12; see also 12.10) but at the same time God oppresses this life that he has given him (10.13-17). For Job, also, God is not only the source of life, his miserable and oppressive life, but also and more especially the source of death.[39] This is alluded to in 6.8-9 where Job wishes that God would kill him, and it becomes more pronounced in Job's later speeches. Indeed, death itself, which God deals out to mortals and for which Job initially longs, becomes in the dynamic movement of the text a source of despair for Job. Thus in 13.15 Job asserts, or at least raises as a distinct possibility, that God will kill him. Following this, in ch. 14, Job expresses a hypothetical wish that he might after death hide in Sheol and be restored to new life, a vindicated life restored in relation to God (14.13-17). But this is rejected out of hand by the assertion, bracketing this wish, of the permanency of death for mortals, for which, what is more, God is

37. This is Habel's interpretation of Job 7.2 (*The Book of Job*, p. 158) with which I agree. For a different interpretation see Pope, *Job*, p. 58, and Clines, *Job 1–20*, p. 184.

38. Although 'life' is not stated explicitly here it is to be understood from the context.

39. See Job 1.21.

Prophets and Paradigms

responsible (14.10-12, 42;[40] 18–22). Permanent death brought about by God, the source of death, becomes here the dashing of hope, a source of despair. This line of thought is found again in 17.13-16 where Sheol is portrayed as a place of no hope.[41] It is again taken up by Job in 30.23 where, following an assertion that God is being cruel to him and persecuting him (30.21-22), Job asserts that God will bring him to death.

So for Job God is the source of both life and death and both are, or become in the progression of the speeches, negative, containing no hope. Job is portrayed as speaking about death and life in these ways whilst he is in a state of, symbolically speaking, embracing death. Job's description of himself in 7.5, 'my flesh is clothed with worms and dust, my skin hardens and oozes', is an assertion that his body bears the marks of death. 'Worm' is often associated with Sheol (for example, Job 17.14; 21.26; see Isa. 14.11) as is 'dust' (for example, Job 17.16), and this, along with his hardened and oozing skin, portrays the appearance of someone close to being a corpse or participating in death.[42] Job sits at the edge of death, at death's door so to speak—or in the symbolism of Proverbs 1–9 at the door of the Strange Woman.

To continue this symbolism, Job, sitting at the edge of death, embraces the Strange Woman, symbol of chaos; indeed can be equated with her, for it can be argued that, in the book of Job, Job is presented not only as embracing death but as embodying chaos. That Job himself embodies and symbolizes the chaotic element in the universe is supported by the following observations. In 7.12, Job asks, 'Am I the sea [ם׳, see 38.8] that you place on me a guard/muzzle?',[43] and this is answered in the affirmative in the Yahweh speeches. In 38.8-11, as we have seen, Yam (ם׳) is born and hedged in (סוך, 38.8), but so is Job in ch. 3 (see 3.23,

40. The permanency of death for mortals asserted here is emphasized strongly by contrasting it with the hope for new life that is possible for a tree (Job 14.7-9).
41. This is in line with the interpretation of this passage by Clines, *Job 1–20*, p. 400; cf. Habel, *The Book of Job*, pp. 269, 278-79.
42. Habel, *The Book of Job*, p. 159. See also the commonly held view that in the Old Testament one who suffers illness and oppression is already participating, metaphorically speaking, in death: for example, von Rad, *Old Testament Theology*, I, p. 387; Wolff, *Anthropology of the Old Testament*, p. 111; Burns, 'The Mythology of Death and the Old Testament', p. 332; Bailey, *Biblical Perspectives on Death*, p. 39; Gese, 'Death in the Old Testament', p. 37; and above n. 4.
43. See Habel, *The Book of Job*, pp. 152-53 for the sense of משמר as 'muzzle' as well as 'watch' or 'guard'. Cf. Pope (*Job*, p. 60) and Clines (*Job 1–20*, p. 165) who translate משמר simply as 'guard'.

סוּף). Hence the Job of ch. 3 who is born but wishes only for death and darkness to blot out the day of his birth is mirrored in, or equated with, Yam who is born and wrapped in darkness (38.8).

In addition, the other symbols of chaos in the Yahweh speeches, Behemoth and Leviathan, can be interpreted as symbolizing Job.[44] The parallels that suggest that Job is mirrored in Behemoth and Leviathan are as follows. The maker of Behemoth draws his sword against Behemoth (40.19): God attacks, or at least is responsible for an attack on, Job (chs. 1–2, especially 2.3, and see 6.3; 16.7-14; 19.7-12).[45] The anger of Behemoth and Leviathan (40.24, אָף; 41.2, אַכְזָר;[46] 41.18-21) reflects the anger of Job throughout the dialogues as he hurls accusations against God, claiming that God has attacked him (6.3; 16.7-14; 19.7-12) and is his enemy (27.7-8). The picture of Leviathan as having no equal or no one to rule over him[47] on the dust and as king (מֶלֶךְ) over all the sons of pride (41.33-34) mirrors Job's pride, especially in the portrait he paints of himself in chs. 29–31 as like a king (מֶלֶךְ, 29.25) and as one who would approach God like a prince (נָגִיד, 31.37).[48] Finally, Job is controlled and limited by God, as are Yam, Behemoth and Leviathan. Yam in 38.8-11 is hedged in (38.8) and restrained behind bars (38.10-11). Behemoth in 40.24 is controlled and muzzled by God, as is Leviathan in 41.1-8. Indeed it is possible to translate 41.12 in such a way that Yahweh is portrayed as silencing the boasting and strong words of Leviathan: 'Did I not silence his boasting?[49] his word of strength...'[50] And Job too is

---

44. For the view that Job is mirrored in the portrayal of Behemoth and Leviathan see Gammie, 'Behemoth and Leviathan', and Habel, *The Book of Job*, pp. 559, 561, 566, 568, 571, 574. Cf. the commonly held and convincing view that in these passages about Behemoth and Leviathan Job is shown that he cannot control Behemoth and Leviathan as Yahweh does. Only Yahweh has power over them. However, since this is poetry it seems to me that both positions can be held simultaneously, as Habel (*The Book of Job*, pp. 559-61) has done.

45. See Gammie, 'Behemoth and Leviathan', p. 219.

46. אָף can mean either 'nose' or 'anger' and probably means both here. See Habel, *The Book of Job*, p. 568.

47. מָשַׁל may connote 'be like' or 'rule' here; see Habel, *The Book of Job*, p. 557.

48. See Gammie, 'Behemoth and Leviathan', p. 225; Habel, *The Book of Job*, p. 574.

49. This is the translation of both Habel (*The Book of Job*, p. 551) and Pope (*Job*, p. 280) who translate בַד as 'boasting' rather than 'part' or 'limb'. See Pope, *Job*, p. 283 for a discussion of this. Cf. R. Gordis, *The Book of God and Man: A Study of Job* (Chicago: University of Chicago Press, 1965), p. 303; and NRSV, 'I will not keep silent concerning its/his limbs'.

silenced by Yahweh, as seen from his response to the first Yahweh speech in 40.3-5. His mouth is muzzled (40.4), like that of Behemoth and Leviathan (40.24; 41.2; and see 7.12), and his mighty words are silenced (40.5). In these ways Job is mirrored in the pictures of Yam, Behemoth and Leviathan. Thus Job like them embodies chaos, indeed is a symbol of chaos.

However, as we shall see, in embracing and embodying chaos, Job does not die, as in the thinking of Proverbs 1–9 where to embrace the Strange Woman as symbol of chaos leads to death. Rather he lives and indeed obtains fullness of life (42.16-17). But before this can be fully understood the reaction of the friends of Job and Yahweh's response to Job need to be explored further.

The friends function as a foil to Job. They respond to Job with a similar outlook and way of thinking to that reflected in Proverbs 1–9. Basically the friends operate with a dualistic view in which life and death, innocence and wickedness are set in opposition to each other. They associate death with the wicked or fools (see for example 4.8-9; 5.2; 4.21; 8.11-12; 11.20; 18.13). Over against this they associate life, a restored and fulfilling life for Job, with his uprightness (for example, 4.6-7; 5.19-26; 8.6) or, as they increasingly perceive Job as wicked, with putting away his wickedness (11.6, 13-19). However, as we have seen, Job embraces death. He does this by hoping for death (for example, 6.8-9); and this for Zophar is a mark of the wicked whose hope is to breathe their last (11.20). Moreover, Job sits at the edge of death, bearing the marks of death (7.5); and increasingly for the friends this condition is associated with the wicked (for example, 18.13).[51]

However, Job is presented by the narrator from the beginning as upright (1.1, see also 42.7). He is portrayed as a figure who embraces death and yet is upright. He is portrayed as one who embraces death and chaos and yet does not die but lives. He is portrayed, therefore, as a figure who stands in contradiction to the dualistic perspective of the friends and Proverbs 1–9.

The response to Job in the Yahweh speeches (38.1–39.30; 40.6–41.34)

---

50. The last part of this line, וחין ערפו, is difficult and there is much debate over its meaning, resulting in a number of widely different interpretations: see Habel, *The Book of Job*, p. 551; Pope, *Job*, pp. 280, 283-84; Gordis, *The Book of God and Man*, p. 303. It seems simplest to omit it here.

51. Job contradicts the friends, claiming that the wicked live and even prosper (21.7, 13; 24.22).

presents a perspective that is very different from that of the friends. As we have seen, the Yahweh speeches present a non-dualistic view of reality in which life and chaos/death are inseparable. The Yahweh speeches, though clearly contrasting with the viewpoint of the friends, are not, however, entirely in line with Job's ruminations on death and life either: rather, they respond to them, correct them and put them into perspective. It remains to explore the way in which they do this in order for it to become clear how it is that Job, who embraces death and embodies chaos, embraces life (42.16-17).

In response to the Yahweh speeches Job admits his ignorance; in seeing God (42.5) and God's universe (38.1–40.2) he perceives that what he had uttered before was limited (42.3b). This includes his words about death and life. The Yahweh speeches reveal that what Job did not understand is that the embracing of death is also the embracing of life; for in the non-dualistic universe that is revealed in the Yahweh speeches, as we have seen, death/chaos and life are inseparable, two sides of the one reality. Job in embracing death saw only death. In wishing for death he rejects life, and even death itself, permanent death, becomes a source of despair for him. The Yahweh speeches take up Job's death wish and show Job that this longing for, and embracing of, death is really a longing for, and embracing of, death and life. In a non-dualistic universe the embracing of death is the embracing of life.

This can be illustrated by taking up once more the symbolism used in Job 38.8-11. In this passage the same symbolism that Job uses to express his death wish in ch. 3, his wish that he had never been born, is taken up and shown to symbolize not only death and destruction but also at the same time life and nurturing.[52] Examples of this have already been touched on in the discussion of 38.8-11 earlier: Job's reference in 3.23 to God 'hedging in' (סוּךְ) humankind, and by implication himself, in an oppressive way, is transformed in the Yahweh speech in 38.8 into a symbol of protection and nurturing in the birthing of life; and the clouds (עָנָן) that for Job in 3.5 are a means of destruction, of blotting out life, are in the Yahweh speech in 38.9 the protective and nurturing clothing/ swaddling bands of a new life.[53] To this can be added that the 'doors' (דלת) of the womb that Job wishes in 3.10 had been shut, making a

---

52. The same can be said of other imagery in other parts of Job 38. See the discussion of the parallels and play on imagery between Job 3 and Job 38 by Alter, *The Art of Biblical Poetry*, pp. 96-102.

53. See Alter, *The Art of Biblical Poetry*, pp. 99-100.

place of no-birth and death, are in the Yahweh speech in 38.8 associated with the womb in bringing life to birth.[54] And the image of birthing as a whole, presented and paralleled in ch. 3 and 38.8-11, also illustrates this. For Job his birth is a symbol of darkness and death; he uses it to express his hope for death and the beginning of the embracing of darkness and misery in life. Job is an infant born against his will, wishing he had never been conceived or born, wishing he had been miscarried or died at birth, that he had never been suckled (3.1-16); he is born into misery, a life hedged in oppressively by God (3.20-26). In contrast, from the divine perspective in 38.8-11 birth is an image of life: the infant is born and hedged in by God for protection and nurture—but the infant that is born is chaos, darkness. Job in birth sees only death and darkness. From God's perspective darkness/chaos is birthed into life. For Job birth is a symbol of darkness and death; from God's perspective birth is a symbol of darkness/chaos and life—the two are inseparable.

In this way, then, Job's longing for, and perception of death is shown to be limited, for it is one-sided. He saw only darkness and death and failed to see that from Yahweh's perspective, in Yahweh's non-dualistic universe, the embracing of such symbols of darkness and death is also the embracing of life. Thus the figure of Job embracing death is, in the divine perspective, taken up, transformed and transcended, to become an embracing of death and life.

There is also a further dimension to this. It has been argued above that Job himself embodies chaos, that the figure of Job is a symbol of chaos, as seen from the parallels between Job and Yam, Behemoth and Leviathan. Thus Job's place in the universe is the same as that of chaos, of Yam, Behemoth and Leviathan as portrayed in the Yahweh speeches. And what is that place? As we have seen Yam, Behemoth and Leviathan are very much alive in Yahweh's universe, but they are restrained and

---

54. See Alter, *The Art of Biblical Poetry*, p. 99, who puts this graphically when he states, 'Job's first speech (ch. 3) begins with birth and conception and circles back on the belly or womb where he would like to be enclosed, where he imagines the fate of the dead foetus as the happiest of human lots. Against those doors of the belly (3:10) that Job wanted shut on him forever, the Voice from the Whirlwind invokes a cosmic womb and cosmic doors to a very different purpose: "[He] hedged in the sea with doors/when it gushed forth from the womb" (verse 8). The figuration of setting limits to the primal sea as closing doors on a gushing womb produces a high tension of meaning absent from Job's unequivocal death wish. The doors are closed and bolted (verse 10) so that the flood will not engulf the earth, but nevertheless the waves surge, the womb of all things pulsates, something is born...'

controlled by Yahweh (see 38.8, 10-11; 40.24; 41.1-8, 12). Furthermore, returning to the imagery of 38.8-11 again, chaos, limited and restrained, is inseparable from life, from the birthing, nurturing and sustaining of life. The birth of chaos and the limiting of chaos are a symbol and embodiment of new life. But Job, also an embodiment and symbol of chaos, is limited and restrained by Yahweh too in his encounter with Yahweh in these speeches. Job, like Leviathan, is silenced (40.35). And in his second response in 42.6 he submits to Yahweh and thus shows himself as limited by and subjugated to Yahweh, when he says, 'wherefore I submit/retract and repent on dust and ashes'.[55] The limiting of chaos is inseparable from the birthing and sustaining of life (38.8-11). And so Job also, limited and restrained by his encounter with God, experiences a birth into life and embodies new life. Thus in 42.6 Job gets up from the ash heap: 'Wherefore I reject and forswear dust and ashes'.[56] For, I would argue, 42.6 can mean here both that Job submits and that he rises from the ash heap as a gesture of embracing life, not only because the ambiguity of the Hebrew allows it, but because in this non-dualistic universe and way of thinking Job, in embodying chaos and choosing to embrace limitation and submission to God, chooses to embody life, for limited chaos is new life. That new life embraced and embodied by Job is described in the epilogue (42.10-17), concluding with the description of a fulfilled life in 42.16-17.

Thus Job embodies and symbolizes chaos, chaos limited by Yahweh,

---

55. על־כן אמאס ונחמתי על־עפר ואפר. The possible translations of this notoriously ambiguous verse are many. For a thorough and detailed discussion of the semantics and grammar of this verse and the possible translations and interpretations of it see W. Morrow, 'Consolation, Rejection and Repentance in Job 42.6', *JBL* 105 (1986), pp. 211-25. The translation given here is the first of three possible translations of this verse given by Morrow (pp. 211-12). The translation of Pope (*Job*, pp. 288-90) is in line with this. For further discussions of translations and interpretations of this verse, see Habel, *The Book of Job*, pp. 575-76; Good, *In Turns of Tempest*, pp. 170-71, 375-77; J.G. Janzen, *Job* (Atlanta: John Knox Press, 1985), pp. 251, 258-59; A. Wolters, 'A Child of Dust and Ashes (Job 42.6b)', *ZAW* 102 (1990), pp. 116-19; C. Muenchow, 'Dust and Dirt in Job 42.6', *JBL* 108 (1989), pp. 597-611.

56. This translation is the third of the three possible translations that Morrow ('Consolation, Rejection and Repentance in Job 42.6', especially p. 212) outlines, drawing on D. Patrick, 'The Translation of Job 42.6', *VT* 26 (1976), pp. 369-71. Other scholars whose translation and interpretation are in line with or close to this are Good, *In Turns of Tempest*, pp. 170-71, 375-77, and G. Gutiérrez, *On Job: God-Talk and the Suffering of the Innocent* (Maryknoll, NY: Orbis Books, 1987), p. 83.

and therefore at one and the same time embodies and symbolizes life. This non-dualistic way of thinking is completed in the very figure of Job.

Conclusion

It has been argued here that Proverbs 1–9 and the book of Job present two very different worldviews, and, within that, two very different positions on the relationship between life and chaos/death. Furthermore, these contrasting views have significant implications for how life is obtained.

Proverbs 1–9 operates with a dualistic worldview. The book of Job, on the other hand, presents a non-dualistic worldview as the authoritative, indeed the divine, perspective on reality. Here life and chaos/death are inseparable—they are two sides of the one reality—and limited chaos means the birthing and sustaining of life. One lives, or obtains life, not by avoiding, but entering fully into, chaos/death. For embracing chaos/death is also the embracing of life; and in embodying chaos as limited by Yahweh, one embodies life.

Both Proverbs 1–9 and the book of Job, with their contrasting positions and implications for living, form part of the canon. The reader and/ or faith community is invited, therefore, to decide—perhaps at different times and in different circumstances—which way leads to life.

GEOGRAPHY AND THEOLOGY IN THE BIBLICAL NARRATIVE: THE QUESTION OF GENESIS 2–12

Yehoshua Gitay

The monumentual call to Abram: 'Go from your country and your kindred and your father's house to the land that I will show you' (Gen. 12.1) is a turning point in the biblical account of the history of Israel. The promise to Abram to be the father of a great nation, and the promise of the land of Canaan as designated for the new nation depend on Abram's moving—to the new land which God shows him.[1]

Given its significant role, the call to Abram is not delivered in the prosaic plain style of the narrative.[2] Rather the call (לֶך לְך) is proclaimed in a poetical, symmetrical language. The opening phrase of the call employs the imperative plus the preposition *lamed*. This combination has a specific function: 'The reference is to someone who goes alone and breaks away from the community or group in whose midst he was till that moment.'[3] The preposition emphasizes Abram's determination.

The double form of words (לֶך לְך), creating a duplicate sound, further strengthens the effect of the call: rush, be decisive. Furthermore, the call, 'Go from your country and your kindred and your father's house', is tied together stylistically by the device of sound effect: a series of

1. Compare B. Halpern-Amaru, *Rewriting the Bible* (Valley Forge, PA: Trinity Press International, 1994), p. 9.
2. For the royal background of the language see J. Van Seters, *Prologue to History* (Louisville, KY: Westminster/ John Knox Press, 1992), pp. 252-57.
3. See U. Cassuto, *From Noah to Abram* (Jerusalem: Magnes Press, 1964 [1949]), pp. 310-12. Among Cassuto's numerous examples see Gen. 22.2. Z.T. Muraoka ('On the So-Called Dativus Ethicus in Hebrew', *JTS* 29 [1978], p. 497), writes: 'Basically it [the *lamed*] serves to convey the impression on the part of the speaker that the subject establishes his own identity, recovering or finding his own place by determinedly disassociating himself from his former surroundings.' Also see B. Waltke and M. O'Connor, *An Introduction to Biblical Hebrew Syntax* (Winona Lake: Eisenbrauns, 1990), p. 208.

assonances and alliterations (ו). By contrast, the destination (הָאָרֶץ אֶל, 'to the land') is disconnected from the remainder of the verse on the basis of its sound. Therefore, the emphasis of the call to Abram is on the land.

Indeed, a close reading of the narrative of Genesis 2–12, the primeval history and the call to Abram, reveals that the dominant theme is the notion of the land. Structurally, the narrative comprises seven events, all of which are concerned with the issue of territory. These events may be classified according to two main aspects of the concept of territory: the first is territory as the heritage given by God himself to humankind; and the second is humankind's desire for territory to fulfill personal need. It is unfortunate that these two notions of the land are not only mutually exclusive, but actually contradict each other.

The two antitheses, God and humankind, are arranged symmetrically, reflecting the literary order of the narrative (of Gen. 2–12) as well. The opening scene takes place in the territory given by God to Adam, while the concluding scene of the cycle is situated in the land given by God to Abram. The literary order conveys a specific concept: the scenes comprising the narrative body are delivered in reaction to the prologue; the epilogue on the one hand contrasts with the narrative body and on the other complements the prologue. Let us look now at the territorial scenes.

In the beginning narrative, the foundation of the prologue rests (a) in the Garden of Eden (Gen. 2–3). There follow the episodes comprising the narrative body's progress: (b) Cain as farmer (4.2); (c) Cain as the builder of a city (4.17);[4] (d) Noah as the planter of a vineyard (9.20-24); (e) the city and its tower as an attempt at unity (11.1-9); and (f) Terah as an interrupted traveler to Canaan (11.31-32). The final scene closes the cycle as it concentrates on the land to which Abram was called by God (12.1).

The first episode of the narrative directs our attention to the provision of living in God's territory—the Garden of Eden. However, Adam, Eve, and their descendants have been sent away from the Garden, forbidden to return to God's territory (3.22-24). Yet God has not designated a new geographical center to replace the Garden. Meanwhile humankind seek a

---

4.   Cassuto (*From Noah to Abram*, pp. 229-30) argues that the builder of the city is Cain's son Enoch. Also see J. Skinner, *Genesis* (Edinburgh: T. & T. Clark, 1969), pp. 116-17, and C. Westermann, *Genesis 1–11* (Minneapolis: Augsburg, 1984), who is convinced that the founding of the first city was originally ascribed to Enoch (p. 12) because 'Cain would be too far away to fulfill this function' (p. 326). That is, Cain the wanderer could not build a city. However, the MT refers to Cain, and this cannot be accidental.

land for themselves; and when the search for the geographical center is initiated by the people rather than by God, a series of misfortunes ensues. Cain toils on the land, but since the land has been covered with Abel's blood it will no longer yield to Cain its strength (4.10-11).[5] Cain must be a 'fugitive and a wanderer on the earth' (4.12): the consequence of his loss of territory. However, on establishing his family, Cain disobeys God's prohibition against his settling in any one place. In building a city for himself he attempts to establish a geographical center. Why does he do this? What is the significance of the fixed location which drives Cain to disobey God's explicit prohibition?

At issue here is the role of territory as necessary for human existence. Historians of religion emphasize the function of fixed territory as a center for human orientation. M. Eliade elucidates the notion of the fixed geographical location thus: 'Nothing can begin, nothing can be done, without a previous orientation and any orientation implies acquiring a fixed point.'[6] The physical need for a geographical center is a deeply-rooted aspect of human behavior.

Nonetheless, Cain's city manifests a denial of the divine command. A tension has been created between humankind's search for a fixed geographical point, and God's charge upon them. That is, God has expelled Adam and Eve from the Garden of Eden, but humankind cannot tolerate the instability of existence without a fixed point. Henceforth, they consistently search for the geographical center.

The tragedy of the Flood requires that humans recommence their search for the fixed point. Ironically, Noah's point of orientation is a vineyard (9.20). In biblical tradition wine has a dual function—as a source of both happiness (see Judg. 9.13, for example) and harm (see Isa. 5.11-13). Regrettably, Noah's drinking results in shameful behavior (Gen. 9.18-21).[7] Humankind's independent quest for a fixed point now has most deplorable connotations.

5.   For God's selection of Abel over Cain as part of a large biblical pattern consult F.A. Spina, 'The Ground for Cain's Rejection (Gen. 4)', *ZAW* 104 (1992), pp. 319-32.
6.   M. Eliade, *The Sacred and the Profane* (New York: Harcourt, 1957), p. 22. Also consult J.P. Brererton, 'Sacred Place', in M. Eliade (ed.), *Encyclopedia of Religion* (New York: Macmillan, 1987), XII, pp. 525-35.
7.   Westermann (*Genesis*, p. 487) regards Noah's vineyard 'as a step forward in relation to agriculture...it yields a product that brings joy and relaxation'. This is a further example of reading a text autonomously without considering its context. The context shows that Noah's vineyard is surely not a blessing.

As the narrative progresses the search for a fixed geographical point continues. The people aim to establish a city and a tower 'with its top in the heavens'. They say: 'let us make a name for ourselves, lest we be scattered abroad upon the face of the whole earth' (Gen 11.4). The selfish human goal to establish a center is portrayed as an explicit challenge to God. Further, the people now seek to seize God's territory. The response is expected: 'So the Lord scattered them abroad from there over the face of all the earth, and they left off building the city' (Gen 11.8). Humankind is divided now into different languages and nations. The unified effort to establish the center has strayed yet further away from its consummation. Nevertheless, the search for the place has been carried on by an individual rather than the entire community. Terah and his son Abram aim to reach a new geographical center by going to the land of Canaan. However, Terah and his family halt in Haran, where Terah eventually dies (Gen. 11.31-32); the desired goal has not yet been achieved.[8]

Abram, Terah's son, continues the journey with the intention of settling in Canaan (Gen 12.1-3). There is, however, a crucial difference between the father's and the son's decision to go to Canaan. Terah initiates the journey, while Abram does not; rather the son responds to God's call to go. That is, Abram, in contrast to his father, depends entirely on God who shows him the new land. The difference between Terah's Canaan and Abram's is illuminating: Canaan is Terah's selfish human desire, while for Abram Canaan is God's designated land.

The events which take place in Canaan following Abram's sojourn there indeed convey the notion of the Promised Land. God has introduced a new means of communication. As a rule, God communicates with human beings through two forms of senses that are not equally graded: sight/vision and sound. The two means of divine communication

---

8.   Source-critical analysis of Gen. 11.27-31 fails to deal with literary matters of content and plot, focusing instead on technical semantic details. See, for instance, J. Van Seters, *Abraham in History and Tradition* (New Haven and London: Yale University Press, 1975), pp. 224-25, and J.A. Emerton, 'The Source Analysis of Genesis 11.27-32', *VT* 42 (1992), pp. 37-46. However, Van Seters revised his position in his *Prologue to History*, pp. 200-205. I am sympathetic to Van Seters's more recent approach, which connects Abram's genealogy of Gen. 11.28-31 to 12.1-3. However, his method does not enable him to see the ideological tension between Gen. 11.32, which reveals that Terah died in Haran and his attempt to go to Canaan (11.31), and God's call to Abram to go to Canaan (12.1-3). See also the discussion below of the wife-sister stories.

do not operate simultaneously. Prior to Abram's settlement in Canaan God communicated with individuals only through utterance (Gen 3.11, 13; 4.5, 9, 15; 6.13; 7.1). God's call to Abram to go to Canaan, which took place in Haran, was also verbal.

In Canaan, however, God reveals himself to Abram: וירא ('revealed to', Gen. 12.7). The verb ראה ('to see', in the *niphal)* conveys God's intimate communication with men and women. (cf. Job 42.5-6, for example).[9] Abram's response is appropriate. In Canaan, where God reveals himself to him, and not in Haran where God first verbally calls him, Abram builds an altar to God (Gen. 12.7) Canaan is not merely another new settlement, but rather, a sacred space. The sacred space reflects 'A primary religious experience that precedes all reflection on the world...The hierophany reveals an absolute fixed point, a center.'[10] The religious experience is manifested through the building of the altar.[11]

The role of Canaan as God's sacred place is expressed in its designation נחלת אלהים, 'the heritage of God'.[12] Consequently, according to specific biblical traditions, the worship of God is confined to the holy heritage, so that Israelites living outside the sacred land must adopt the foreign god of the land in which they reside. Thus, for instance, David, pursued by Saul, blames the king of Israel for forcing him to serve a foreign god: 'It is men, may they be cursed before the Lord, for they have driven me out this day that I should have no share in the heritage of the Lord, saying, "Go serve other gods"' (1 Sam. 26.19). Remarkably, the episode that immediately follows Abram's settling in the sacred place of Canaan concerns the issue of his sojourn outside Canaan. Gen. 12.10-20 deals with the danger of famine in Canaan. The issue is the fear of God (the promise) versus fear of nature (famine), and the fear of nature controls Abram's actions: he leaves God's designated land.

9. Note that the verbs ראה ('to see') and ידע ('to know') appear regularly as a pair. See, for instance, Lev. 5.1; Deut. 11.2; Josh. 24.31, and more. Cf. I. Goldberg, 'The Poetic Structure of the Dirge over the King of Tyre', *Tarbiz* 58 (1989), p. 281 (in Hebrew).

10. See Eliade, *Sacred and Profane*, pp. 20-21.

11. The first to build an altar to God (וישן מזבח) was Noah (Gen. 8.20). The profound difference between Noah and Abram is that Noah desecrated the land through his vineyard and his drunkenness.

12. For the formula 'the heritage of God', see also 2 Sam. 14.16; Ps. 68.10; 74.2; 78.62, 71; 79.1; 106.5. For further biblical references and a detailed discussion regarding the formula, consult S.E. Loewenstamm in S. Japhet (ed.), *Studies in the Bible* (Jerusalem: Magnes Press, 1987), p. 4.

Abram descends into Egypt owing to the famine in Canaan. However, in Egypt Abram fears for his life, believing that the Egyptian king may take his beautiful wife, Sarai, away to his palace and kill him, the husband. Abram consequently tells his wife to pretend to be his sister. Sarai is indeed taken by Pharaoh, but God intervenes, and Pharaoh releases Sarai, sending both husband and wife back to Canaan, enriched with gifts. God's intervention on behalf of Abram and Sarai is clearly linked to his promise to establish Abram as a father of a nation in the land of Canaan. The promise was threatened by the incident in Egypt, and God acted.

Strikingly, two further similar stories concerning Abram and then Isaac going away from the promised land, risking their lives, and then pretending that their wives are actually their sisters appear in the book of Genesis (ch. 20; 26.1-11). The triple repetition of a single motif in one book has caught the critics' attention. The diachronic approach, searching for the original source, regards the triple repetition as an indication of a sporadic, mechanical and inconsistent editorial process. The following conclusion is characteristic: 'It is possible to lift each of these stories (12.10-20; 20; 26.1-11) out of its present context in the book of Genesis and to regard each as giving us a different version of one traditional theme.'[13] Furthermore, the similiar literary pattern of the three stories indicates to C. Westermann that they constitute an independent entity.[14] How should we explain this? The diachronic school responds: 'As the first basic narrative was being formed many other early traditions were incorporated...Including short stories (Genesis 12.10ff.; 20; 26)'.[15]

The premise of the literary 'surgery' of Gen. 12.10-20; 20; 26.1-11 is that the repetition is an indication of an earlier self-contained story, and the critics' aim is to reconstruct the original narrative.[16] Methodologically, and for the sake of demonstration, we may apply the analytical method to the structure of other biblical compositions such as the book of Proverbs. We may assume that in its original oral stage of transmission,

13. See R. Davidson, *Genesis 12–50* (Cambridge: Cambridge University Press, 1974), p. 4.

14. See C. Westermann, *Genesis 12–36* (Minneapolis: Augsburg, 1985), p. 174.

15. See G. Fohrer, *History of Israelite Religion* (Nashville and New York: Abingdon Press, 1972), p. 120.

16. For a critique of the comparative cross-cultural study, seeking to find the 'real' social norms of the 'events' behind the wife-sister stories, see T. Thompson, *The Historicity of the Patriarchal Narrative* (BZAW, 133; Berlin and New York: de Gruyter, 1974), pp. 234-48.

each proverb was independent, an axiom in itself. However, in the inscribing process, that is, the literary editorial operation of collecting the random proverbs and arranging them as a list or a book, the compilers have established a new text. Each proverb is now no longer an independent unit, but a link in a chain:

> By taking the proverb out of the context of speech, by listing it along with a lot of similar pithy sentences, one changes the character of the oral form. For example, it then becomes possible to set one proverb against another in order to see if the meaning of one contradicts the meaning of another; they are now tested for a universal truth value...[17]

One may conclude from this example that the incorporation of Gen. 12.10-20; 20; 26.1-11 into the patriarchal narrative has created a new discourse. The readers (listeners) respond to the narrative as a whole rather than to each independent episode. The tripled scenes relate to one another both thematically and formally. And the audience perceives the triple related scenes as a literary code, which communicates a specific message or concept.[18] Gen. 12.10-20 is perceived now in relation to the preceding event (Abram goes to Canaan by God's order).

A new literary context has been established: Gen. 12.10 (Abram descends into Egypt) contradicts Gen. 12.1 (Abram goes to Canaan). Similarly, the other two wife-sister situations (Gen. 20; 26.1-11) are now read according to their new context.[19] The previously proposed autonomous self-contained story of a wife-sister motif is no longer valid. The

17. See J. Goody, *The Domestication of the Savage Mind* (Cambridge: Cambridge University Press, 1977), p. 126.

18. For the poetics of the repetition, consult M. Sternberg, *The Poetics of the Biblical Narrative* (Bloomington: Indiana University Press, 1985), pp. 365-440. Also see I.N. Rashkow, *The Fallacy of Genesis* (Louisville, KY: Westminster/John Knox Press, 1993), pp. 34-48.

19. For the theoretical principles of reception theory, 'what is involved in the act of reading', see T. Eagleton, *Literary Theory* (Minneapolis: University of Minnesota Press, 1983), pp. 74-90. I support D.J.A. Clines's call ('The Ancestor in Danger: But Not the Same Danger', in his *What Does Eve Do to Help?* [JSOTSup, 94; Sheffield: JSOT Press, 1990], pp. 67-84) for a contextual reading of the stories of the ancestress in danger. However, I reject his claim that Abram 'cannot believe that Sarai will have anything to do with the fulfilment of that promise. Her barrenness is a datum of both their lives' (p. 69). This is a rational argument foreign—as I argue above—to the internal dynamics of the narrative. For another, intelligent reading of the wife-sister stories, see R. Alter, 'Interpreting the Bible', *Commentary* 89 (1990), pp. 52-59, esp. pp. 57-59.

reading of the whole presents the scenes of Gen. 12.10-20; 20; 26.1-11 in
their contextual focus: the risk taken by the patriarch while going out of
the promised land. The risk is double, both personally (the threat to the
husband's life) and religiously/nationally (denying God's promise of the
land).

The unity of a complex narrative is determined by the sequence of
events, in which each event is the result of the one before it. Aristotle
observes that 'The mutual relationship between cause and effect should
result from the actual structure of the plot in such a way that what has
already happened makes the result inevitable or probable' *(Poetics,*
1452a). The issue therefore is that the event concerning Abram's
sojourn in Egypt has no validity without the preceding event. The conclusion of the preceding episode (Abram dwelling in Canaan) indicates
that Abram settles in the southern region of the land—the Negeb, a
semi-desert (12.9). The themes of the shortage of water and the search
for it are characteristic of the patriarchal narrative. Stories with related
themes are Hagar's despair while she is wandering in the desert with her
son (21.14-16), Abraham's struggles with Abimelech regarding the well
(21.22-34), the famine in Isaac's time (26.1-5), and Isaac's struggles with
Abimelech regarding the well (26.14-16, and others). The famine of Gen.
12.10 is not therefore particularly unusual. The issue at stake is the
problem of migration and the fixed geographical center: hence the reference to the drought as motivating Abram's migration out of Canaan is
thematically significant in the narrative. Furthermore, the famine that
takes place in the promised land corresponds thematically with the childless Abram, who is promised by God to be the father of a great nation.[20]
The two divine promises are challenged by both geographical conditions
and humanphysiology. The problem concerning Abram is therefore
following transcendental belief versus yielding to natural needs.[21]

Gen. 12.10 tells of Abram's going to stay in Egypt. The Hebrew verb
גור indicates the status of an alien (see Gen. 19.9, for example) that might

20. My reading questions the thesis that the two elements of the promise—nation
and land—were originally mutually independent. See H.W. Wolff, 'The Kerygma of
the Yahwist', *Int* 20 (1966), p. 140. The analysis above suggests that this distinction
is too mechanical and even artificial.

21. H.C. White *(Narration and Discourse in the Book of Genesis* [Cambridge:
Cambridge University Press, 1991]) raises the theological question whether 'faith in
Yahweh's promise requires of Abram a total passivity' (p. 176). White seeks to
resolve the issue on literary grounds rather than theological considerations: 'If God
will protect him there will be no opponents, hence there will be no story' (p. 176).

be permanent (see, for instance, 2 Sam. 4.3; Jer. 35.7).[22] Thus the employment of the verb גור in connection with Abram's determination to go to Egypt does not necessarily impose limits on the period of residency in Egypt.

In this respect, a comparison between Jacob's reaction to a famine in Canaan and Abram's response is quite illuminating. Jacob sent his sons to buy grain (לשבר) in Egypt, but they were told to return to Canaan (Gen. 42.1-2). Abram, however, went to stay in Egypt.

Let us look at the language of the sentence describing Abram's migration to Egypt (Gen. 12.10):

וַיְהִי רָעָב בָּאָרֶץ וַיֵּרֶד אַבְרָם מִצְרַיְמָה לָגוּר שָׁם
כִּי־כָבֵד הָרָעָב בָּאָרֶץ׃

Now there was a famine in the land. So Abram went down to Egypt to sojourn there, for the famine was severe in the land.

This sentence has two 'meanings': one is literal, the other is literary. The literal is solely confined to semantic meaning in its strict sense, ignoring all problems of context and connotation, which comprise the literary meaning. This literary meaning responds therefore to the question, 'What does the text signify?'[23] The literal meaning of the sentence is clear: Abram went to stay in Egypt to escape the severe famine in Canaan. Now, the structure and form of the sentence are conventional, and a similar situation is expressed in very similar language:

וַיְהִי בִּימֵי שְׁפֹט הַשֹּׁפְטִים וַיְהִי רָעָב בָּאָרֶץ וַיֵּלֶךְ אִישׁ מִבֵּית לֶחֶם
יְהוּדָה לָגוּר בִּשְׂדֵי מוֹאָב הוּא וְאִשְׁתּוֹ וּשְׁנֵי בָנָיו׃

In the days when the judges ruled, there was a famine in the land, and a certain man of Bethlehem in Judah went to live in the country of Moab, he and his wife and two sons (Ruth 1.1).

The literal meaning informs us that because of the famine a certain man from Bethlehem in Judah went to sojourn in the country of Moab, he and his wife and two sons. Nonetheless, a specific syntactical change has taken place in this linguistic convention. The destination of the journey is

22. In Ugarit *gr btzl* is one who dwells in the temple possibly as a fugitive. Consult D. Kellermann, 'גור', *TDOT*, II, pp. 439-49. Also see G.J. Wenham, *Genesis 1–15* (Waco, TX: Word Books, 1987), p. 287, who regards the use of the verb גור in this context as 'striking'.

23. On this question see T. Todorov, *Introduction to Poetics* (Minneapolis: University of Minnesota Press, 1981), pp. 16-20.

the issue in question. In Genesis the destination, Egypt, is attached to the subject Abram, preceding the verb גור. In Ruth, however, the geographical goal, Moab, is placed at the end of the sentence, following the infinitive, and unattached to the subject. Now, the implication of Gen. 12.10—its literary meaning—can be perceived. The syntactical structure of Gen. 12.10 signifies the theological concern: Abram's destination is Egypt. God's destination is Canaan; Abram, however, goes down to Egypt.

In Egypt, Abram fears that Sarai's beauty will attract the Pharaoh of Egypt who will kill him, the husband; hence Abram asks his wife to pose as his sister. However, Sarai is taken to Pharaoh's palace although Abram escapes. A complex situation emerges. Sarai now lives with Pharaoh, separated from Abram. God's promise to Abram to be a father of a great nation may be threatened. Therefore, the move to Egypt causes Abram to deny Sarai's right as his wife, also jeopardizing God's promise. Consequently, God intervenes (v. 17), and Abram and Sarai are sent back to Canaan.

In short, Abram failed. He failed in his transcendental belief in God, yielding to earthly conditions.[24] He also failed concerning his commitment to his wife. Abram's immoral behavior might have motivated the author of the Qumranic scroll, the *Genesis Apocryphon* (1QapGen), to introduce the following passage:

> And on the night of our entry into Egypt, I, Abram, dreamt a dream...I saw in my dream a cedar tree and a palm tree...men came and they sought to cut down the cedar tree and to pull up its roots, leaving the palm tree (standing) alone. But the palm tree cried out saying: Do not cut down this cedar tree for cursed be he who shall fell [it]. And the cedar tree was spared because of the palm tree and [was] not felled...[The interpretation] of the dream...that they will seek to kill me, but will spare you...[Say to them] of me, he is my brother, and because of you I shall live, and because of you my life shall be saved...[25]

The dream and its interpretation are perceived by B.J. Lisotzky as an attempt to defend Abram's unfaithful behavior. Abram is not to be accused; the responsibility for his actions has been transferred to the

---

24. Compare K.A. Deurloo, 'Narrative Geography in the Abraham Cycle', in A.S. van der Woude (ed.), *In Quest of the Past* (*OTS* 26; Leiden: Brill, 1990), pp. 48-62. Deurloo condemns Abram for his sojourn in Egypt, which Deurloo construes as bad faith: Abram is the one 'who set out to go to the land of Canaan, a shameful experience' (p. 54).

25. The translation is by G. Vermes, *The Dead Sea Scrolls* (London: Penguin, 1987), pp. 253-54.

initiator of the dream, God, who acts in a different moral sphere from that of humanity.[26] The notion of Abram's failure has been pursued by the Ramban (Rabbi Moshe, son of Nachman, the Nachmanides, 1195–1270?) as follows:

> His (Abram) leaving the land, concerning which he had been commanded from the beginning, on account of the promise, was also a sin he committed, for in famine God would redeem him from death...In the place of justice there is wickedness and sin.[27]

In conclusion, Genesis 2–11 and 12–24, that is, the primeval history and the stories concerning Abram, share a common theme that establishes a sequential narrative. The conceptualization of the sequential narrative is unattainable through a random reading of the narrative, which isolates the events concerning Abram's sojourn in Egypt, regarding them as a folk-tale.[28] The present paper shows that a sequential reading, based on the structure and composition of the narrative, reveals a thematic unity.

The common subject is the search for land. The narrative reflects the unceasing tension between God's assigning land to humankind, and humankind's inability to keep this land. Humankind's independent search for a fixed point is ruled out by God. The narrative reaches its climax when God calls Abram to go to the land which God will show him. Abram obeys, and a new chapter concerning the land has been opened. However, the old problem of humankind's inability to keep God's land continues. Abram descends into Egypt, but is led back to the promised land by God.

The story of the land continues further, however. The division of the land between Abram and his nephew, Lot, leaves Lot with the better portion, questioning again Abram's ability to keep the land:

> Then Abram said to Lot...Is not the whole land before you? Separate yourself from me...Lot looked about him, and saw that the plain of the Jordan was well watered everywhere like the garden of the Lord...(Gen. 13.8-10).

---

26. See B.J. Lisotzky, *Reading the Book* (Garden City, NY: Doubleday, 1991), pp. 58-59.

27. Ramban, *Commentary on the Torah—Genesis* (translated and annotated by Ch.B. Chavei; New York: Shilo, 1971), pp. 173-74.

28. For a sophisticated folkloristic study of the motif of the wife-sister consult S. Niditch, *Underdogs and Tricksters* (San Francisco: Harper & Row, 1987), pp. 23-69. Nonetheless, given her diachronic approach, Niditch defines the episodes of Gen. 12, 20 and 26 as 'Tales'.

The promise of nation and land is thus problematic. Abram is childless, and the land (kept by Abram) is subject to natural disasters, such as drought. This land is however the promised land, God's heritage. In order to keep God's promise a transcending of human nature is imperative. The tension between human nature and belief is the objective of the narrative.[29]

29. The issue has been raised and discussed in the present paper and will be continued in a comprehensive study of the entire patriarchal narrative and the Deuteronomistic historiography. Meanwhile see my article, 'Reflection on the Poetics of the Samuel Narrative: The Question of the Ark Narrative', *CBQ* 54 (1992), pp. 221-30.

PSALM 50: PROPHETIC SPEECH AND GOD'S PERFORMATIVE UTTERANCES

Stephen Breck Reid

G.M. Tucker described form criticism well: 'The aim of this literary-sociological approach is to analyze the typical features of biblical texts, especially their conventional forms or structures, in order to relate them to their sociological contexts.'[1] Form criticism, which emerged in this century, forged a set of assumptions about the nature of language which informed the interpretation of the ancient texts. This assumption that language is being shaped by social location in institutions, such as prophecy and law (to name just two), has yielded helpful insights. Nonetheless, the understanding of social roles and language in form criticism requires re-evaluation through an examination of phenomenology of speech which places rhetoric in newly configured categories of social institutions. Each of the proposals for the *Sitz im Leben* of Psalm 50 will have its own plausibility but ultimately will seem inconclusive because each assumes a rigidity of social roles and rhetoric that is no longer existentially coherent to the contemporary reader. Form-critical and tradition-historical work on Psalm 50 point to the promises and limitations of form criticism while establishing a route to a better understanding using the phenomenology of language. The equipoise of the reader of Psalm 50 breaks under the attack of a particular type of speech, a speech which does more than describe: a speech that acts, performs.

A modern reader must stand vigilant, so as not to get lost in the dogmatic concept of law or sacrifice generated by some systematic theology.[2] Protestant prejudice makes the world of the Bible less accessible in areas where the matters of law and sacrifice come to the fore because of the

---

1. G.M. Tucker, 'Prophetic Speech', *Int* 32 (1978), p. 32.
2. H. Gese, 'Psalm 50 und das alttestamentliche Gesetzesverständnis', in J. Friedrich, W. Pohlman and P. Stuhlmacher (eds.), *Rechtfertigung: Festschrift für Ernst Käsemann zum 70. Geburtstag* (Tübingen: Mohr, 1976), p. 56.

polemic left over from the Reformation. A discussion of sacrifice provides the rubric for our understanding of the concept of law in Psalm 50. An example of a later prophetic liturgy, Psalm 50 represents a radical deepening for understanding the law without the smallest break with the total tradition of Torah. Nonetheless, it clearly rejects the older legal tradition.[3]

This article will explore the phenomenology of language through an examination of the Yahweh speech (divine discourse) and the use of the divine first-person speech in prophetic dialogue as seen in Psalm 50.[4] Some have located the use of prophetic speech generally and divine first person particularly to a process of spirit mediumship.[5] This article will demonstrate that at the level of speech this may, in fact, be the case but at the level of text, the social context of the Yahweh speech is performative language. In other words, if we follow the *Gattungsgeschichte* of the Yahweh speech we discover that the shift from *ad hoc* speech to ritualized speech, what I will call text, indicates a different social location. However, each social location functions to authorize the speech, and, sometimes but not always, the speaker.

Form-Critical and Tradition-Historical Readings of Psalm 50

Gunkel designated Psalm 50 as a non-liturgical psalm.[6] More importantly, he connected Psalm 50 to the prophetic and legal traditions. We can also see his romanticism as he describes these so-called spiritual songs: 'These Spiritual Songs, as much as anything in the Old Testament, stand closest to the Gospel.'[7]

Mowinckel frames a discussion which continues to this very day: 'The whole psalm is cast in the mold of prophetic speech, with a hymnal description of the glory of theophany for an introduction.'[8] Broad

3.   Gese, 'Psalm 50', p. 58.
4.   Tucker, 'Prophetic Speech', pp. 40-45.
5.   T. Overholt, *Channels of Prophecy: The Social Dynamics of Prophetic Activity* (Minneapolis: Fortress Press, 1989); R.R. Wilson, *Prophecy and Society in Ancient Israel* (Philadelphia: Fortress Press, 1980); S.B. Reid, *Enoch and Daniel: A Form Critical and Sociological Study of the Historical Apocalypses* (Berkeley: Bibal Press, 1989).
6.   H. Gunkel, *The Psalms* (Philadelphia: Facet Books/Fortress Press, 1967).
7.   Gunkel, *Psalms*, p. 26.
8.   S. Mowinckel, *The Psalms in Israel's Worship* (Nashville: Abingdon Press, 1962), II, p. 70.

parameters are set by Mowinckel, but this form-critical designation in no way generates a consensus. Gerstenberger notes the use of legal and prophetic traditions but then argues that this is a sermon.[9] Craigie notes the same rhetorical similarities to legal and prophetic tradition, but designates this as a covenant liturgy which directs the reader into a way of understanding the use of the divine first person.[10]

G. von Rad labels the divine conveyance of the Decalogue as the center for Psalm 50: 'Indeed, the whole authority of the cultus itself stands or falls by the Sinai narrative, which is, in other words, the cult-legend of a particular cultic observation.'[11] While von Rad may have overstated his case regarding the centrality of the Decalogue for the cultus, he nonetheless understands the rhetorical logic of Psalms 50 and 81. 'We recognize commandments six through eight in 50.18ff. and the first commandment in 81.10. The cry in 50.7, and 81.9 also underscores the kinship between the two psalms.'[12]

The language of Ps. 50.7 resonates with Ps. 81.9. Psalm 50 shares some points in common with Psalm 81 by using first-person speech, but the two psalms are derived from different tradition-historical roots. One comes from the Priestly Narrative and the other from the Holiness Code. In Psalm 81 Moses is an actor amidst the divine first person. We hear the word, as it were, without other explicit actors or mediators. Psalm 81 develops from Holiness Code traditions; whereas Psalm 50 presupposes the context of the Decalogue, Priestly formulations.[13]

Connections with legal traditions notwithstanding, several scholars have explored the cultic prophet as the socio-literary context of Psalm 50. 'In short, the cultic prophet is summoning his [*sic*] fellow country-men to a great act of repentance and as a result of this, to a resolute renewal of that initial pledge of obedience which had been so often and so wilfully neglected with the passing of years.'[14] Aubrey Johnson notes

9. E.S. Gerstenberger, *Psalms* (FOTL, 14; Grand Rapids: Eerdmans, 1988), p. 210.

10. P.C. Craigie, *Psalms 1–50* (WBC; Waco, TX: Word Books, 1983), p. 363.

11. G. von Rad, 'The Form Critical Problem of the Hexateuch', in *The Problem of the Hexateuch and Other Essays* (trans. E.W.T. Dicken; New York: McGraw-Hill, 1966), pp. 21-22.

12. W. Zimmerli, 'I am Yahweh', in *I am Yahweh* (ed. W. Brueggemann; trans. D.W. Stott; Atlanta: John Knox Press, 1982), p. 24.

13. Zimmerli, 'I am Yahweh', p. 24.

14. A. Johnson, *The Cultic Prophet and Israel's Psalmody* (Cardiff: University of Wales Press, 1979), p. 22.

that Psalm 50 represents a prime example of such a rhetorical agenda. According to Johnson the poetry of Psalm 50 is more than a case of being influenced by prophetic traditions. Rather it is the presentation of a 'professional prophet'.[15] Jörg Jeremias, working with the same rubric of cultic prophet, follows Mowinckel and von Rad in claiming that Psalm 50 is not cultic prophecy *per se* but levitical preaching based on prophetic and legal rubrics. Jeremias makes such a judgment because the date of this psalm appears to be after the exile and cultic prophecy did not extend past the monarchy.[16]

Form criticism of Psalm 50 concurs with Gunkel in many points but it definitely does not agree with his rendering of Psalm 50 as a non-liturgical psalm. On the contrary, Psalm 50 is considered the great psalm of covenant renewal.[17] The cultic prophet would, of course, have a liturgical psalm. The use of divine language provides a clue to the liturgical or non-liturgical context of the psalm.

Use of divine language distinguishes Psalms 50 and 81 from the entrance liturgies of Psalms 15 and 24. Psalms 50 and 81 'contain ordinances binding upon human conduct for the *future*, and must therefore be distinguished from the laws governing admission to the rite...'[18] Behind von Rad's comments that Psalm 50 differs from Psalms 15 and 24 stands a sense of liturgy. The ethical requirements are appropriate at the point of entry, hence Psalms 15 and 24 are properly liturgical. But Psalm 50 does not present itself as an entrance liturgy and locates its ethical material in a place that would be liturgically unacceptable. Thus von Rad argues that Psalms 50 and 81 'are not liturgical manuals, but secondary poetical compositions which retain their characteristics of original *genre* only in their form'.[19]

Jeremias notes the theophanic introduction to the divine speech in vv. 5 and 7 through 23. Jeremias states that whether we characterize this as cultic prophecy or not the theophanic elements nonetheless come through clearly. He appears to link the theophany as an element in the divine speech rhetorically buttressing the moral exhortation.[20] This

15. Johnson, *Cultic Prophet*, p. 29.
16. J. Jeremias, *Kultprophetie und Gerichtverkündigung in der späten Königszeit* (WMANT, 35; Neukirchen–Vluyn: Neukirchener Verlag, 1970), p. 127.
17. Jeremias, *Kultprophetie*, p. 125.
18. Von Rad, 'Form Critical Problem', p. 25.
19. Von Rad, 'Form Critical Problem', p. 24.
20. J. Jeremias, *Theophanie: Die Geschichte einer alttestamentlichen Gattung*

relationship between moral exhortation and divine speech comes into better focus with a change in nomenclature.

Ernst Würthwein describes cultic moral exhortation as an antecedent of prophetic speech. The sociological origin of prophetic speech, according to Würthwein, is legal. Hence the *Yhwh mlk* psalms and Psalm 50 which blend the magisterial and legal depictions of Yahweh seem to be natural reservoirs of tradition for prophetic speech.[21]

The form-critical style of reading complements a tradition-historical approach. However, as we try to track the rhetoric and social institution of the psalm, attempts to locate Psalm 50 in the Ephraimite tradition on the basis of vocabulary and its association with the broader collection of the Asaph psalms are not helpful.[22] Nonetheless, we see points of continuity between this orphan Asaph psalm and the Asaphite and Korahite psalms, which are often connected to cultic prophecy. Psalms 50, 75, 81 and 95, designated by Gunkel as prophetic psalms, share the same use of divine first-person speech.

We shall be able to chart the points of contact by checking the use of the divine first person in the Korahite and Asaphite psalms. The phrase 'I am God' occurs in the Psalter only twice (Pss. 46.11; 50.7). Another case of divine first person occurs in Ps. 87.4 where the divine first person 'remembers'. The Hebrew term *zākar*, with the first-person inflected form, occurs five times (Exod. 20.24; Pss. 71.16; 77.12; 87.4; Isa. 63.7), but only in Psalm 87 and Exodus 20 do we have cases of literal divine first person. Interestingly, both of these are covenant-making circumstances.

Psalm 75 is full of first-person language: 'I will set the time/appoint'; 'I will judge'; 'I will keep'; 'I say'; 'I will declare'; 'I will sing'; and 'I will cut off'. The question arises whether all of these are divine first person. The declaration and praise in v. 10 are clearly human.

We find the divine first person in Psalm 81 framed with the first person of human witness: 'I hear a voice I had not known' (81.6b). 'I will relieve' occurs in Ps. 81.7 and 1 Chron. 17.13. In both cases God is the actor. The term for 'deliver' occurs elsewhere in the Psalter but this

(WMANT, 10; Neukirchen–Vluyn: Neukirchener Verlag, 1965), pp. 132-33.

21. E. Würthwein, 'Der Ursprung der prophetischen Gerichtsrede', in *Wort und Existenz: Studien zum Alten Testament* (Göttingen: Vandenhoeck & Ruprecht, 1970), p. 123.

22. H.P. Nasuti, *Tradition History and the Psalms of Asaph* (SBLDS, 88; Atlanta: Scholars Press, 1988), pp. 59-63.

appears to be the only time it appears in the first person. 'I answer you' occurs four times (Job 14.15; 33.12; Ps. 81.8; Nah. 1.12). The term 'I tested' (*bāḥan*) in the first person occurs here only. The term for 'admonish' (*yādâ*) occurs five times (Deut. 31.28; Neh. 13.21; Pss. 50.7; 81.9; Isa. 8.2) including one time each in two of the prophetic psalms (Pss. 50.7; 81.9).

The self-presentation formula 'I am the LORD your God' occurs five times (Exod. 20.2, 5; Deut. 5.6, 9; Ps. 81.11). The 'I will fill' language only occurs here (Ps. 81.11), but it parallels the language at the end of the Psalm (81.17). The language in all three terms for eating has no parallel in the same inflected forms.

Use of the divine first person appears to occur in the Asaphite psalms and in the covenant-making texts as well. A correlation of Psalm 50 language and the vocabulary of covenant confirms the research of von Rad and Zimmerli. In order better to understand the use of such rhetorical devices the philosophy of language on performative speech might be instructive.

Performative Speech as a Category

The philosopher John L. Austin pioneered the study of speech-act theory. His discussion of performative language is an example of his theory. This groundbreaking work comes from his 1955 William James lectures at Harvard University published 'in his jocosely entitled *How to Do Things with Words*'.[23] The basic model of performative speech has three components. (1) Performative sentences contain 'verbs in the first person singular present active indicative'. (2) They do not describe or report. (3) 'The uttering of the sentence is, or is part of, the doing of an action, which again would not *normally* be described as, or "just", saying something'.[24] It is called performative because the utterance of the sentence itself is performing an action.[25]

A second and derivative model of performative speech also exists. Characteristics of the second-order performative speech include verbs in

---

23. T. Eagleton, *Literary Theory: An Introduction* (Minneapolis: University of Minnesota Press, 1983), p. 118; J.L. Austin, *How to Do Things with Words* (ed. M. Sbisà and J.O. Urmson; Cambridge, MA: Harvard University Press, 2nd edn, 1975).

24. Austin, *How to Do Things with Words*, p. 5.

25. Austin, *How to Do Things with Words*, p. 6.

the second or third person (singular or plural) in a passive voice.[26] However, in more informal speech, mood and tense break down as absolute criteria.[27]

Some performatives are primary; they do not define the action to come. Other performatives are explicit.[28] Explicit performatives have a number of characteristics but I shall only list those relevant for written speech. Explicit performative speech often uses the imperative mood. It uses connective articles such as 'that' and often has adverbs.[29]

Austin does not describe sociological setting as one might expect in a form-critical argument. Rather, as a philosopher, he sets up the necessary ingredients for successful performative speech. The ingredients articulate the setting of performative speech as a set of grammatical rules. (1) 'There must exist an accepted conventional procedure having a certain conventional effect, the procedure to include the uttering of certain words by certain persons in certain circumstances.'[30] (2) 'The particular persons and circumstances in a given case must be appropriate for the invocation of the particular procedure invoked.'[31] (3) 'The procedure must be executed by all participants correctly.'[32] (4) 'The procedure must be executed by all participants completely.'[33]

Austin developed a typology of verbs which indicate different tasks for performative speech acts. (a) *Verdictives* are verbs which pronounce a verdict, such as 'acquit', 'correct', 'declare', 'judge', etc. (b) Certain verbs embody the act of exercising power, right or influence; these Austin calls *exercitives*. Examples would be 'appoint', 'adopt', 'bless', 'choose', etc. (c) *Commisives*, which are promises and commitments, employ verbs such as 'acknowledge', 'adopt', 'pledge', 'promise', etc. (d) *Behabitives* are 'a kind of performative concerned roughly with reactions to behaviour and with behaviour towards others and designed to exhibit attitudes and feelings'.[34] 'Appeal', 'confess', 'cry', and 'complain' are some behabitives. (e) Expositives 'make plain how our utterances fit into the course of an argument or conversation, how we

26. Austin, *How to Do Things with Words*, p. 57.
27. Austin, *How to Do Things with Words*, p. 58.
28. Austin, *How to Do Things with Words*, p. 69.
29. Austin, *How to Do Things with Words*, p. 73.
30. Austin, *How to Do Things with Words*, p. 26.
31. Austin, *How to Do Things with Words*, p. 34.
32. Austin, *How to Do Things with Words*, p. 36.
33. Austin, *How to Do Things with Words*, p. 36.
34. Austin, *How to Do Things with Words*, p. 83.

are using words, or, in general, are expository'.[35] The vocabulary of expositives includes verbs such as 'affirm', 'mention', 'inform', 'testify', etc. 'The biblical texts abound in examples of occurrences of these verbs in institutional, situational, and inter-personal contexts which render them performative speech-acts. One such context is that of *liturgy or worship*, of which the Psalms contain many instances.'[36]

The work of Austin was employed effectively by T. Mettinger by using these rubrics to assist in the interpretation of Psalm 50. Mettinger was the first to make the connection between Austin's work on performative language and the language of the Psalter. He noted this in connection with the first-person divine speech in narrative as well as the Psalter.[37] We see the use of performative utterance in the Succession Narrative concerning Solomon's designation as *nāgîd* (1 Kgs 1.35). Mettinger quite helpfully designates performative language through the designation 'hereby', so we should read this passage 'I hereby appoint him *nāgîd*...'[38] This speech is an excellent example because the very speaking of the words brings the political reality into being by the speech itself.[39]

The divine performative speech legitimates the royal functionary in the speech of Samuel (1 Sam. 10.18). Divine performative speech also delegitimizes (1 Sam. 16.1ff.).[40] Mettinger indicates that the performative divine language matches the confessional first person of the petitioner, in this case, Solomon. In fact, the performative utterance in this case legitimizes the different style of charisma that comes about with the more bureaucratic style of Solomon.[41] Performative language undergirds royal charisma, such as in Isa. 42.1ff.[42]

The divine performative language also occurs in the Psalter in order to designate sacrally the cachet of the monarch. We see this in Psalm 2

---

35. Austin, *How to Do Things with Words*, pp. 151-52.

36. A.C. Thiselton, *New Horizons in Hermeneutics: The Theory and Practice of Transforming Biblical Reading* (Grand Rapids: Zondervan, 1992), p. 299. For a different assessment of Austin see Eagleton, *Literary Theory*, pp. 118-19.

37. T. Mettinger, *King and Messiah: The Civil and Sacral Legitimation of the Israelite Kings* (ConBOT; Lund: Gleerup, 1976), p. 261.

38. Mettinger, *King and Messiah*, p. 23.

39. Mettinger, *King and Messiah*, pp. 161-62.

40. Mettinger, *King and Messiah*, p. 176.

41. Mettinger, *King and Messiah*, p. 240.

42. Mettinger, *King and Messiah*, p. 249.

where it conveys a sense of divine sonship of the king.[43] One wonders about Psalm 110 as well.[44]

Psalm 50: A Close Reading

Genre follows the communicator's overall purpose, a purpose most transparent through stylistic observations.[45] Psalm 50 is a single psalm with three parts which can be easily discerned. The first part contains vv. 1-6, a theophany description, which leads into a two-part sacrifice speech made by God (vv. 7-23). The first part of the divine sacrifice speech (vv. 7-15) closes with a Torah saying (vv. 14-15). This first section of the divine sacrifice speech focuses on the sacrifice itself. The second section (vv. 16-23) focuses on the human response and goes from a rebuke at the end with a 'count the cost' expression in the admonition (v. 22). The section ends (v. 23) with a Torah statement reminiscent of the Torah statement of vv. 14-15. All of the structure argues, according to Gese, against H. Schmidt's hypothesis of two original psalms which were later joined together. Allen describes the psalm as a unity with an overall chiasmus using the name Elohim to connect all three strophes. The deliverance in v. 15 is not available for the reprobate in v. 22. Connecting the second and third strophes is the term 'deliverance'.[46] The connectedness of the human reference to God and fellow humans must be appropriately observed in Psalm 50.[47]

The Genre and Setting of the First Strophe
Kenneth Kuntz also examined Psalm 50 with regard to the theophany genre. He recognizes that the theophany (vv. 1-6) introduces the divine speech (vv. 7-23). More importantly, Kuntz sees the connection of the *hieros logos* with the reprimand and exhortation. This theophany contains three strophes, with the emphasis falling on the concluding colon of each strophe in vv. 2, 4 and 6. These join the epiphany of the divine shining forth to the judgment culminating in the confession (set

---

43. Mettinger, *King and Messiah*, pp. 259-62.
44. Mettinger, *King and Messiah*, pp. 264-65.
45. L. Allen, 'Structure and Meaning in Psalm 50', *Vox Evangelica* 14 (1984), p. 19.
46. Allen, 'Structure and Meaning', pp. 18-21.
47. Gese, 'Psalm 50', p. 62.

off by the deictic particle *kî*) that God is judge.[48]

We can describe the theophany as being in three parts. The first section of the theophany (vv. 1-2) begins with the language of the appearance of God with verbs such as 'speak', 'summon' and 'shine forth'. The basic stronghold for Psalm 50, the speech-event of the God of Gods, is in the first verse. The second verse describes the *Doxaerscheinung* (appearance of glory) from the center of the universe, namely Zion.[49] If the first section describes a theophany as speech-event, then the second section, using traditional metaphors of devastating fire and storm, describes a theophany as judgment. The third section confirms this reading. The divine instruction of v. 5 describes a gathering of the faithful. For the judgment is, in fact, an eschatological reconciliation signaled by the disclosure to the heavens of God's righteousness. The faithful described here are the culticly constituted covenant partners.[50]

Gese reminds us that this resonates with the *Yhwh mlk* psalm (97.6).[51] This is part of a larger question for Gese: is Psalm 50 an expression of eschatological witness? Deliberations on this question must examine the parallel text in Psalm 97 but also the material in Deutero-Isaiah. While that is an intriguing question, it goes beyond the scope of this paper. Gese argues that this new Zion Torah replaces, or at least remodulates, the Sinai Torah.[52]

When one pays attention to v. 5, the unity of Psalm 50 becomes clear. The theophany benefits those designated as the righteous by virtue of sacrifice. The material in Ps. 50.7-23 continues the theme set out in the theophany.

Psalm 50 does not exhibit the pristine form of the *Gattung* theophany. It nonetheless compares favorably to Psalm 18 which is more closely a theophany. Two aspects of the theophanic traditions come to the foreground. First, the technical language 'shine forth' (*yp'*) in v. 2 occurs in seven other Hebrew Bible contexts. Five of these describe a divine subject (Deut. 33.2; Ps. 80.3; 94.1; Job 10.3; 37.15). All of these, with the

---

48. J.K. Kuntz, *The Self Revelation of God* (Philadelphia: Westminster Press, 1967), pp. 192-93.

49. Gese, 'Psalm 50', p. 65; Gese includes v. 3a in this section, but this does not seem persuasive.

50. Gese, 'Psalm 50', p. 65.

51. Gese, 'Psalm 50', p. 65.

52. Gese, 'Psalm 50', p. 66.

exception of the Job passages, are theophanies.[53] Secondly, the theophany connects to the divine speech by means of the self-asseveration, or self-presentation, formula ('Yahweh, your God, am I'). The function of the psalm is the cultic reappropriation of the Sinaitic *Urtheophanie*.[54] Here Kuntz and Gese seem to be following the same path though without knowledge of each other's work.

The legal conflict background of the psalm has been noted. J. Harvey argues that this is a *rîb*.[55] Even though E. Beauchamp argues that this is a theophany he nonetheless makes the connection between theophany and prophetic legal speech.[56] The conflict inherent in this section is typical of theophanies/epiphanies.[57]

The Genre and Setting of the Second Strophe
While the first strophe fails to use performative language, the second strophe brims with it. The second strophe is the divine speech in vv. 7-15. It begins with an introductory prophetic formula and a self-presentation formula. After a 'call to hear' formula followed by divine first person we find the *rîb*. The basis of the complaint derives from the self-presentation formula, 'I am the LORD your God', accompanied by the Torah. Gese reminds us of a fuller form of this combination in Ps. 81.9-11, which is also a prophetic liturgy psalm.[58]

The performative language in v. 7 signaled by the verbs 'speak' (*dbr*) and 'testify' (*'wd*) demonstrates the verdictive type of performative speech. The verdictive performative language rests on the foundation of the self-presentation formula. The self-presentation formula, 'I am your God', anticipates the end of the strophe, 'I will deliver you', forming an inclusion (vv. 7, 15). The self-disclosure language of the self-presentation formula introduces a section of negatives (vv. 8-9) followed by a *kî* clause of ownership and knowledge (vv. 10-11). The verdictives embody the negative message of the psalm and connect to the term 'sacrifice' which forms an inclusion in the strophe (vv. 8, 14). The images of bulls

53. Kuntz, *Self Revelation*, p. 197.

54. Kuntz, *Self-Revelation*, p. 203.

55. See J. Harvey, 'Le "Rib Pattern" requisitoire prophétique sur la rupture de l'Alliance', *Biblica* 43 (1962), pp. 172-96.

56. E. Beauchamp, 'La Theophanie du Psaume 50 (49)', *NRT* 81 (1959), pp. 897-915.

57. F. Schnutenhaus, 'Das Kommen und Erscheinen Gottes im Alten Testament', *ZAW* 76 (1964), pp. 1-22.

58. Allen, 'Structure and Meaning', p. 21.

and goats also form an inclusion (vv. 9, 13).[59] The verdictives of vv. 8-9 give way to the *kî* clause where we find our next divine first-person speech in v. 10. The first section of the second strophe (vv. 7-11) is closed with the expositive performative speech.

The speech moves to a modal quality introduced by *'îm* (vv. 12-13) but the negative sense still pervades this piece of the psalm.[60] Here the psalmist uses irony.[61] The use of negation with the use of irony in the passage sets up the positive assessment of sacrifice pronounced in the Torah (v. 14). The first-person speeches of vv. 12 and 13, introduced by the conditional particle 'if' (*'îm*), do not carry the performative force but rather these rhetorical questions prepare the way for a series of three imperatives. A careful reader notes that the first-person performatives are sometimes complemented by the imperative (second-order performatives).[62] All of the imperatives point to the subject matter of the strophe as identity and sacrifice.[63] The strophe ends with second-order performatives, 'call on me in the day of distress', connected to the commissive performative verb 'I will deliver'. These commissives replace the verdictives earlier in the strophe. In summary, we note that the final verse of the strophe moves from second-order performative to commissive performative speech, then returns to second-order performative speech. We can think of this as an A-B-A pattern. The statement 'you will honor', is a second-order performative speech. The way this imperative of honor anticipates the contrast of the honor in v. 15 with disregard in v. 17 might lead one to think of this as the chiastic center of the entire psalm.[64]

The positive understanding of sacrifice and the translation of v. 14 stand together. Gese rightly grasps the situation as a question of whether this is literal or metaphorical.[65] The key to this reading is the term *tôdâ*. Lev. 7.12 describes the *tôdâ* as a thanksgiving meal offering. For Gese the *tôdâ* has its existential roots in the danger of death and persecution that prompts a thanksgiving to the one who delivers the threatened person from these threats.[66]

59. Allen, 'Structure and Meaning', p. 21.
60. J. Bos, 'Oh When the Saints: A Consideration of the Meaning of Psalm 50', *JSOT* 24 (1982), p. 68.
61. Bos, 'Oh When the Saints', p. 71.
62. Austin, *How to Do Things with Words*, p. 58.
63. Allen, 'Structure and Meaning', p. 21.
64. Allen, 'Structure and meaning', p. 21.
65. Gese, 'Psalm 50', p. 70.
66. Gese, 'Psalm 50', p. 71.

The Genre and Setting of the Third Strophe
The third part of Psalm 50 is the counter-speech to the wicked. The final strophe uses the term 'Elohim' as an inclusion (vv. 16, 23). Within this strophe we find three sections. The text uses the first-person divine possessive in vv. 16 and 17 in the context of rhetorical questions which refer to the Decalogue. The divine speech uses a particular construal of the Decalogue to shape the rhetoric of accusation. The second part of the strophe uses the second-person singular suffix to bind v. 18 to v. 21. The third part of the strophe uses a contrast between those who forget God and those who bring thanksgiving. The antithetical parallelism unites vv. 22 and 23.[67] However, the enemies here are within earshot.[68] The irony of the previous section is now replaced by bitter sarcasm. Gese correctly understands the conclusion as a summary of entreaty and Torah which provides the rationale for the exhortation. Further, we notice that the first-person divine speech is not performative but rather simply descriptive.

M. Mannati questions the designation *rîb* for this text. She concurs with Mowinckel in construing this as part of the covenant renewal festival.[69] The use of the *rîb* makes the *Tendenz* clear, directing the divine speech as revelation to be fully understood and found in the salvation in 'right', *Gericht*.[70] The accusations of vv. 18-20 echo the tone of the theophany that described the coming of the great God of judgment (see vv. 1-6). The prophetic divine speech observed in Psalm 50 requires the reader to pay attention to its parallels in Psalms 81 and 95. These two describe not a theophany *per se* but rather the divine presence amidst the cultic event. Such a comparison indicates a concurrence between the Zion theophany of Psalm 50 and the Sinai traditions.

Gese sets as his frame of reference the question of the understanding of law in the Hebrew Bible. Allen, in his examination of the structure and meaning of the psalm, comes to a similar conclusion. The issue is ultimately moral behavior demonstrated through the appropriate practice of the cult. What prophecy and liturgy have in common is moral

67. Allen, 'Structure and Meaning', pp. 23-24.
68. See G.T. Sheppard, '"Enemies" and the Politics of Prayer in the Book of Psalms', in D. Jobling, P.L. Day and G.T. Sheppard (eds.), *The Bible and the Politics of Exegesis* (Cleveland: Pilgrim Press, 1991), pp. 61-82.
69. Gese, 'Psalm 50', p. 63; M. Mannati, 'Le Psaume 50 est-il rib?', *Sem* (1973), pp. 27-50.
70. Gese, 'Psalm 50', p. 64.

exhortation. An examination of the psalm with an eye to the performative language indicates the intersection of prophecy and cult.

What Zimmerli noted before, concerning the formula of self-introduction, is confirmed with an examination of the divine performative speech in Psalm 50. Performative speech tenaciously adheres to proclamations of maxims.[71] Allen used the chiasms of Psalm 50 as his guide for the meaning of the text. Allen, Gese and Zimmerli all agree that the psalm persuades the reader about behavior by the use of moral exhortation. But the ground of that exhortation derives its poetic power from divine performative speech.

When one discovers moral exhortation and divine speech in Hebrew prophetic speech or liturgical material one often discovers performative language. That is language which shapes the world by organizing power. In this case the moral exhortation has the divine sanction and therefore is worthy of social reorientation.

What does this mean for the understanding of language? Early form criticism understood the relationship between language and institutions such as prophecy and worship in too wooden a way. Language conventions about power relationships span institutions. We see this with a proper understanding of performative speech.

It is an honor to contribute to this volume. The areas of prophetic speech, form criticism and theology of the Hebrew Scriptures have been interests of Gene Tucker. His insight and skilled instruction have made me a better interpreter.

---

71. Zimmerli, 'I am Yahweh', p. 28.

INDEXES

INDEX OF REFERENCES

OLD TESTAMENT

JOURNAL FOR THE STUDY OF THE OLD TESTAMENT
SUPPLEMENT SERIES